THE TROUBLED SEMINARIAN

A young man's struggle with his faith at
the time of the Protestant Reformation

Neal Grey

Published in the USA
Printed in the United States of America
ISBN: 978-1-7327110-0-6 (paperback)
         978-1-7327110-1-3 (ebook)

Book & cover design by Darlene Swanson • www.van-garde.com

CONTENTS

FOREWORD

The central characters of this story and their actions are fictitious. The background characters, however, those who held significant positions of political and/or ecclesiastical authority, as well as their fundamental actions, are real.

The most outlandish and unseemly instances portrayed, as well as the bizarre rationale attributed to them, are taken directly from Malleus Maleficarum, the official ecclesiastical text on the heresy of witchcraft at that time; they are not the fabrications of the author. Malleus Maleficarum has been subject to revisionist history but the underlying fact is, legitimate adjustments or not, Malleus was disseminated as stated for generations and civil authorities took their direction in prosecuting pertinent matters from the Church. Also, historically speaking, it is impossible to deny the existence and power of evil spirits and pacts with the devil yet still follow the teachings of the Church.

People were killing in the name of God during that era, just as they are doing today, albeit now as isolated occurrences. This is born out of ignorance, institutionalized conditioning and poorly examined faith led by religious extremists who have appointed themselves surrogates of God. Will mankind ever come to its senses? Perhaps we should focus on temporal injustices and leave retribution for perceived spiritual deviations to the deity of one's faith.

CHAPTER I

SEEDS OF DOUBT

Never did that obscure Augustinian priest think that he would spark a revolution. But on Saturday, October 31, 1517, some say that he was so outraged that he nailed his theses to the doors of the castle church in Wittenberg. This miner's son from Saxony changed the course of history; the sway and universality of his own Church would be forever diminished. It is a date which is easy for me to remember, for it is the date on which I was born. Rafer is my name.

The Schilling family has been legendary for generations as providing the premier mountain guides from the Tyrol area of Austria. My father was overjoyed to have a son and he had every expectation that I would live up to my heritage. We live on the outskirts of Innsbruck and, as with all European families of this era, the religious schism created by Martin Luther has had its effects on my family, especially so for me. You see, I was to skirt tradition and enter the seminary.

Sunday church was mandatory while growing up; Mother is a devout Roman Catholic and she made sure of that. I was well drilled in my catechism and dutifully received the sacraments. My father, Erich, the most renowned of all the guides in my lineage, is still a member of the parish but in name only. To him there is a major disconnect between faith and reason. He accompanies us to Mass when he is not traveling but it is a facade to accommodate Mother and deflect the suspicions of the more militant clergy. Religious conformity is demanded and woe to wayward Christians or Muslims. Unrepentant heretics and apostates are put to death. Muslims execute their heretics and infidels by cutting off their heads; Christians burn them at the stake.

In my early youth I had heard reports of such happenings but was assured by my teachers that, as appalling as this appeared, it was only right in the context of the magnitude of the perpetrators' offenses to God. After all, what could be more heinous than defying the will of our creator? This, I was told, demanded the most severe of penalties. What else was a youth to think, I took my lead from my superiors, my teachers, my protectors.

I've kept a diary throughout the years of my extraordinary life's journey at this extraordinary time. Reminiscing with a friend and scholar at the University of Vienna, he asked me to write an account of my experiences as an historical biopic. In so doing, I find myself reliving it so I'll stick to the present tense for the most part. It was an unforgettable winter when I first began that extended diary…

I awaken to the mournful moaning of a worsening wind racing across the torn face of the mountain. A fine sleet is thrashing the hard crust on the naked fields. My father is returning from the stable, the icy needles stinging his discolored cheeks. On a foul morning like this the winter sun is not to be found; the bent trees denied any solace. A lone horse, pulling a lone sleigh, is trotting on an unreal horizon. The light shivers in the troubled air disturbed by an occasional clap of thunder. On my way to the morning meal I overhear…

"Some said it was the cardinal himself, his volatile temper," volunteers Mother, who had visited the butcher shop the preceding day. "Can you imagine the audacity of some people, suspecting the cardinal of such a thing? After all this time the rumors get more and more preposterous. Next they will be saying that little Manfred, our tiny sexton, had killed her; he gets blamed for everything else around there. Though he is very forgetful, I must admit."

"Klaus Heibel said that? I always thought he was a bit perverse himself; seems to take an eerie pleasure in hammering the meat, chopping things up."

"Nein, not him. Some of his help. He shushed them up."

"Apparently it was someone in the chancery, either a member of the clergy or the staff. Snow had fallen after she had arrived. Only Manfred's footprints leaving the chancery were in the snow when he returned with the sheriff."

"Before Luther split the Church no one would dare suggest such a thing. Besides, the killer must have hid in the cathedral. The sheriff just didn't find him. Snuck out later."

"Maria, I spoke with deputy Seidel later that very day; he said that a half dozen deputies spent hours covering every inch of the chancery, where the killing took place, and the rectory and the cathedral."

"The cathedral is full of nooks and crannies, hidden staircases, underground tunnels, above ground walkways to the other buildings. All those rebuilds after earthquakes and fires over the centuries. You could hide a legion in there."

"Don't exaggerate. Those tunnels were sealed years ago. And St. James is far from a cathedral; it's a church. People just call it that because it's the biggest church in the area and because a cardinal has taken up temporary residence here. But Gerhardt doesn't know the definition of temporary, how long has he been here?"

"It's big enough. And there was another set of footprints, ones outside the cathedral. My goodness, after all these years we have to go through this again."

"All the cathedral doors and windows were bolted from the inside. The footprints showed someone approaching and then retreating back to the mish mash of traffic. They were made when the cathedral was still locked down. Except for those footprints and the ones of Manfred leading from the chancery, that was it."

"The cardinal and none of the good fathers were involved in such a thing."

"Good fathers? I'm not talking about those in Innsbruck so much but the clergy in general? Priests with concubines! Avaricious cardinals and popes using contributions to the Church to enrich themselves and kinsfolk! How can one believe in the Church anymore? Where is the Holy Spirit?"

"Don't talk like that Erich! Rumors, that's all. It upsets me so… I'm worried that Father Frankhauser suspects your, well, weakness of faith as it is."

"Well, I suspect Father Frankhauser of weakness of character, a splinter of a man and worse for wear. He is not stupid but you have to look hard to be sure. Much of the Church is corrupt. How else do you account for the groundswell of support for Luther? Even his nemesis, Johann Eck, had to ease off his attacks on him because of it."

"Enough of such talk!" Dad knows when to shut up and he does.

All this gives me pause as to my own convictions. Of course, Mother never gives me a choice. I am being raised a Catholic and practice the faith regardless of any doubts. Dad doesn't interfere, perhaps for my own safety in these strident times. But a clergyman involved in a murder?

Sheriff Werner Mitlstrasser has been on the case from the start. Short, muscular, shoulders on a slant, broad face weathered by a penurious upbringing, equipped with a razor sharp mind, his authority emanates as much from his personal presence as from the power of his office. Wolf, his recently acquired German shepherd, is constantly at his side longing for loving strokes that Werner is pleased to give.

Self-educated but still prone to errors in grammar, a product of the commonplace illiterate family, he shrugs off slights of the pretentious nobility who are quick to remind him that he is not of privileged birth. Mention "*The Peasant*" in those circles and they all know who you mean, resentful of the authority the emperor chose to invest in him. But the case has been as cold as an Alpine night. He has his suspicions but no incriminating evidence.

❧

In a verdant valley at the crossroads of Central Europe, Innsbruck takes its name from the Inn River, which meanders northeast across western Austria, and the bridge that spans it. Born of a far off Swiss lake to the southwest, and capturing the frigid waters dripping off the snowcapped mountain peaks, the Inn is narrow and fast as it departs the town twisting, turning and dropping for the better part of two hundred miles, penetrating the German frontier and eventually contributing to the majesty of the Danube. Aside from tropical, along the way one can experience virtually any other climate imaginable. Depending on which side of the mountain you are on, high and low pressure areas, the differences can be dramatic. Warm air is carried from the lower regions to the upper elevations where it is thinned and cooled, often producing rain or snow. Forecasting this and how to cope with it has allowed the Schillings to prosper for generations.

Flowing north through the Wipptal valley to the Inn, and situated a bit east of town, is the less prominent Sill River. It helps encompass a population by recent estimates of almost five thousand people. The townhouses and arcaded shops, most of which are four or five story structures, are adorned with pointed arches, ribbed vaulting and colorful frescoes inside and out. The frescoes, composed of subdued and vibrant pigments and applied by our local artisans, liberally dress our gothic architecture. The towering, limestone Alps volunteer protection to the town itself, which was first recognized as a political entity only three centuries before; initially under the auspices of Bavarian counts but now the Habsburgs rule. Austria's central government has been historically located in Vienna about 300 miles overland to the east but the emperor himself, Maximilian, took up residence here until his death in 1519.

❧

We first met as schoolboys, Johann Carberry and I did, taking instruction at the Wilten Abbey. Our teachers, Premonstratensians, are Augustinian canons whose main orientation is preaching and pastoral administration but each year they accept a few boys for instruction; boys recommended to them as having *"abilities and potential for religious service."* Catholicism was central but with a heavy emphasis on languages as well as history, geography and mathematics.

To say Johann is chubby is a somewhat discreet way to put it. As long as I've known him he has been... well, hefty. Chubby and jolly. A big belly and a big laugh. He lives in one of those townhouses I mentioned, most of which are set upon narrow cobbled streets and practically shoulder to shoulder with nearby shops. He keeps his schoolbooks on a strap and delights in spinning them until they refuse to go no further, then accelerate in the opposite direction. When not in class, he runs errands for the shopkeepers, often helping customers tote their purchases. Frugal but not parsimonious, he is quick to drop a coin in a beggar's hat. Hungry himself, I've seen him take a cold, roasted turkey leg he was about to bite into and give it to a boney, stray dog whimpering in the drizzle of a sunless morning.

And he takes great delight in the holiday street performers, especially the magicians, whom he trails relentlessly to uncover their tricks and make them his own. Johann's father is the bookkeeper at the Boar's Head Inn, the most prestigious lodge in the Tyrol, and he has found it convenient to house his family of two just a stone's throw away. Neither talk of his mother. I once asked of her but the conversation was quickly diverted. Rumor has it that she ran off with a soldier of fortune; some women opt for the rogue over the dependable.

People tell me that they know that I am a Schilling without a second glance, a predisposed exaggeration, of course. A somewhat dark complexion with blond hair is not uncommon in these parts but I suppose the hardy lives of my forbearers navigating mountains on foot and horseback gave impetus to the metamorphosis into the tall and sturdy frames characteristic of our clan.

Academics come easy to me but there is a methodical, personable fellow straddling two cultures in our class who captures top honors from time to time. Being competitive, I'd be lying if I said that this doesn't irk me a bit. His name is Basil Jaborowski. Recently of Poland, he is a consummate student. He and his family would remain in Innsbruck for less than a year. His father, an architectural engineer by training, had been hired by the town to design a bridge across the Sill River. Part of his compensation package was for his son to receive Premonstratensian schooling.

My association with nobility comes through a fellow classmate, Franz von Clausen. Innsbruck is home to but one extension of this prominent family. Franz is a bit hard to know; has his moods, taciturn one might say, yet with an intensity lurking beneath. He is lanky, almost skinny, a counterpoint to Johann, prominent jaw, but you know that someday he will grow into his substantial frame. Johann and I never really felt accepted by his parents, that class thing that is so important to the nobles but Franz's alternatives for companionship were limited.

Franz's former nanny and part-time family staffer, Frau Keller, dotes on us and often has tortes and juices at the ready. "Now you boys need your nourishment. Don't go rushing out without something to eat!" The truth be known, we were more anxious to go rushing in to her culinary domain of heady aromas and homemade pastries.

The von Clausen castle is a bit smaller but more formidable than the Schloss Ambras, a Renaissance castle which will be built by Archduke Ferdinand II several decades from now. Atop the semi-circular stone towers, on a clear day, we can witness the Brenner Pass about 20 miles to the south as the crow flies, much farther by trail, as well as the nomadic Inn River nearby. There is a stately reception room with aloof portraits and an adjoining dining hall with a considerable, sculpted oak table and stately, cushioned chairs. Gilded, ornate ceilings are complemented by priceless sculptures and tapestries. To our joy the castle has a dungeon where we cast imaginary villains and murder holes in the parapets where we dump buckets of water, in place of boiling oil, on the invaders laying siege to the formidable outer walls.

It was at the castle that we first heard some detail about that murder a few years past. The adults were talking querulously about it in the next room and at the same time trying to keep their voices down, almost as if they were embarrassed to discuss it. It was Effie Eberle, the bookkeeper for St. James at the time. She had her own key to the chancery, which is contiguous with the rectory and cathedral, and had always arrived an hour before the others were up and about. She had trauma to her head, as though it was smashed violently against the wall, which was blood stained. On her desk was a closed copy of the New Testament, the bookmark at John 20, and the verses relating to Thomas' interaction with Jesus following the resurrection were underlined. The priests and the cardinal himself were not exempt from Sheriff Mitlstrasser's pointed interrogation but lacking definitive proof the case wallowed in limbo.

The von Clausens have managed the finances of the archdiocese for decades on an almost pro bono basis. They knew Effie very well and were quite distraught that such a thing could happen at all, let alone on church property, although some sneered that their distress was a bit ingenuous. Franz's older brother, Willem, who is many years his senior, had been particularly upset as he was engaged to her. About five feet tall, long lashes over flashing green eyes, curvaceous, she was stunning. His parents had not been thrilled, however, that he wanted to marry a commoner. She was very nice but the line was always drawn sooner or later. They would come up with all sorts of remote aspersions; an eye was always tearing for no reason and she was always blotting it, so unseemly; she was too friendly with the riff raff; her taste in clothes was pedestrian; she pouted too much. Willem knew she had good reason to pout and he balked at every barb.

Shortly before her death, her relationship with Willem had gotten rocky, possibly because of the perfunctory way she was treated by Willem's parents. Many suspected that their marriage would be called off but sentiment pulled for love winning out.

☙

"That was the day you were to go to the chancery to pick-up the prior month's books as I recall," his mother says to Willem. "What reason had you given that peasant, what's his name, Mitlstrasser, as to why you didn't go?" Her sun starved face is almost as white as her lace collar.

"I had put it off on account of the inclement weather."

"Then why did you leave the castle? He knew you did. Someone saw you near here. Now they say you were seen over there."

"When I started out, there were just flurries. I had gone just a half mile or so when it started coming down hard. The wind kept getting stronger and the cold was piercing. I didn't think it worth the trip. You know how quickly conditions can change in these parts. It was getting more miserable by the minute. I was as concerned for my horse as well as myself. You could hardly see your hand in front of your face."

"They do have stables over there. And what of Effie? You loved her you kept telling us. You could have seen her home. Wasn't that the line of questioning?"

"I had told him that we were going through a rough patch. Besides, she'd be better off staying put; they'd put her up at the rectory."

"Do you think he believed you?"

"How do I know what he was thinking? I told you all this ages ago."

"His ambivalence is only natural, my dear. Leave Willem alone. Mitlstrasser didn't charge him with murder then and he won't now," the Baron finally chimes in. "After all, he didn't do it. Why would he? What are you worried about?" He appears to address his glass of wine more than his wife.

"I am worried Ulrich. And where were you that morning?" she says testily. "I came down to fruhstuck and you were nowhere to be found once again. All that food going to waste." She suspected Ulrich of having marital ambiguities then and now, that nobility tradition so to speak.

"Don't start an inquisition on me Louisa; you're not going to spoil my day," he voices in a cadence. "I'm sure that the food wasn't wasted; undoubtedly Frau Keller put it in the hole in the wall.[1]"

"It is a shame all the same. She did come from a nice, educated

---

1   A small hole in the castle wall where leftovers, unable to be preserved, are routinely passed to the poor.

family, her father a biblical scholar and all. And him predeceasing her by only a matter of months. The poor girl." The Baroness rises from her ornate chair and, still limping from a tumble on a stone staircase the previous winter, comes to Willem to embrace him. She could turn from testy to charming with the suddenness of a vagrant spark.

"She was a wonderful girl," adds the Baron sporting a pomaded salt and pepper mane with matching moustache and chiseled beard; his coat as usual draped over his shoulders like a cape.

"I can't deal with this hypocrisy," Wilhem mutters as he abruptly takes his leave. An awkward pause engulfs the parents.

"Ulrich, you must get that boy to rethink his priorities." With the baroness money, power and heritage supersede love and affection.

୧୨

A rumor had recently gained momentum that a passerby had seen Willem walking up to the cathedral door and then slowly back again that fateful morning. Mitlstrasser traced it to a timid store clerk. She found it odd that Willem didn't even try the door. Willem was questioned again…

"No one could be identified that blizzard-like day, regardless of who says what, unless they were nose to nose," said Willem.

"There are lulls in intensity," the sheriff retorts.

"I wasn't there, period. You know these peasants, some real or imagined slight by nobility and the need for revenge seethes until they devise a way to retaliate."

"You offended this woman?"

"I didn't say that."

"But you know each other?"

"This is a small town. You encounter everyone sooner or later."

"A tryst with her perhaps?"

"You're into wild speculation, sheriff! I wasn't there! She can say what she wants but I wasn't there."

The incident itself could very well be true, the sheriff surmises, who would make up such a convoluted observation, *"didn't even try the door?"* Didn't try the door because it dawned on whoever it was that the cathedral doors were always locked that early in the morning? But wouldn't he try it anyway? Or perhaps the murderer, upon exiting the cathedral and being clever, made sure there were footprints leading in both directions thus disguising a telltale clue. But the door was bolted from the inside. Or was there an accomplice? And why would Willem kill his fiancée? Was her death an accident of rage? What the sheriff also didn't know was that Effie's father, on his deathbed, revealed something to her that could undermine the very foundation of the Church itself. But I'll deal with that in due course.

Another persisting rumor is that an incubus[2] killed her. The clergy certainly won't deny the possibility. Dad says that the perpetrators of such rumors are just ignorant, superstitious. Then he has second thoughts, even many educated and intelligent people don't question it.

ℰ𝒟

In our teen years we occasionally hike to an abandoned, horseshoe shaped quarry. Late one summer morning, Franz and I decide to scale its face once again, ascending by fingertips and footholds. As we rise, so does the sun and the accompanying heat. Franz discovers as he is near the top, about sixty feet up, that he has no place to go. Worse yet, he has no room to maneuver.

---

2   Incubus - a devil that descends upon and has sexual intercourse with a woman.

"Rafer!" he calls. "Rafer!"

"What?"

"I'm in big trouble. I'm stuck. I can't even turn around."

"Go back down!"

"I can't. I would but I can't."

About two yards above and four to his left, I look down and survey the situation as best I can. His forehead is alive with perspiration, how much from heat and how much from fear I do not know. I can clearly see the red laces of both leather shoes, almost all of which are standing on air. The left hand clings to a tiny bare root that snakes from the dry, light brown dirt smearing the face of the unforgiving rock. Small lines of residue sporadically trail downward as he tugs it to keep his balance. His right hand appears to be just resting against the wall, unable to find anything to clutch.

"Johann!" I shout. "Johann!" I scan the floor of this man-made canyon. When last seen, he was dozing against a boulder. "Johann! Where the hell are you? Johann!" The silence is sickening. Even if I can get close to Franz, which I doubt, there is nothing that I can do for him. "Franz, hold on! I'm almost at the top. Two yards. I'll get help."

"No time. I can't hold much longer, Rafer. I'm going to fall."

"You're not going to fall, damn it. I'm almost up."

Just then Johann appears at the rim. He had already gone the long way around to meet us at the top. "Did someone call?" he asks facetiously.

"You dumb S.O.B. We have an emergency here. Franz is teetering. Get the rope from our old tree house!" I was desperate. I didn't even know if it was still there.

"What rope?"

"The one on the ladder. And bring the ladder too. Hurry! Hurry!"

Johann can only see the top of Franz's head; the latter's face buried in the wall. To his credit, Johann ascertains instantly that the rope would provide our only access and he is off. The tree house is near but I worry as the seconds pass.

I reach for the top but the bone dry ground breaks away. Instinct and a well-placed vine stop my fall almost at once. I glance at Franz; he has ignored the commotion, a leg is quivering on its tentative perch. My skin is burning from the abrasions and blood trickles into my left eye. I start back.

The ladder slides by me in the direction of Franz. The rope is still tied to it with the other end twisted around Johann's wrist. Franz eases his right elbow between some rungs while grimacing in pain. Hand over hand Johann pulls the rope towards himself and then the ladder rung by rung. Clearing the lip is a problem.

"Rafer, I need you," Johann shouts.

"I'm here. I'm here." As Johann makes a final tug I grab Franz by the belt and we drag him onto the top. All collapse, exhausted.

"Jesus!" I gasp.

"Amen," replies Johann.

"You guys," gushes Franz. "You're unbelievable."

"Johann, if I'm ever in a crisis, I want you beside me," I say.

Franz leans towards Johann and grabs his hand. "Johann, I am forever in your debt." He then reaches across and takes mine. "Both of you, thanks, I... I thought I was going to die."

"The Lord was with us," says Johann. Our vigor comes back about the same time and we sit up, extending our arms behind us as props. "We better not mention this to our parents," says Johann. They'd skin us alive for getting into this predicament in the first place."

"My mother knows we had been climbing here; she told me that I wasn't to do it anymore. Boy, was she right," says Franz.

"Then it's our secret," Johann says. "Let that be the end of it."

"Come on!" I say, standing up. "Let's go into town and get some tortes mit schlag. I want to celebrate being alive." Apollo butterflies flutter past us as if in affirmation.

"I'm for that," Johann says, hurriedly joining me.

"I'm buying! I'm buying!" Franz insists, digging his hands into his pockets. Ten steps later, he says, "Hey! Can anybody lend me some money?"

☙

Thereafter, we are inseparable. In fact, friends and neighbors refer to us as "*The Troika.*" But trips to the quarry are no longer on our agenda. Our inclinations turn to competitive activities. The merchant guild holds trade fairs intermittently from spring through autumn coupled with sporting contests to attract crowds. Teams are sponsored to promote their businesses.

Herr Carberry is instrumental in getting the Boar's Head Inn to sponsor our gang. It is, also, about the time that we become acquainted with the owner's son, Albert Freihofer. Albert isn't "*one of the boys*" so to speak. Likable enough but not outgoing and gregarious like his father. This is a major disappointment to Herr Freihofer since he expects his son to eventually take over the inn and such qualities in a proprietor are important.

Herr Freihofer, Fritz to his friends, is a fair complexioned, portly bundle of energy who walks with feet pointed at a nine to three, the ultimate factotum who fusses over his cliental like a doting grandparent. His partially bald pate wreathed in graying black hair is set off by joyous hazel eyes and a hearty spirit, a handkerchief frequently mopping his brow. Never a swear word to be voiced. He agrees to sponsor our team if we will befriend and encourage athleticism in his son, whose build seems to be progressing towards that of his father. Part of the reason, he confesses, is his guilt in not being more involved in a personal way with Albert. The inn is a jealous mistress further complicated by Albert losing his mother in childbirth.

Johann knows Albert from previous visits to the inn to see his own father. While known to each other, a relationship never developed. After being introduced to the deal, however, the rest of us are anxiously looking forward to meeting this curious character. Johann is the bait and after ostensibly coming to see his father once again, and receiving the good news about the sponsorship, he invites Albert to join him and some of his friends to roam the trade fair. Albert's father is on hand to release him from his restaurant duties and Albert accepts tentatively. Three of us are at the wrestling venue, as prearranged, when Johann and Albert come waddling up.

"You guys, this is Albert Freihofer. His pop owns the Boar's Head Inn and he's agreed to sponsor us."

"Ja! Ja! Wunderbar!" the chorus goes up.

Albert shuffles his feet a bit, waves his right hand in a semi-circular motion at us, and says, "Yo!"

There are a few sheepish grins. Tongue in cheek I wave back in kind and give voice with my own "Yo!"

The others quickly follow in unison. "Yooo!" Some try to stifle smirks. I thought that we may have killed the golden goose right there but Albert takes it in stride. After names are traded, we soon learn that physical activity is not one of Albert's priorities.

"Albert, we could use another wrestler," says Franz. "We don't have any depth there. Rafer is our sole entrant so far; he could train you."

"No desire to interlock my limbs with a sweaty, smelly body. Offend my nasal sensitivities, I should say. Nothing personal, Rafer." Eyes widen; Albert certainly has a distinct way of expressing himself.

"How about the foot races?" is volunteered, although he certainly isn't built for speed.

"Wouldn't think of it my good fellow, hasten only under threat of physical impairment."

"He could compete in the log toss with me," says Johann.

"Wouldn't climb a tree let alone pick one up my boy."

His singular manner of speech aside, he does convey exactly where he stands. There is no question that he has no enthusiasm for sports and he doesn't proffer input as to how he might fit in. I do detect, however, a real desire for camaraderie.

We make our way to the archery stalls where a half dozen targets stand at the base of a berm. Bows and arrows are available for the taking since the event isn't in progress. Each position has a small wooden barrel containing nine copper tipped arrows. This has real possibilities for Albert, I say to myself, more a matter of skill than rigorous activity. For all his flabbiness, he is deceptively strong and he can bend the stiffest bow with relative ease. His arrow hits the bullseye on his first try. Mission accomplished.

Franz is our sprint man. He is very fast and never places less than third. Being a contender, he is a valued member of the team but I always have a sense that the others feel a bit discombobulated around him. It isn't that he ever says or does anything that one could reprove; he is principled to a fault. It is just that at times he is a castaway adrift, unsure if he wants to be rescued. I suppose it is more that he is uncomfortable around others and they sense it. Not adept at repartee, he opts for reticence.

Reggie Snuffle, born of unsettled times and orphaned at ten, navigated the North Sea and an uncertain traverse to reside in Austria with his maternal aunt, who did so a few years prior as the bride of an Innsbruck commodities broker. Snuff complements Franz in the running events. A slight, wiry guy with a craggy face and prominent nose that arrives seconds before he does, he scampers long distances over hills and valleys like a gazelle romping across an African plain. A mischievous fellow, who embellishes our native tongue with his East End London accent, he is the antipode of Franz. Quick with a joke or story, he will have people contorted in laughter within minutes of his appearance. Outrageous, one might say, hyperbole being his method of communication. The only other confederate brandishing such a wit is Harry Schmidt but years will pass for him to declare his presence. As with so many others, Harry will stop in Innsbruck for respite from his journey; decide to extend that respite, and discover that there are more reasons to stay than continue on.

At a corner of the tavern of the Boar's Head, at off hours when the place is virtually empty, Herr Freihofer will let us congregate and he will treat us to cheese, olives, fresh bread and chunks of baked cod not long from the cold waters of the Baltic and occasionally to slices of prized cold meat. The beverage is usually water with chopped ice from the ice house but now, in the fall, a pitcher of sturm will be put on the table. Grape juice emboldened by a yeasty fizz and part way on its journey to wine, this murky concoction is tasty nevertheless and one of our favorites.

Wine making in these parts can be traced back to Celtic times, long before the arrival of the Romans. Many monasteries make wine on their premises and, in addition to quenching the monks thirst, provide some needed income. Our wines are fresh and usually drunk young and are not as sweet as those of our German cousins. Now that their wine is being heavily taxed, the Bavarians are brewing more and more beer instead. But the demand for wine is still dominant at the Boar's Head and white is favored over red since our climate isn't kind to the latter.

Assembled there during such a confabulation, and having woofed down some of these low charged libations, I abruptly announce that my father and I have all but finished building a canoe. And at the close of the year's games next weekend, I am taking Elsa Obernesser on its maiden voyage. Girls haven't been our focus and the response is indicative of the adolescents that we are.

"Whoa! Whoa! Whoa!"

"Oooh! Oooh! Oooh!"

"Hey! Hey! Hey!"

"Can she swim?" Franz asks, being practical in nature. Everybody laughs.

"I saw her in the Herr Heibel's butcher shop. You know, Chop Chop Klaus. I said, '*Hey babe, care to join me on a cruise down the Inn?*' She swooned and the deal was done."

"Yeah, right! And I guess we'll being seeing less of Rafer from now on."

"You got that right," I say. "It's eye candy from now on. Besides, a man's got to do what a man's got to do."

"Which is?"

"Snuff, take him aside sometime!"

"Taking her to the dance for the close of festivities?"

"Certainement."

"Yo Rafer! You are something else."

"Leaving you guys in the dust bins of frustration, as usual," I respond.

"Not sa fast. Not sa fast. I avn't mentioned this to anyone but Rafe. I've asked Stella Chiapparelli tah thuh dance," says Snuff.

"Whooah!"

"That fast Italian model, I'm still not sure you can handle her?" I say.

"Shiiit! Wimmen, once they knows me they can't live wit out me." Johann and Franz flush a bit, two straighter guys don't exist. Both are awkward around the opposite sex. Albert shuffles uncomfortably.

"Albert, reserve a table for us. In fact, Elsa plans to bring three of her girlfriends. Snuff, if Stella loses her allure for you, let me know and I'll see if she can make it four."

"Thar's a better chance the sun wunt cum up tammarah."

"Right, lover boy! Are the rest of you all right with it?" I'm met with vacant stares. "Well, I don't want anyone to be stood up."

Johann and Franz look at each other. "Yeah, alright," they say, not brimming with confidence. Albert remains silent, although he will be there by default.

⁕

Elsa is tentative as I hold the canoe alongside the bank of the Inn but she manages to make the transition from shore to craft with poise and grace. There are seats in the bow and stern, each about three inches below the gunwale; Elsa takes the bow seat. I step in and push off with my paddle. The river moves slowly here and there isn't a ripple to be seen.

"This is special," Elsa says. "You and your Dad made it. Wow! Tell me more, Rafer."

"The toughest part was steaming and shaping the wood ribs and planking. Then we covered them with birch bark and bound everything with natural sinews. Gums and pine pitch were used to make the canoe watertight."

"It seems to handle easily enough."

"It handles best if we keep it on a level trim; I'm told."

"You're told? Rafer, is this the first time you have been in the boat?"

"Well, as you said, it seems easy enough."

"Yes, it does, but it I get the feeling that it wouldn't be hard to tip over."

"Think positive."

"Alright, I'll go with the flow," she giggles. Elsa is substantially lighter than I causing the bow to tilt up a bit but we glide along just fine.

"Grab your paddle. I'll paddle on the starboard, the right side, and you paddle on the port, the left side, unless I say otherwise. I'll do most of the steering." Elsa is a quick study and is feathering the paddle by instinct, adding to our efficiency of movement. The only shakiness is when she turns her head to look at me during our chatter back and forth. Her smile is like stolen sunshine.

A bit west of town, we glide downstream on the mirror like surface as though we have been a team for years. We are okay until I decide to leave the right bank and steer towards the outside of an upcoming bend. I soon learn that the current is quicker there and we pick up speed. The water becomes a bit choppy and even faster as the river drops off as we get closer to town. The current pushes us broadside and exposes my inexperience. The flow works to tilt us over, the starboard gunwale being licked by the river, some water spills into the canoe.

"Lean a bit to port, to the left," I say. The stern is being nudged more downstream than planned. In short order we are careening downstream backwards with my feeling sillier by the second.

"It's more exciting this way," Elsa says, laughing, her comment going a long way to restore some of my dignity.

"That's why I did it," I respond, laughing in contradiction of my words.

"There are some rapids a ways down," she laughs again. "I'm not sure I'm ready for that much excitement."

"Not to fear. I'll get us back on course. Let's both paddle starboard." Some chop catches the bow and we turn one hundred and eighty degrees. At least we are going forward I confide to myself. Somehow I'm not concerned. Elsa looks soft and beautiful and I am falling in love while sitting in a runaway canoe.

"My hero!" she exclaims.

"Shall we sail onward to the Danube?" I jest.

"I don't think we'll make it, Rafer; we are taking on water up here."

"Water coming in? Oh boy. Not good. Better head for shore. Long, hard, steady strokes," I say. "We're an experienced team, now."

"I'm so confident when I'm with you," she laughs. "And the cool water inching up my legs is so refreshing."

"All part of my plan to show you a good time." With a fortuitous drift of the current we glide to the river bank. Just as we pull alongside, the canoe settles down into shallow water and rests on the bottom. We start laughing at our circumstances. "It doesn't get any better than this," I say.

Suddenly, Elsa starts bouncing about with sounds of alarm. "What is it?" Without even turning to me, she raises her left hand, holding a frog by the foot. She flicks it into the river and then gasps in relief. Once again, we start laughing.

I wade forward, put my arms under hers and lift her to her feet. Feeling her close to me gives me a rush. She grabs some brush to pull herself up the embankment as I keep the canoe steady and lend a hand. After tipping the canoe over, Elsa helps me maneuver it onto the river bank.

The sun helps but with our clothes sopping wet we are a bit chilly as we walk along the river path. She is tall with a fair complexion and a sculptured body. Her golden hair now straight with wetness. She has an inner strength and a tipped-up smile. No other girls compare. I put my arm around her small waist under the pretense of providing warmth. "This is nice," I say.

"You mean strolling along listening to our bones rattle."

"Music to my ears."

"Was this part of your plan?"

"Am I that transparent?"

"I'm glad to be part of it," she says as she leans into me.

"Are you up to jogging? It might warm us up."

"I'll race you to the edge of town," she says.

"You're on," I say, bursting into a trot. Each time a shoe hits the ground it is answered with a squish. Our clothes, blotched with sediment, present quite a sight to the passersby.

ᏨᎧ

The athletic events long over, the merrymaking is in full swing. Outdoors and in, everywhere you turn there are tables covered with sautéed fish and cheeses, vine ripened fruits and exquisitely crafted Bavarian desserts. Hand held mugs of beer and glasses of wine bob like corks on the sea. The lowering sun plays hide and seek among the rooftops and puts the towering mountains into silhouette as torch lighters make their way to prepare for the inevitable night. Deep bass sounds rumble from the bands and Tyrolese bedecked in colorful costumes dance in the streets and in the taverns coaxing others to frolic with them. Elsa lives in town but our date isn't for another hour. It had become easier to keep track of time now since clocks made in the metal working towns of Augsburg and Nuremberg had become fashionable and many businesses were proud to display them. Many clocks just have one hand moving among the numbered hours. Strolling about, I bump into Snuff.

"I didn't get you a girl, lover boy. You're all set with Stella, I take it?"

"No need, me mon. Wimmen find me irritable."

"I think you mean irresistible. Let's snatch a couple of libations."

"Yah goht it."

We literally swipe beers off a table from the unsuspecting. On this occasion, antics from the boys are part of the entertainment and manage a forgiving nod. The air is filled with the smell of fresh made bread as we pass a bakery. We wander down the streets and alleys, beers in hand, talking about the recent contests, girls and the night ahead of us. Inescapably, the conversation turns to sex.

"Owld dyah fairst lairn bout thuh act?"

"The act... from a visiting cousin, he's three years older."

"Shock yah?"

"I told him he was gross and weird. Let's face it. Kind of bizarre when you first hear it. Thought he was putting me on, older cousins will do that. But he persisted, gave me a biology lesson. Still wasn't sure about believing him."

"If yuh add trouble withe at, whoat of homosexuals, two men goin at it?"

"Snuff, give me a break; it's not something that I've given any thought. You get on the damnedest topics."

A conversation with Snuff is always stimulating. The topics invariably border on the lusty, illegal or outrageous. Franz, in particular, will often outwardly cringe at his flamboyant observations. But Snuff gives toxicity to our otherwise antiseptic group. And he never misses an opportunity to tweak people's sensibilities, which is another bonus. So I enjoy myself thoroughly as we walk, talk, swipe more beers, and drink away the waning daylight to the beat of the Oktoberfest percussions.

❧

Elsa's mother, a stately and polite woman with a lenient voice, answers my knock and invites me into her home. She leads me to the common room, where Herr Obernesser sits facing the hearth; at first I thought he was dozing. His legs are stretched out and arms crossed at the chest. I want to make a good impression so my mind is racing. The beers haven't helped.

"Ernst, this is Rafer Schilling. He's the young man who will be taking Elsa to the Oktoberfest," she says trying to hide an amused look knowing his lack of enthusiasm for the encounter. He turns to take suitable if postponed notice of my being; his manner doesn't convey warmth.

"Guten abend," he grumbles with prickly undertones. His good evening doesn't convey sincerity as it takes its place in the inventory of my mind.

I respond with the same salutation but more heartfelt, adding "Sorry about the canoe, hic." *Oh boy, that last beer was one too many,* flashes across my mind.

"What canoe? Sorry for what?" looking straight at me, a thing he had not considered before. I was briefly unsettled by the directness of his gaze.

Now I did it, I thought to myself. Elsa evidently made it to her room without being seen. "Elsa didn't tell you about the canoe? My father saw one some months back on Lake Constance. But it's a long story... are you going, hic, to the festivities?"

"So what is there to be sorry about?"

"Well, everything didn't go as planned,"

"Didn't go as planned? Your father saw one on Lake Constance and you apologize to me?"

"Well, we built one and eh…"

"You took Elsa in it out on the river?" he glares at me searchingly. "You may have drowned her? Didn't you know that those things are unstable? I know about canoes."

"Nein, sir. I mean ja sir. Not really. I mean, hic... Elsa knows how to swim."

"Elsa knows how to swim! That river is dangerous, boy. It's narrow and swift… and cold. Do you have any sense at all?"

"Nein sir. I mean ja sir. I mean, it's not all that cold now."

"Elsa!" her mother calls, fully aware of the pregnant pause.

"Ernst, Rafer is the son of Erich Schilling for goodness sakes," as if this is enough to excuse my perceived indiscretions.

"Is that so," he says rhetorically. "Your father is quite a man," he adds, leaving the impression that I am not a chip off the old block. "Why do you take my daughter out?" I am not sure where to go with this one. I fidget in silent perplexity. I redden. My jaw sags. I have flashbacks to my discourse with Snuff. *I have good intentions,* I insist to myself.

"To show her a good time. I mean… I think we'd enjoy each other's company. Oktoberfest and all." His look isn't comforting. Frau Obernesser gives me a bolstering, sympathetic glance. Elsa comes down the stairs. My heart leaps; she is gorgeous.

"Hello! Rafer. Sorry to keep you. Thought my hair would never dry," she winks.

"You look lovely, Dear," says her mother. "Doesn't she Ernst?"

"Ja," says Ernst glancing at her, making sure she is appropriately attired.

"Well, nice meeting you Herr Obernesser. Frau Obernesser, hic," I say, moving with purpose to the door.

"Frau Obernesser and I will be at the festivities," says her father almost as a warning.

Elsa doesn't react to the chill in the air. She nonchalantly kisses her parents goodbye before joining me at the door.

"Be back here by ten thirty!" her father scolds. I hear him mumble under his breath, "That boy must have had too much bratwurst."

"Ja. Ja," I say. I feel much better when the door closes behind us. Elsa smiles and takes my arm.

"Is it me, hic?" I ask.

"It's any young man," she replies. "Fathers are very protective of daughters. Do I smell beer on your breath?"

"Ya, it's Oktoberfest you know."

"It's Oktoberfest!" she acknowledges. "The girls are to be at the river by the Boar's Head. If all goes as planned, we should meet up with everybody about the same time."

The heady scent of burning autumn leaves suspended in the dwindling dusk makes for an auspicious start. The town folk are in a jolly mood as we join them ambling through the streets. A black cat with white paws takes it all in from the secure shadows of a vacant alley, unsure if he wants to be a participant.

"There they are," I say, when the Boar's Head comes into view. To help Elsa register who is who, I point out that Johann Carberry is the hefty one standing there rather rigidly with his hands in his pockets but, nevertheless, chatting away. Franz von Clausen is the taller one on the periphery, almost as a spectator. His shy counterpart on the distaff side, I am about to learn, is coy little Frieda. She wears a vulnerable smile and appears despairing of love, her visage seeming to dither between plainness and cute. Albert Freihofer is the one with the sneezing fit, which seems to be triggered by any contact with teenage girls. As we approach, Albert is throwing a few high priced words around between snorts and the girls don't quite know what to make of him. Their eyes drift about and, when they do focus, it is with expressionless stares.

"Are these jokers unsettling you ladies?" I say. "I can see how you would be troubled; they don't seem to have much going for them."

The girls snicker as they spot Elsa. Joanna, who seems to have taken an interest in Johann, responds with some warmth in her kind eyes complemented by blushing cheeks. "Oh, I don't know; I see potential."

I turn to Elsa and say, "Your friend is very compassionate."

"You are not being very nice," Elsa says, laughing.

"This guy thinks he's a prize!" responds Johann. "Why, no one has figured out yet."

"Well, the night is young. Maybe you ladies can unleash that potential but I'm not optimistic," I retort. "Shall we venture into the inn?"

"One dunking is enough today, thank you," Elsa whispers with a twinkle in her eye.

The white and grey marble terrace of the Boar's Head Inn reaches handsomely off the main dining room towards the river. The surrounding lawn and clay pots blossom with thirsty edelweiss and multi-colored wild flowers, some transplanted from the greenhouse. Herr Freihofer reserved a choice dining room table near the terrace perimeter for us. By default, the other young lady, dimple cheeked Adelais, is paired with Albert.

"Aey yuh rhowdies," Snuff yells as he bursts on the scene with petite Stella at his side. Black hair, deep dark eyes, lunging breasts, nothing happens slowly with Stella. Both have mugs of sturm in their hands. The observers' eyes pop at the sight of these two.

"Yea!!! Snuff," I yell. With the exception of Elsa, the other girls sink into self-consciousness. Snuff drapes his right arm over Stella's shoulder, still holding his mug in his left hand.

"Laidies. Gennlmin... Stel...lah," he says pointing towards her with his mug. I em Snuff."

I volunteer the names of the others, going clockwise around the circular table. Stella and Snuff take their seats, their feet struggle to reach the floor. A bartender is polishing a glass while a waiter comes by and lights the candles at the center of the table giving Albert an acknowledging wink at the same time. Another pours a citrus drink in all the steins and leaves another pitcher on the table. As the waiters are retreating, Snuff pulls a flask from his pocket and goes about pouring a sprig of distilled spirit into everyone's drink. The surplus he dumps into the pitcher. The girls look wide-eyed. "Atl puht aire oin yer chests, boyz." Then he adds, "Yooh too, goils." The girls giggle. "To thuh Boar Heads!" he says, raising his mug. After some surreptitious glances, all follow his lead and drink the fortified beverage.

A bass drum leads the band back into action and the girls look at their opposites trying not to look too hopeful. Elsa takes the initiative by going around the table and pulling each guy up by the arm. "Let's go! Outside! Onto the dance floor!" as she motions to the terrace with her head. A good part of the evening is spent with the girls giving dance instructions to their counterparts. This makes for a mixture of levity and frustration as often the messages don't get from their brains to their feet. Most eventually take refuge at the table inside.

Stella proves to be down to earth and is soon accepted by the other girls. She, Joanna and Frieda, during a break in the music, step out onto the far end of the terrace for some confidential girl talk. Under a waxing, crescent moon, they catch the attention of four boys ambling along the road just steps from the river. These boys start walking up the embankment making advances as they go.

"She looks like a gypsy to me," one of them says, gawking at Stella.

"Hey, gypsy! Need a man to take care of you?" says another in a surly voice.

"Yeah! But I don't see one," she replies.

"Wise bitch," is the retort just as Snuff happens on the scene.

"She looks tough, Walker," are you sure you can handle her?"

"All my bitches submit in the end; I'd say it's her turn now," it is the same churlish, gruff voice. His hair is knotted in the back which tightens the skin at his hollow eyes and contributes to an unforced, melancholy smirk. He is taller than the others with a broad back and long, loping arms. He is only a few yards from Stella and still closing.

"Walker, you're my man," says one of the bunch smiling deliciously to divulge his chipped teeth spaced like headstones in a country churchyard. The trailing two middleweights swagger in his wake touting their toughness.

"Ehs thair ah probe lem, eahr?" inquires Snuff.

"Look at the runt! Is that your idea of a man?" the boisterous one that they refer to as Walker asks. He and his abbreviated militia laugh.

"Talks funny, too," says the one in serious need of dental work.

"Yeah, that's my idea of a man. What about it?" Stella is not one to retreat.

"Obviously, you haven't been on my couch." Hess looks back at his buddies and snickers.

Snuff abruptly hands two flagons to a startled partygoer and runs head first into Hess' stomach leaving him curled up and gasping for air. He then wheels and brings his right elbow up into the chin of Mr. Tooth Decay fracturing another tooth and forcing his withdrawal to spit blood. As Snuff looks for his next victim, each arm is grabbed from behind by the other bounders. Walker Hess, shaking off the hit, gets up and moves in for the slaughter. A series of punches to Snuff's body and head smashes his valor and nose turning his face into a bloody landscape and splattering Stella's dress. Stella, arms whirling, propels herself at Hess only to be shoved to the ground. Snuff is dropped like a sack of flour next to her.

"Stupid bitch," Hess snarls, wiping the back of his bruised hand across his mouth.

"Knave," Joanna replies, joining the altercation as she stoops to help Snuff.

"I'll get the boys," yells Frieda as she races back towards the dining room. Bystanders drawn to the commotion are milling about bewildered by the ferocity and suddenness of it all. With some parting obscene gestures, the antagonists shuffle back down the slope into the quasi darkness. By the time Frieda blurts out what's happened and we rush to the scene, they are gone.

"It all happened so fast," explains Frieda as Joanna comforts Stella. "It's just crazy."

We take Snuff to the lavatory to get him cleaned up. He no sooner looks somewhat presentable than he pukes into a basin. We aren't sure if he got sick from the beating, the spirits, or both. Herr Freihofer arranges for some medical attention and then I escort Snuff home. When I return to the inn, we commiserate with each other and try to remain upbeat. Elsa and I dance the evening away nonplused by lack of proficiency. My feelings for her grow stronger with every touch. From this day forward, we only date each other. Neither of us are ready for marriage but without any formal commitment, we still consider each other that special one.

❧

Another remarkable incident during these teen years would impact our lives. During an unusually warm spell in mid-February, Johann, Franz and I decide to take an afternoon hike in the woods. Buoyed by the spring-like weather, like migrating geese we set off towards the quarry that we used to frequent some years past. We saunter along taking in the stark beauty, telling jokes and trading friendly insults. We happily amble our way among the evergreens, which are every-where, still defying the elements regardless of season. Our slow pace brings us to the quarry at dusk so Franz, being the most practical, suggests that we turn about so as to avoid the whole trek back in total darkness. But I notice a delinquent light flickering beyond the tangled brush.

"There's a fire deep in the horseshoe," I say.

"I don't see anything," says Johann.

"Come on, follow me!" I say as I start jogging down the dirt path.

Advancing a hundred yards further, the glint becomes a spectral glow accentuated by the fast approaching night. We press on as howling sounds now grip our ears. Quietly we approach the edge of a clearing and crouch behind a fallen tree. To our astonishment there are eleven half naked women circling the fire in buoyant chasse steps. All wear knee length skirts of black leather strips with a few blood red strips interspersed here and there; masks partially cover their faces. Hands almost touching and with trance-like movements they float with an eerie quiet. Easing to a graceful stop, the quiet is broken when, in unison, they emit low and mournful howls. If I wasn't seeing this with my own eyes, I would be hard pressed to distinguish the sound from an itinerant wolf pack wandering the wilderness. The dance is repeated yet again in the opposite direction.

A woman enters from obscurity and kneels as the others form a semi-circle behind her. She raises her arms as if pleading to the gallant moon and loudly proclaims, "Call me Purveyor of Purgatory." She continues with what at first I think is gibberish until I realize it is a transposition of words. "Us against trespass who those forgive we as trespasses our us forgive and, bread daily our, day this us Give."

At the conclusion of this dyslexic prayer, a young, bare chested male acolyte in goat skin pants and wolf mask appears from nowhere and lights an array of candles on what we ascertain to be an altar of boards set upon piled rocks. As he withdraws we see movement from the rear periphery as an imposing figure rises in the shadows from a roughhewn throne and, with slow, measured steps, proceeds up a slope to a position behind the altar. He wears an iridescent goatskin robe which shimmers in the light of the fire and a grotesque goat-like mask with horns. He places something on the altar and we have to tax our eyes to recognize a tiny black lamb with its mouth bound shut and legs tied together.

"Beee Elzebub, our most high," he implores, raising his arms with palms extended upwards in supplication. "We gather here to offer you sacrifice and to baptize by fire a new servant for your legions." The priest, what else should I call him, slits the throat of the lamb and collects its blood in what appears to be a wooden chalice. With considered steps he moves down the slope and leans the chalice against the lips of the kneeling woman, who in turn sups from it. He then tosses the chalice into the fire; we watch it roll to the edge and then down an embankment. He withdraws a branding iron from the fire and, pointing it directly at us, the tiny red hot tip appears to read *coc* in the blackness. The acolyte pours water on it, the steam absorbing a cluster of heat.

"Purveyor of Purgatory," he commands, "touch your forehead to the Earth, the preserve of the Satan."

Remaining on her knees, the woman places her forearms and forehead to the ground. In one swift motion, as her skirt parts, the iron is lightly touched to her left buttock. With a shriek she falls forward gasping and groaning before falling into semi-consciousness. A liquid is poured on her buttock.

"Bring the Roll," the priest commands, throwing the branding iron aside. At the ready, a woman with parchment and quill in hand comes forward and in turn offers her back as a writing surface. The priest puts quill to paper and at the same time makes another declaration. "Purveyor of Purgatory, be admitted to the Coven of Constance and receive all powers and benefits appurtenant thereto."

The acolyte puts the parchment in a black, tube-like case and then twists the branding iron into the dirt presumably to extinguish its scorching residue. The priest points to two of the women who dutifully come forward and each takes one of his hands. They walk into the shadows and disappear as the others tend to the branded woman and disassemble the altar.

Perhaps thirty minutes pass when the priest's distaff selections scurry back to the others. He reappears and summons everyone to him. Turning his back on them, he raises his arms once again and requests, "Spirits of the Dead, do not deny us your solace, when our time shall come." His words no sooner leave his mouth when vagrant clouds shelter the full moon darkening the sky and a wrathful wind begins to stir. The temperature falls, flurries of snow swirl amid claps of thunder.

Visibility is cut to just a few feet. The lee of the fallen tree is our only shelter. Shivering, in only light clothing, we huddle together for warmth, gawking at each other in disbelief. Five minutes or so later the sky begins to clear and the winds wane. We aren't in a hurry to leave the womb of the tree or be discovered so we wait another ten minutes. I am compelled, however, not to miss anything, so I poke my head above the fallen tree and am surprised to see all gone except for the acolyte and a man holding a bag with part of the iridescent robe sticking out. Startled, I sit back down. Johann and Franz look at me inquiringly. "What is it?" Franz asks. I just shake my head and motion them to be quiet.

We bide our time waiting for the random sounds to cease. I look about again. I see and hear nothing. Uncannily, the moon reappears in full color and the temperature softens. My friends join me for a look around. A dampened fire covered with wet ash and dirt are all that remain.

Stories of such gatherings, of course, have been told for centuries. And there are persons, mostly old hags, who people say cast spells. But these women were not old and this is the first time that I ever came across a so called sabbat, a gathering of witches from near and far. I say far because Constance is a bit over a hundred miles away as the crow flies, or should I say as a witch flies.

Bernard of Como's *Tractatus de Strigiis*, written not long ago, in 1508, comes to mind. This Dominican inquisitor proclaimed the reality of sabbats and transvections (witch flights). Witches, he said, are given to night rides and the bewitching of children. The devil comes to them in human form; they deny the faith and pledge their allegiance to him. Since I was old enough to know of such tales, my father would ridicule them as nonsense. My mother, on the other hand, would shudder and make the sign of the cross. My mind is racing. Franz breaks the silence.

"All those stories of witches, they are true." No one immediately replies. "They were worshiping the devil; they were."

"That they were," Johann finally acknowledges Franz.

"It's all true. We saw it with our own eyes!" says Franz. Again, there is no immediate response. "They flew here from Constance. We have to report this to the Church. This is scary."

"We saw a cult; it was an initiation ceremony," I finally reply. "We didn't see anyone fly in or out. We saw nothing supernatural."

"But it was dark. The storm," Franz answers.

"It's scary alright," says Johann.

"I never came across anything like this before. I have always been skeptical of such tales. But what did we actually see? It was a ceremony. A weird ceremony... but still, when it comes down to it, it was just a bizarre ceremony." I then threw the ball to Johann. "What say you, Johann? Did you witness the supernatural?" Both Franz and I look at him as he hesitates.

"The whole context favors what Franz says... but technically you're right. We didn't see anything supernatural... most likely there was debauchery, the leader and the two women going off together. And the dancing."

"There will be an inquisition in Innsbruck within a month if this gets out. This is how rumors get started. What I know of inquisitions... not to my liking," I say.

"Rumors! We saw it with our own eyes!" Franz almost shouts.

"What did we see, Franz? A few crazies running around in the dark," I reply.

"But the devil invoked a storm."

"It was a snow squall. Not that uncommon around here; you know that. And it wasn't the devil," I add.

"How can you be sure?" Franz shoots back.

"How can you be sure that it was the devil?"

"But the debauchery?" Franz insists.

"Cults often center on sexual gratification; so Snuff tells me anyway. He seems to be way ahead of us on all things bizarre."

"It was sacrilegious, a distortion of the Mass," Franz insists.

"He has a point," says Johann.

"Sacrilege alright, but did either of you actually see anything supernatural?" I ask.

"We didn't see everything because of the storm," replies Franz. "Or the storm cut things short."

"But did you see anything supernatural? Did you?"

"Nein!" he answers almost angrily.

"Then if we report this all the superstitious nuts will come out of the woodwork," I add. "And we will be at the center of it."

"Rafer makes a good point, Franz. Which is worse? Us not reporting a weird gathering or possibly unleashing a bogus inquisition. If something else happens, maybe then we should say something."

"Franz?" I challenge, for added emphasis.

"The town will be turned upside down, that's for sure. It seems that every time that we come to this place we have to keep our mouths shut."

"Let's get out of here; it's getting late," I volunteer. I pick up the singed chalice and wipe it off; it has an obscure symbol. I wrap it in my handkerchief and worry that Franz won't be able to keep his mouth shut.

"What disconcerted you?" Johann says to me on the fly.

"Not now, I just want to get out of here." I reply.

CHAPTER 2

THE MIDWIFE

Mostly, she was simply referred to as *"Anna the midwife."* Living alone in the countryside certainly didn't enrich her public persona. Hardship was her companion, if she had one at all. I come to know all this from her own lips, long after the fact. What struck me was her ability to absorb the hurt and persevere with dignity, although she had every excuse for melancholy.

The modest piece of land that she takes over when her father passes away contains a small apple orchard, which generates some income. An ample garden provides some food, which she jars for herself but some is sold, a few chickens for a few eggs. An exceptional talent as a seamstress enables her to wholesale hand sewn frocks, sweaters, scarves, quilts and the like to the town general store but this is time consuming and production is meager. Her main income derives from her midwife fees. She works dawn to well after dusk. As rugged an existence as it is, what she fears most is illness and old age. A husband would come in handy, her practical side tells her, as well as a few able bodied children. She is really a very young woman but her mature bearing and hard life makes her seem much older.

To be quite frank, Anna is rather plain. She knows that she is more substantial than the vain world will acknowledge but is still self-conscious about her slightly bent nose and situation.

If pretty is the initial attraction for men, nothing ever really gets started. That is until a young itinerant laborer passes by in early March, the year being 1517, some months before the Reformation ever gets underway and before I am born. He offers to perform some manual tasks for food, lodging and a small stipend. Itinerants don't have a good reputation as to dependability and trustworthiness. Anna is intelligent and usually knows better but he has stirred a mischievous spark in her and she decides to take a chance on him. He too is far from dull minded, rather good looking, clean shaven, and a couple of years her junior, it turns out. He speaks well for a drifter and she figures that he is a young man with wanderlust in his heart rather than someone who can't make something of himself. He owns a horse, assuming it isn't stolen, so he has some means. And so it begins.

"Frau!" he yells from the road.

"May I be of assistance?" she replies.

He dismounts and walks his horse down the path; it is less intimidating than addressing someone while mounted, he has learned. "People know me as Karl and I'm working my way to Rome. Perhaps I could be of assistance to you and your family somehow?"

She likes what she sees. "But we know nothing of you. One must be careful."

"I do have some references. From my pastor and the burgermeister of my town." He pulls two somewhat crinkled envelopes from his coat pocket and hands them to her. Each document lists his vital statistics and vouches for his character and industry. Official stationery and wax seals attest to their authenticity.

Anna looks him over. "Winter has been hard on the property. Repairs need to be made and things readied for spring. We can feed and house you for a day or so, if that is to your liking. Plus a customary wage."

"A couple of days is quite satisfactory."

"Done. You can begin by clearing some brush. Then I will give you some dinner. You can bed in the loft."

"Wunderbar! And what may I call you?"

"Anna will suffice."

"Well, Frau Anna..."

"As I said, Anna will suffice. Besides, it's Fraulein. It is just my brother and I who live here," she lies. "He's been away on business. I expect him back this evening."

"Danke, Anna," he says with a smile.

"Put your horse in the barn. You will find plenty of hay in a corner. The water trough is over there near the well." Once his horse is settled in a stall, he knocks on the farmhouse door, saddlebags in hand.

"Come in." Anna points the way to the loft. "Do you need work gloves?" He has his own; he tells her.

Anna shows him around the place and where the tools are kept. By the end of the afternoon he has stacked large, somewhat symmetrical piles of brush, branches and debris making the area around the house and garden much tidier. The grey winter sky is quickly sliding into blackness and Anna calls to him that goulash will be served very shortly.

He draws some water from the well and takes off his shirt despite the brisk air. As she is going about her business in the house she catches a glimpse of him splashing the water on his face and neck and then she lingers to watch him wash his hands and arms with the bar of soap she left in a niche of the stone well. She has never seen the bare, broad shoulders and hardened muscles of a young man before and something in her stirs. He takes the towel that Anna left on the top of the well for him and, as he dries himself, she continues to stare. He turns unexpectedly and sees her at the window and against a backdrop of glimmering candles; she beats a hasty retreat.

Karl knocks before pushing the ajar door open and stands there indecisively, doubtful as to where he should go now. "Sit down," she says, pointing at the table. Anna had gone back and forth in her mind as to whether he should dine with her.

Three place settings have already been set. Warm bread, a mini tub of butter, Vorarlberg cheese, and a decanter of red wine are on the table near two red candles, the flames swaying to the rhythm of a slight draft. Anna places a colorful ceramic bowl of hot goulash on the trivet, lifts the cover and ladles some onto their plates before taking her seat at one end of the table.

"I can heat more quickly enough… for my brother. I'm not going to wait, however. I can never be sure when he will turn up." She bows her head and gives thanks for their meal; he follows her lead. "Why don't you pour the wine," she suggests.

Karl pulls the stopper. Maintaining wine etiquette, he only half fills the glass that Anna proffers, and then his own. This doesn't go unnoticed by Anna, who despite her social status has come to know the conventions of polite society. Raising his glass he says, "To the gracious lady of the household, I thank her for facilitating my trek to Italy, this delightful meal, and allowing me to sup with her this evening. I am most honored."

"Danke, and may your journey be tranquil and safe."

After touching glasses ([1]) and taking a sip, they place them back on the table. He waits for her to start eating before he breaks some bread and scoops some butter onto his plate. *His manners are impeccable*, she muses.

---

1   The Origin of Clinking of Glasses: poisoned drink had been a common way of dispatching one's enemy. A practice came about in that the host would hold up his glass to allow the guest to pour some of his drink into that of his host's. They would then partake simultaneously. If the guest trusted the host, he would only clink glasses.

"You are a wonderful cook; I've never had better goulash."

"Danke. Would you like it again tomorrow night? I would like you to prepare the garden for spring planting in the morning." Karl seems to fight off a pained expression. Hard labor is apparently contrary to his nature.

"I could eat goulash like this every day of the week."

"You had said you are making your way to Rome; how is that?"

"The marvels of the Eternal City. And I hear that the Tyrrhenian Sea is beautiful. I've seen enough of what's behind me."

"That's it! No other plans?"

"I expect to settle there. What then? We'll see," he smiles. Anna tries not to show her disappointment. *Too good looking and too much going for him to be interested in me anyway.*

"I'm glad that you stopped. It's hard to find someone to help."

"What of your brother?"

"His business takes him away quite a bit."

"What does he do?"

"He's a farrier. Travels a circuit." She knew this question would come up sooner or later so she was prepared for it. "He thought he would be back by tonight."

"What about you? All this fabric." He is taken by her smile, how it narrows the void between them. The conversation doesn't last much past supper; they both need their sleep.

Karl spends the next day clearing the garden of surface stones and undergrowth and going to town with Anna in a horse drawn wagon to haul back supplies. Then a day and a half loosening it with a pickaxe, more pulling and picking, and establishing rows for seeding. Glad to put that behind him, he turns to carpentry work on the barn and patching the roof.

It is becoming apparent that there is no brother. No men's clothes are to be seen anywhere, no male accessories, and only a cursory mention of him since that first day. And then the fact that Anna playfully tosses her chestnut hair in front of him or puts her hands behind her head to thrust out her bosom. She sways her hips in a deliberate, provocative way. *There may be yet other compensations to this job*, he ponders.

A week has gone by ever so quickly. More work must be done but Anna picks up signals that Karl is ready to move on. Except for breakfast the next morning, this supper would be their last meal together, she realizes. She had already paid him several groschen as a gesture of good will. She had second thoughts about that, might he leave even sooner? He hadn't. She is impressed that he is well versed in many subjects though, and surprisingly up to date on current events.

"Sultan Selim is in control of most of the Arabian Peninsula and Egypt; undoubtedly his territorial appetites will lead him westward. Our emperor, Maximilian, is already expressing concerns. If the Muslims conquer this country, there will be radical changes," Karl volunteers.

"How so?"

"Their culture and religious customs are quite different. Women, for example, have much less freedom of action. Muslims believe in one God. They chastise Christians for claiming three."

"But our Church says there is only one God, with three divine natures. Like the three leaf clover, three leaves on one stem."

"According to Islam, a Christian rationalization to explain away the polytheist conundrum of their doctrine. But St. Thomas of Aquinas in his *De Rationibus Fidei* counters that God is a spiritual being having an intellectual nature and that his word proceeds from that intellect and that love proceeds from the word. Keeping in mind our limited vocabulary attempting to define the Almighty, we refer to God himself as God the Father, the Word of God as the Son of God and the Love issuing from the Son the Holy Spirit. All are of a spiritual nature, having an unseen presence, and are of each other and thus co-eternal. The three persons of this Blessed Trinity are interrelated as to their essence and comprise one divine nature and are not distinct per se. I'm not saying that Thomas originated that rationale but he certainly reiterated it. Christians are commanded to adhere to this teaching."

"An extraordinary rationale. Jesus was the Word made flesh we are told. But Jesus was distinct."

"Ja, the Incarnation. It does seem to make him distinct, doesn't it? I'll have to ponder that." Karl pauses before continuing. "The Muslims, however, are of immediate concern. They take young Christians boys from their families for conversion to Islam and service in their army, they are known as Janissaries."

"They wouldn't take my son, if I had one. I don't like this talk." Anna rises from the table and takes her dishes to the sink. "Bring me your dishes!" He does so and tries to put them on the right sideboard but it is already crowded. "No, over here, on this side." The space is tight and he brushes against her. He has to lean into her to put them down. Anna doesn't flinch.

Should I or shouldn't I, he thinks? His mind races. He puts his hands lightly on her hips; she still doesn't flinch. He gently kisses her neck. Still no resistance. He wraps his arms around her and kisses her cheek and then back to her neck. They turn to each other and their lips meet. The embrace becomes more passionate as her lashes close over her submissive eyes.

He unbuttons her blouse and to her own surprise she unbuttons his shirt. She kicks off her shoes and he eases her skirt to the floor. Both striped to the waste, he carries her into her bedroom. He slowly and deliberately unravels the stockings off her legs as her eyes remain locked on his movements. His shoes and trousers are off in an instant and he lies next to her on the bed. His hand slides up her inner thigh and lingers there for an eternity. *He obviously has had experience with other women,* she thinks, *but so what, this isn't about fidelity.* Her need to be wanted tugs at her heart.

The next morning Karl awakens to an unhurried dawn tip-toeing through the window; he always prefers the sun to revive him. He slowly rises and retreats to the well to shave and freshen up as Anna begins to stir. The morning is brisk but not as cold as one would expect at this time of year. He then proceeds to the barn to prepare his horse for the journey.

Anna wistfully leaves the window and draws some water from the cistern pump at the kitchen sink to ready herself for the day. The sun is well up by now so she snuffs the candles as she finishes dressing.

She is pouring some grape juice to complement the breakfast when Karl returns from the barn. She hastily puts the pitcher down and pulls a purse from her pocket. "Put out your hands!" she commands. As he does so, she deposits the balance of the groschen that is due into them. "Now, sit down! Frühstück is ready." Both endure an awkward silence until… "When we were in town, I asked about Erich Schilling. He's a guide, the best. It so happens that he will be taking a party to the Brenner Pass today; departure scheduled two hours from now at the town square. Explain your circumstances, I'm sure he won't charge you much. He is kind and flexible. I intended to tell you last night but..... I, I never got around to it," Anna looks down.

"I've gotten this far alone. I'll be alright."

"You really should take advantage of his expertise. Some areas are just not safe. I know these parts. Just do it."

He stands and walks to her. Taking her hands, he pulls her to him and kisses her gently on the cheek. "You're terrific Anna. I'll never forget you."

"Yes you will." She reaches for a sack. "Here, I packed you a lunch. Put this in your saddlebags!" The bags are on the floor next to him and he does so, ever so carefully. He precedes her through the door and after securing the bags to his horse, Karl climbs onto the saddle.

"Take care mon petit chou, my little cabbage."

As his horse trots down the path to the road and then into a gallop, she desperately watches from the front steps. Unprompted tears lay neglected on her cheeks as he fades from her sight along with her dreams. "Auf Wiedersehen, Karl," she whispers to a love lost. Returning inside, her steps a bit uncertain, she slumps into a chair, crossing her forearms on the table and then resting her head on them. Solitary and despairing, living on the periphery of society, she begins to sob.

☙

Seeing a gathering under the empty sky, obviously the Schilling party, Karl decides to explore the possibilities. He introduces himself to the man clearly in charge, the one with the high square shoulders and rugged jawline; they quickly come to terms.

The hills are steep and the travel arduous. The occasional rattle of recalcitrant leaves which haven't let go of their branches mark their passing. Several hours go by before they pause for the mid-day meal. Karl opts to sit alone by a clump of evergreen trees to partake his lunch. Taking Anna's sack from his saddlebags, he discovers sliced salted ham, cheese, bread, olives and a torte carefully wrapped in a cloth. But also, to his surprise, there is a blue silk handkerchief with a small, gold, broken heart embroidered in one corner; it is more sartorial than practical. He carefully unfolds the handkerchief to discover several coins; this is in addition to what he had been paid that very morning, money that is just as dear to Anna as it is to himself. *Danke once again, Anna,* he says to himself with an unforeseen twinge of loss.

Travel resumes with mostly single-minded faces of Italian silver merchants on their way back from the mines of Schwaz and Rattenberg. Passing through Innsbruck and then the well-traveled

Brenner Pass will be just the initial steps to their hometowns in the Papal States. With the darkening sky they make camp with good natured banter in what seems to be the middle of nowhere, tying the horses and donkeys in a string line. Hired guards are posted on the perimeter and will take shifts through the night to sound the alarm as to any furtive raid from bandits.

Yusuf Sahin, Joseph to the outside world, cook and jack of all trades, roasts some lamb on a spit and at the same time tends to a large kettle hanging over the campfire that is simmering with cut carrots, chopped sauerkraut and diced beets in a tasty broth. Using a ladle, he tastes the concoction and decides to throw in three more pinches of salt. One of the merchants plays tunes on his flute. Karl, being quite gregarious and with a good sense of humor, is soon accepted by the group. And, as with any gathering of men regardless of the era, the conversation eventually turns to religion and politics.

"I don't care what you say," asserts one they call Tiziano. "Witchcraft is real and witches can fly over great distances; the Church says so." His black hair is slicked down giving the illusion of a protective helmet capping his wiry body.

"Who are you going to believe, the old Church or the new Church?" replies Vito, who has a refined air about him and manages to stay fastidious even in the wilderness, even his boots retain a splendid polish.

"I can't believe that it changed its position. The Church is consistent on matters of faith and morals."

"Witchcraft is associated with heresy. Heresy is a matter of faith and morals. The canon *Episcopi eorumque*, brought to public attention circa 900 by the abbot Regino of Prum, and incorporated into Gratian's authoritative text of canon law, the *Decretum*, around 1140, says that transvections are in one's imagination, delusions of the devil, and to believe in the reality of such flights is heresy. St. Augustine, the pre-eminent Doctor of the Church of the 4th and 5th centuries, thought along similar lines. So once it was heresy to believe in them and now you are a heretic if you don't."

"There must be an explanation," replies Tiziano.

"There is, at least according to one source. The inquisitor Bernard of Como asserts that this canon speaks only of witches from the first millennium and that the witches of today are of a different sect."

"You answered your own query."

"Did I? How dexterous of Bernard. On what authority is this self-serving explanation based? It just goes to show that if one wants to adhere to something bad enough some specious argument will be coughed-up." Vito shrugs his right shoulder front to back as if shooing a bug.

"May God have mercy on us all," repeats the bewildered Tiziano. "What say you, Karl?"

"Pope Innocent VIII's papal bull *Summis Desiderantes Affectibus* of 1484, which is a formal announcement affixed with a seal, a bulla, affirmed the actuality of claimed witch practices in the provinces. The bull was written to fervently refute those clergymen who said that witchcraft was not being so practiced and accordingly there was no legal right for Dominican inquisitors Henry Kramer and James Sprenger to exercise their powers of inquisition. Thus the bull also confirmed the inquisitional powers of these men. Two years later they authored Malleus Maleficarum, translated as The Hammer of Witches, which affirms transvections. Malleus now is the universal and official Church text on identifying and punishing witchcraft. So Tiziano is right in that Catholics are very much obliged to believe in transvections."

"Karl knows some Church history," observes Vito. "Does he know what specific powers are ascribed to witches in this bull?"

"It cites witches raising storms, slaying infants/women/men/animals or afflicting them with diseases, causing impotence and infertility, destroying crops, and having sexual intercourse with devils. It gave new energy to the inquisitions to seek out so called witches and destroy them."

Karl settles himself at the edge of the campfire; the dusk is turning to dark. "I might add that references to sorcerers, in the Old and New Testaments, are frequent. Also, the renowned 13th century Doctors of the Church, the Franciscan, St. Bonaventure, and the Dominican, St. Thomas Aquinas, believed in transvections. The theological faculty of the University of Paris in 1398 adopted twenty eight articles regarded as unanswerable arguments against skeptics of magic."

"You know what that means. Those who persist in this heresy are to be burned at the stake," counters Vito. His shoulder shrugs front to back again.

"Burned at the stake!" says Erich, who opts to listen rather than participate in such discussions. "You fellas might wish to change the subject before you yourselves find things too hot to handle." There is nervous laughter.

"What about you, Joseph? Or is it really, Yusuf?" Vito readily sees through the façade. "What say you of these things?"

"I agree with my boss. We best change the subject."

"Yusuf," persists Vito, in a friendly manner, "what nationality are you?"

"I am Austrian." He looks over his shoulder for a place to escape.

"Yusuf?" says Vito raising an eyebrow.

"I was born in Istanbul… I mean Constantinople. But I grow up in Austria," he answers with an underpowered voice. Erich decides it would be worse to interfere.

"Then you must be familiar with the Qur'an," says Vito. "What does it say of witches?"

"It condemns sorcery. But I am not the one to ask such things. As I said, that was long ago. I am Austrian." There is a strong smell of sauerkraut and he glances at the simmering kettle.

"Shouldn't we fear the Muslims, Yusuf?" Vito persists. "After all, the Qur'an says believers are not to take unbelievers as friends. And Muslims should slay the idolaters wherever you find them, unless they repent and become Muslims, of course. Must we be ever wary of the sultan?"

"Muslims slay only if attacked. The Qur'an commands that '*whoever slays a soul, unless it be for manslaughter or for mischief in the land, it is as though he slew all men.*' "

"Does being a brother, being a nephew, and being a son constitute mischief in the land? Selim had all his brothers, all his nephews and four of his own five sons killed to preempt any of them from possibly usurping his power. If there be mischief in the land, it falls at the feet of the sultan Selim himself. Only one son, Suleiman, was spared and was designated heir apparent. And what of the thousands of fellow Muslims, the Safavid tribesman of eastern Anatolia, that Selim slaughtered? He even carried his aggression to Egypt and Syria, Muslim countries. Is being a relative a criminal offense? And when is invasion of brother nations tantamount to self-defense?"

"As to the latter, the guiding principle is to insure the integrity of the faith and root out heresy, heterodoxy. But now I am Austrian, so please don't ask me to defend the sultan. It is not my place to do so."

"Ah" says Vito, "so it is alright to kill heretics even though they are not aggressors. Please note, however, that Selim, the Sunni Muslim, gains more territory, power and wealth by overcoming the Shia Muslims."

"Please excuse me, I have work to do. Let me take your utensils," he pleads with scarcely concealed anxiety.

❧

"Has Joseph been with you long, Herr Schilling?" asks Karl out of ear shot of the others.

"About a year or so. Says he grew up near Vienna. Fluent in German, of course, and knows these parts well. Wonderful with animals. Travels well. What do you think of him as a cook?"

"I'm impressed." *And what a wonderful job to gather intelligence for an Ottoman invasion*, thinks Karl. "And what do you know of Vito? He is reckless with such outspoken heresy. Does he have a death wish?"

"Vito is vocal in select circles only. Considered an amusing eccentric within his powerful Medici family but savvy enough not to roil his brethren. I'm sure you know that our current pope, Leo X, is a Medici. No one dares make an issue of Vito, who has clout of his own."

"I hear that Pope Leo is very generous and a patron of the arts."

"Oh, he is all of that, generous in alms, generous to the arts and generous in frivolities. It is not so jokingly said that he has consumed the treasuries of three pontificates, his predecessor's, his own and his successor's. He's been trying to replenish it by selling ecclesiastical offices and spiritual indulgences with reckless abandon. It seems the Medici are more concerned with the here and now than the hereafter. Where is the guiding Holy Spirit I ask myself?"

"What of Herr Eberle? He didn't join the discourse but I noticed an occasional wry grin under that shock of white hair and myopic gaze. I understand that he is a retired university professor."

"Yes, and it's Dr. Eberle; he has a PhD. And don't mistake that rumpled appearance and slight stoop for signs of decline. He has a prodigious memory. A biblical scholar. He knows more about these things than any of us. Apparently you and Vito have your facts right, if not your opinions. He found no need to correct you."

"Or was he being discrete?"

"He is not reticent to speak up to set the record straight. On the other hand, he is wise enough not to speak heresy."

"Are you saying that he secretly harbors heretical beliefs?"

"You were speaking of being discrete."

"Have you known him long?"

"He has made many trips to the Muslim world over the years. We have become friends."

"Is that where he is heading now?"

"He is going to Venice. From there he will sail to Egypt. He is well known and respected there, a man of letters. Muslims can be practical also. They have not challenged his faith."

"What will he do in Egypt?"

"Not many are aware that there were dozens of gospels but only four made the canonical or official list in today's Church, namely Matthew, Mark, Luke and John, which are not traceable to the Evangelists themselves but rather inferred. The faithful, not so well informed, don't realize that these four gospels were anonymous until decades after they were written. While in the process of sorting things out, priests and bishops were accusing each other of heresy. *Bishop Eusebius of Caesarea*, a favorite of the Emperor Constantine, lived from about 263 to 339, if my memory is correct, *is known as the 'Father of Church History.'* Even he was accused of heresy by Alexander, Bishop of Alexandria.

"According to Eusebius, Papias, Bishop of Hierapolis and an early Christian author, attributed circa 130 the Gospel of Mark to John Mark, an associate of Paul. The Gospel of Matthew came by that name, once again, through Papias. Matthew is believed to also have been known by the name Levi, the tax collector; he was an apostle. Papias named the Gospel of Matthew as the first gospel. The Gospel of Mark, according to many scholars, is the first gospel, not Matthew, and it wasn't even written until circa 70. And as I said, many decades had passed from the time they were written until the time they were named. Eusebius penned that Papias had been influenced by a false millenarian teaching, namely believing that Christ would establish a one thousand year reign on earth, and disparaged Papias as a man of small mental capacity."

"The professor seems to have made you into something of a sage yourself or is this part of a personal quest?" asks Karl.

"He taught me a quite a bit. Tradition, for example, holds that Luke was a friend of Paul and a physician, both so called facts are considered unlikely by some biblical scholars. As to the Gospel of John, which John was the author? Some say it was John the Elder of Ephesus; some say it was John the apostle, son of Zebedee; some say it was John the beloved disciple; others say that the latter two are the same person. The Gospel of John was written at the end of the 1st century and many maintain that we just don't know who wrote it. Also, there is no way for us today to ascertain just how, from a multitude of tomes attributed to an Apostle or just titled a gospel, only four made the official canonical list. And only two of these were attributed to Apostles. Also, we can surmise that just because something is traditional doesn't necessarily mean it is correct."

A curious quiet descends on the camp causing Erich to pause. Seeing that all is well, he proceeds.

"We do not have any of the original texts. And as important as it is to know who wrote what and when, the obvious question being, if God took it upon Himself to inspire the gospels, would their authorship be left in doubt?"

"Jesus was about preaching and instructed his Apostles to do the same. He did not transcribe his own teachings and did not direct others to do so," Karl adds as if paired in synchronization.

"*Logion kyriakon exegsis* was composed of five books and written by Papias. According to the Church, based on the fragments of these books which survive, St. John the Presbyter vouched for the correctness of St. Mark's Gospel, which embodies the teachings of St. Peter, even though Mark's order of events is incorrect. Keep in mind that Mark was not a disciple of Jesus; his writings, according to Church tradition, are based on the explicit discourses of Peter. And one might ask how this supports the contention that his gospel was inspired? If anything, it points to the Gospel of Mark being simply a historical religious text?"

"I hear what you are saying," says Karl, "but what bearing does this have on Dr. Eberle's trip to Egypt?"

"Now we come to the Gospel of Thomas," replies Erich, "Coptic copies of which have been found near Nag Hammadi, Egypt. He is going there to examine the documents for himself and hopes to have the good fortune of bringing back a copy. This gospel is attributed to Didymus Judas Thomas, one of the twelve apostles, and not to be confused with that other apostle, Judas Iscariot, the betrayer of Jesus. Once again, notice that I say attributed to. Well, the Gospel of Thomas is a sayings gospel in that it is a collection of sayings and parables that coincide with many found in Matthew, Mark and Luke. This gives it an aura of commonality and possibly authenticity with those synoptic gospels regardless of who all the authors are. There is quite a contrast, however, between those gospels and the Gospel of John, which is peculiarly devoid of parables. Instead, Jesus partakes in long discourses of a theological nature. John contains a majority of material found only within itself which leads scholars cognitive of this to question the objectivity of the author."

"Care to elaborate?"

"I'm saying that possibly or even probably it is replete with the author's bias."

"If some of the Bible is questionable, wouldn't that raise doubts as to the rest of it?"

"In the early Church, we know that the Gospel of Thomas was condemned and its destruction ordered. Obviously, it was at variance with other doctrine but what? In light of today's exegesis, it might be a legitimate challenge to accepted dogma. This could be a very sensitive document for the Church. If so, would the Church want to suppress it again?"

"Your suggesting that skullduggery on the part of Church officials might even come into play?"

"Who knows how things might play out? But let me get back to the Gospel of John. John differs from the synoptic gospels in other ways. It portrays the public ministry of Jesus as three years, not one year as the synoptic gospels do, which is quite a departure to say the least. Also, John contrasts with Mark in that John portrays Jesus as being open about his divinity; Mark indicates the opposite; they can't both be right."

"John is known as 'the spiritual gospel,' " says Karl.

"Well, Dr. Eberle has been told that the Gospel of Thomas doesn't even refer to Jesus as the Lord or the Christ."

"So either the Church or its critics would love to get their hands on this for different reasons."

"As far as the professor knows, prior to further examination, the Gospel of Thomas may just be another affirmation of the multiplicity of beliefs in the early days of Christianity. It is another aspect pointing to the fact that the public in general and congregations in particular are ignorant as to the real development of the New Testament, which they accept without question."

"What are Dr. Eberle's hopes?"

"That it may give today's biblical scholars, who must be very circumspect as it is, some support in rectifying some arguments one way or another. Assuming, of course, that there are open minded members in the hierarchy."

"What doctrine does the professor have in mind? And when do the scholars believe it was written?"

"It was written sometime between the mid-1st century and the mid-2nd century but most favor the latter. Dr. Eberle is particularly disturbed by the belief in witchcraft and its alleged link to a pact with the devil. The Gospel of Thomas makes no reference to witchcraft or even the devil. One would think, if Satan and his minions were so prevalent and diabolical, it would be a dominant topic for Jesus."

"Are you suggesting that Dr. Eberle feels that maybe this gospel might provide a premise that dismisses such a connection? At present it is heresy to say otherwise."

"He would be pleased to find something, especially in relation to the canonical gospels, that will tip the balance in favor of those theologians who challenge such packs…those who say that witchcraft is nonsense. Not that it is, of course."

"Of course."

CHAPTER 3

KATARINA

My name is Katarina.
I was born 10 December 1517.

That is all anyone needs to know, Anna decides, as she pins this note to the baby blanket. Gently, she puts Katarina on the top step and to the side. *Am I doing the right thing? This is not what I want. I don't. I don't... It isn't about you. It's about Katarina. Just do it. You must do it. You must. Oh, dear, Katarina, forgive me, forgive me.* Imprisoned tears escape without warning. Anna slams the door knocker of the small, Premonstratensian convent house above the Inn Valley several times then quickly scurries to the tree line; the hem of her dress is wet from the morning dew.

The unfriendly grey sky adds to her melancholy as she pulls up her collar to offset the swirling breeze. Her heart pounds as a diminutive nun thrusts open the large door but seeing no one, puzzled, begins to retreat. A fortuitous coo brings her back. Spreading her arms in bewilderment, she rushes to the child. Sister Marlena von Mauer nestles Katarina in her soft, delicate arms and walks about the area searching, pleading, while caressing the infant. "Is anyone there," she calls out time and again. "Please come forward. We can help. Please let us help."

The pleas are tearing Anna apart. *Help? How can I remain part of Katarina's life? I've worked this over in my mind a thousand times. This is the way it must be. Don't be selfish, Anna. You must be strong. You must go. You must go. Go now. I will always keep track of my baby; I will.*

Her slender fingers resisting the chill, finally the good nun looks into the baby's eyes and whispers, "three months old and already an orphan." Just as quickly she corrects herself. "Nein, you are now the newest member of our family of sisters... my, what an exquisite blanket!"

The pink and blue ([1]) wool is interwoven yet the border of the blanket is of solitary blue silk; Anna had started knitting well before delivery. As a last minute gesture of love, to bridge another separation, a gold, broken heart had been stitched into one corner. A whole year has passed since Karl left but not a day passes without thinking of him. *Will he ever come back? What if he does?*

Sister von Mauer is from a family of German nobility with relatives on the German side of Lake Constance, many miles to the northwest, their residence being an imposing castle on a hill well above the shoreline. She had recently received notice that her distant cousin, Baroness von Hoffen, lost her daughter due to a late term miscarriage. Sister decides that Katarina will take her place in the world. Katarina will be now known as Katarina von Hoffen and this little cherub will become the darling of the convent house.

Two other nuns of noble origin also are in residence and are quite learned for the times. Many books had been donated to the convent in these start-up years and the whole congregation has voraciously devoured them. This formidable library is not lost on Katarina. She proves to be a student gifted with intelligence, high spirits, and is a handful for her exceptional family as she passes into her teen years.

"The other day, Naunie," this is what she had come to call Sister

---

1   Blue was associated with the heavens and thought to ward off evil spirits lurking above and seeking to enter the bodies of infants; particular importance given to boys. Pink later evolved to distinguish girls.

von Mauer, "Sister Thomasena's shouting that there is no God, then hastily leaving the convent in an awaiting carriage. Not unlike Sister Elizabeth leaving some years ago. Why did they say that?"

"The devil is always at work, dear. It is as simple as that. It is unfortunate that the devil has occasional victories."

"You talk of the devil, Naunie. If I wasn't taught that there is a devil or God for that matter, I probably would not believe in them. I know of the village people. I know of our sisters and Father Schoedler. I know of the trees, the grass, the flowers and the mountains. But where is the devil? Where is God?"

"Katarina, for shame, you experience God in the Blessed Eucharist, which is the presence of Christ under the appearance of bread and wine. Jesus instructed that we take bread and wine, which is consecrated by a priest, in commemoration of Him. We do that here every day. You know that. Sometimes you shock me," she replies with animation and at the same time shocking herself with the realization of the uncertainty of it all.

"But where is God? Not just a representation of Him. If one generation after the next wasn't so taught, why would anyone think God exists? The Jews adhere to Judaism because they were raised in it. The Muslims adhere to Islam for the same reason and the same with Christians. From what I ascertain, whom we become as adults is largely a product of how we were raised and educated. The religion we grow up in establishes our norm, our foundation, and we just accept it as being right. We never even consider let alone adhere to another religion. There are exceptions to everything, of course, but who is to say which religion is right, if any? Am I wrong that such things come to mind?"

"God is God no matter what the religion;" she pauses. "Although they may have different interpretations of what God expects of us. Regardless, how else do you explain the order and design in nature? It presupposes a higher intellect. And what I say isn't what counts; it is the Bible that matters. It is God's word, set down in the Bible." Sister von Mauer fails to distinguish between the Old and New Testaments let alone the Qur'an.

"If God loves us and we are important to Him, why doesn't He interact with us? We pray but it all seems so one sided."

"Jesus is the Son of God. He did come to us so that we may know Him."

"It was so long ago."

"God works in mysterious ways, dear. Who are we to comprehend the supernatural? It is not within our capacity."

"If I could create the universe, I wouldn't need people praying to me. You must think me awful, Naunie. I am so confused." Katarina goes to her and they hug.

"All will be revealed to us someday. You will see. Pray for God's grace!"

"By the way Naunie, I spotted that woman again."

Rarely does Katarina see Anna. Although tempted so many times to risk a *chance encounter* and strike up a conversation, especially when Katarina was very young, she didn't. The risk of Katarina deducing her true identity is too great. Children can be very intuitive. And there is a resemblance. What of the emotional and practical consequences if she does learn of their relationship? *Katarina, my daughter, if only I could have been your mom.*

സ

Katarina's dress naturally is given to plain and shapeless. Abetted by a small waist, narrow hips and close cropped hair, there is hardly a hint of femininity. Her favorite attire is riding britches with a loose top masking an ample but less than buxom bosom. She has heard much of Innsbruck and longs to see it but something had always gotten in the way. Usually the excuse was that the trips were strictly business and she was too young to be left on her own. She has been to closer hamlets but never Innsbruck. This August, however, would be different. Sister von Mauer, now Prioress von Mauer in recognition of her increased responsibilities, will be assisted by Father Schoedler in presenting the financial circumstances of the convent to the cardinal; the diocese has been significantly subsidizing the order. Father Schoedler thinks the trip for Kat, as he likes to call her, is long overdue. The good nun and Kat can share a room at the Boar's Head Inn so the extra expense will be minimal, especially since Herr Freihofer always gives clergy substantial discounts. Albert Freihofer is behind the front desk when they check-in that Friday evening. He puts aside the financial statement that he is reviewing.

"Fr. Schoedler! It has been awhile, so good to see you." The priest has the round face and round body of a snowman. In character with other chubby people, he seems perpetually jovial. Accustomed to wearing a cassock, his stride kicks forward from the knees down.

"And you, Albert. You and your father always make my visits here such a wonderful experience. Going over the books I see."

"Ja, checking the month's expenditures; profits seem to be low for some reason. The von Clausen firm is doing them now. We sure miss Herr Carberrry; he died so unexpectedly. You heard, of course? He seemed to be in excellent health. You wouldn't believe all the condolences that have been expressed."

"I don't doubt it at all. He was such a friendly and kind man. And your father held him in high esteem. Yes it was sudden, one never knows. I sent young Johann a Mass card. He is alright, I pray?"

"Johann seems to be doing satisfactorily. Herr Carberry was a frugal man and managed his affairs well; he had money put aside.

Besides, everyone likes Johann; he is never at a loss for odd jobs. Hasn't decided on a career, however."

"Oh, I'm so glad to hear that. That he is managing well, I mean. He will do well at whatever he sets his mind to," Fr. Schoedler says with avuncular ease; his head inclines as he speaks.

"There are three of us this time, Albert. Prioress von Mauer and Kat over there with the luggage. I need two rooms." Albert thinks he said Jack, not Kat, and registers Fr. Schoedler and Jack to the same room. The porter takes the luggage to the respective rooms while the three proceed to the dining room.

Fritz spots them and greets them with a flourish, fussing over them even more than his usual attention to his guests. The good father has been there before on occasion, the others have not. With his signature stride, Fritz waddles his way to a candle lit table with a magnificent view of the Inn River and its famous bridge a bit down river. He seats his guests attentively and then signals to a waiter. In short order a complimentary bottle of fine, chilled white wine appears, not long from the cask. Fritz takes the bottle and pours it, twisting it with a flourish as he does so, into the priest's glass. Father Schoedler swirls the wine, puts his nose to it and then takes a measured sip. Exhilarated, he blushes as if he undeservedly stumbled upon the nectar of the ages and Fritz continues to provide for all.

"The best Riesling in Austria, Fritz. Always the best. Just the right amount of chill too. I don't know how you manage that. Your ice house is still packed from last winter I'm sure," he says rhetorically as his black, crescent eyebrows rise in unison.

"Enjoy your meal my friends."

"May God bless you," responds Prioress von Mauer with heartfelt modesty.

After hot rolls and butter, warm bowls of borscht are the next delight laid before them. Katarina keeps looking about in wonder of the grand furnishings, hardly able to contain her excitement as more and more diners sit down at the quickly filling establishment. She studies their dress and manner and is taken by their interaction as apparent friends and acquaintances dally at nearby tables to converse and cajole. Her benefactors smile to themselves in amusement.

This evening features a Heringschmaus, a buffet feast packed with every fish and salad specialty imaginable, a far cry from convent food. "Naunie, this must have been the fare in the Garden of Eden," Katarina exclaims.

"I wasn't there but this will certainly do, dear," as she blots the edges of her moist, pale lips.

"Amen," Father Schoedler concurs with a contented smile.

All make several trips to the buffet, a highlight making their journey both delicious and memorable. Malakoff Tortes followed by glasses of Welschriesling top off the meal. Finally, all good things do come to an end. After strolling around town under the slate sky they head for their rooms. The luggage mix up is sorted out and they settle in for a sound and comfortable sleep.

❧

Fruhstuck is had the next morning on the partially roofed veranda. Diamonds of light bounce off the river surface only to be absorbed by the fresh mountain air.

"Could anything be more beautiful?" Katarina asks.

"Well, maybe a bit," says the priest. "I must bring you back in the spring when more flowers are prevalent. The white and pink azaleas, purple rhododendrons and yellow edelweiss underscored with their star shaped white leaves are without equal. They surround the veranda."

"Oh, how wonderful! Yes, we must come back again," adds the nun.

The setting is magnificent. A waiter unobtrusively appears and places empty cups with saucers in front of each of them. Fritz, approaching with a nimbleness unique to portly men and holding a steaming pot, graciously fills each cup and waits for their reactions. Father Schoedler, having tasted the treat before, nods to Katarina and the good nun urging them to drink up.

"What is this?" they say almost simultaneously.

"Tea," says Father. "From the Orient."

"From the Orient!" both women exclaim.

"It is special to us. No other place in the area has it as far as I know," says Fritz. "A friend, Erich Schilling, is acquainted with a Venetian sea captain who gives him a respectable quantity from his private stock from time to time… in exchange for business that Erich sends his way. Erich gives much of it to me… in exchange for the business I send him."

"It is one more thing that makes the Boar's Head special," adds Father, his pudgy fingers wiping the napkin dormant on his protruding belly.

"Oh! It is special," exclaims the nun. "I've never had anything like it. It is stimulating."

"Ja! Ja! Everything is so wonderful. I'm in heaven," says Katarina.

"Now, now, that's a stretch," replies Fritz, playfully nudging the priest. "I'll leave the pot. Enjoy!"

To their delight the hotel is hosting a plum dumpling contest and they watch the participants wolf down dozens of the gooey things. After a bit, Fritz comes back to the table, always the attentive Herr Ober, and announces that more substantial fare is on the way.

"Fritz," says Fr. Schoedler, "Prioress von Mauer and I have business at the chancery. Kat here may find it boring just sitting and waiting for us there. Would there be anything here in town that might better occupy the day for this youngster?"

"My son Albert and some of his friends are involved in some athletic events this morning. They've been doing it each summer for several years now. Albert competed in an archery event once but he prefers to just manage the team now. Kat, he would have checked you in at the front desk when you first arrived. He's there now. When you finish here, tell him I said that I'd like you to accompany him this morning," giving her a wink.

When we arrive, Albert remembering checking her in as Jack, tells us that Jack will be joining us. Albert only gives our names to her when he waves her over. With her husky voice, we are none the wiser. Reserved but eagerly attentive, Kat watches the competition and asks a lot of questions of the other spectators. She also minds the lunches prepared for us by the hotel's kitchen staff. Johann finishes 3rd in the senior log toss event. Snuff wins the cross country race. Franz places a step behind the winner in the sprint. I place 3rd in heavyweight wrestling. We regroup and Kat has an ear to ear smile on her face.

"The river's crook," I suggest.

"The river's crook!" the Boars reply in unison. Hot and sweaty, we hike into the woods eating our late lunches on the go and rudely interrupt a covey of quail.

"Owl be doing sum heavy neckin tuh night," says Snuff. It is the first time that Kat has heard that term but she doesn't want to appear un-cool so she doesn't ask.

"You better be careful," Johann admonishes.

"I know ow far I kin go," Snuff replies. Franz, as usual, flushes. "Besides, yuh should be chastening Rafer, ee only dates Ellie anymore. Ee's likely to be the first un to marry, voluntary ur not."

"What about it, Rafer?" asks Johann.

"I'm not going there and I wouldn't take you with me if I was. Franz, any of your inclinations kick in yet? Dancing with Frieda. Smelling her perfume. Touching her soft skin. Doesn't that get a rise out of you?" The other guys laugh. Kat is intrigued. And so the dialogue goes until we reach the crook in the river where the water pools at a bend. I am conversing with "*Jack*" as the others rush forward ripping off their clothes and jumping into the water. I start to take mine off and say, "Come on, this is how we freshen up after the games."

"Certainly not," she blurts out wide-eyed.

"In this heat?" Bare chested, I hop on each foot to pull off my shoes. "Nein!"

"Don't be a spoil sport. If you don't, I'll throw you in."

"Don't you dare!"

"You're bashful; aren't you? I'll help you get over that." A wrestling kick to the ankle and a take down. I tug the bottom of Kat's shirt and pull it up taking the loose vest with it. "Whoa!" Rolling off and then walking a few steps away I say, "I didn't realize. Albert said you were a... well you know."

"You've never seen a girl before?" she said, tucking in her shirt.

"Well, you don't look like a girl."

"What's that supposed to mean?"

"Your hair... and stuff."

"What's that supposed to mean?"

"What are you guys waiting for?" Johann yells from the river. I wave him off. I pick up my shirt and shoes and move behind an ash tree out of the swimmers' line of sight. As I dress, neither of us speaks or makes eye contact. I unsuccessfully try to stifle a raffish smile.

"What was I supposed to think? Your name being Jack, for crying out loud."

"Jack! Who's Jack?"

"Isn't your name Jack?"

"My name is Kat, for Katarina. Who said it was Jack?"

"This is embarrassing for me."

"For you?" More silence.

"Well don't mention this to anyone. I have a reputation."

"You have a reputation! You're a self-centered, egotistical jerk." She doesn't sound very bashful at the moment. More silence. We both sit and listen to the frolicking at the river. After what seems an eternity, the others exit the water.

"Don't peek!" I say. Katarina stifles a smile.

Albert is the first to finish dressing and is in the lead. "What's wrong with you two?" he shouts. "The water is great!" The words no sooner leave his mouth when an arrow slams into his chest.

᪥

Sheriff Mitlstrasser theorizes that someone had shot an arrow randomly into the air and, unfortunately, when it came down, it struck and killed Albert. The arrow being identical to those used in the tournament, anyone could have come by one. And, after all, who would want to kill Albert, a friendly young man in his late teens without an enemy in the world. Still quite bizarre, I thought.

Katarina's liberating excursion had ended in tragedy and solemn departure back to the convent in Reith. All of us were devastated, of course, especially Fritz. The inn kept operating in fine fashion since Fritz's employees made an extra effort to compensate for their boss' depression. It was his patrons' turn to be solicitous of him and he was taken by their concern. He continued to sponsor the team and went out of his way to be sure we kept coming to the Boar's Head for our team get-togethers including complimentary snacks. I'm convinced that part of this was because it kept him vicariously connected to Albert. And it's funny how certain things stick with you for the rest of your life. Whenever I think of Albert, I think of his last words, "The water is great!"

CHAPTER 4

THE SEMINARY

A watershed moment arrives with the approach of my nineteenth birthday. I am in love with Elsa but at the same time I am intellectually challenged to champion the cause of God. All my training and education tells me that God comes first, my desires are secondary. My Premonstratensian mentors tell me that I am gifted and that those talents should be used in the service of God. Since the Church demands celibacy, I now face the first major dilemma in my life.

Father Geissler, in particular, is always selling the Church, if I may put a commercial spin on it. He encourages all his students to carefully examine the priesthood as a career path. To what greater calling might one aspire to, he will ask? What greater service than to do the work of the Lord? Should anything come before God? These are turbulent times for the Church and it needs all the troops it can muster to combat the forces of the devil and his heretical surrogates. Every family should give one of its children to God. The priesthood is first among all vocations, then comes medicine, the caring for the sick. Father Geissler doesn't equivocate. These are weighty words to someone not yet out of his teens and I have given much thought to them over the last few months.

The year is 1536 and there are other pressing issues; I am much conflicted. I read Protestant reformer John Calvin's just published

Institutes of the Christian Religion, a critical statement of biblical theology. This book, written in Latin, appears to be propelling him to great prominence in the Protestant movement.

The Protestant Reformation tumbles on and I try to make sense of it. Not long after much of Germany had rebelled against the Roman Catholic Church nearly two decades ago, so too significant segments of the population of France did the same, springing up like dandelions in country meadows, particularly those in financial distress or oppressed by government. The French Protestants became known as Huguenots, how is not entirely clear but the name of a leader of the Geneva movement, Besancon Hugues, may have contributed to it. In 1534 the Huguenots had posted placards attacking the Mass all over Paris, one wound up on the king's bedroom door at Amboise. Their persecution had been going on for many years but this accelerated it and many fled the country, including Calvin, who had collaborated with them.

Calvin had first studied for the priesthood at the University of Paris but then left to study law. Later he was influenced by Renaissance humanism, defined by rigorous classical scholarship, intellectual freedom, individual expression, an increased faith in the capabilities of man but retaining a firm devotion to Christianity. It advocated that the New Testament be studied in its original language, Greek. Manuscript variants were used by scholars to reconstruct the original readings of the Bible. A century before Lorenzo Valla used this technique in his investigations into the textual errors in the *Latin Vulgate* translation of St. Jerome, the translation the Catholic Church embraced. Valla's historical philology approach caused him to comment that *"none of the words of Christ have come to us, for Christ spoke in Hebrew and never wrote down anything."* Desiderius Erasmus, perhaps the most prominent Renaissance Humanist and a contemporary of Calvin, in 1505 published the corrections that Valla had made as the *Annotationes*. Erasmus' edition of a Greek New Testament in 1516 relies on this text as do other contemporary Protestant editions.

Adding to my confusion were *the actions of King Henry VIII, the sovereign of England. Henry, who had been named "Defender of the Faith" by Pope Leo X in 1521 for his book chastising Martin Luther for breaking with the Church, broke with the Church himself in order to divorce his wife, Catherine of Aragon, and marry Anne Boleyn in 1533*; Pope Clement VII had refused to grant an annulment from Catherine. The Archbishop of Canterbury, Thomas Cranmer, then annulled the marriage to Catherine. By 1534, the religious supremacy of the Catholic Church, at its head the Pope, was renounced and Parliament declared the king Supreme Head of the Church of England. The Reformation now has an antagonistic companion of sorts in England. In 1536, Henry began confiscating religious properties and their assets, adding greatly to his coffers.

જી

A retreat has been scheduled for a four day weekend in mid-September with a special segment for those contemplating a religious life. Held at the Augustinian seminary established in 1384 on the outskirts of Rattenberg, northeast of Innsbruck, I register this Friday afternoon as a possible future seminarian; I emphasize the word possible. There will be over three hundred men arriving. Bread, wine, cheese, fruit, and slices of cake will be our only repast until the following Monday morning. Prospective seminarians are placed in two small, stone buildings across the campus green from each other. We are on our own to get acquainted before retiring for the night.

Set groups come together at their assigned places for the remainder of the weekend. Confessions for those considering the priesthood are penitent/priest peripatetic strolls about the grounds followed by the communal Mass. The lecturers rotate among the groups rather than vice-versa. Time is set aside throughout the day to meditate on the instruction just given, for private prayer, and for communal prayer when the chapel bells signal vespers.

The priests conducting the retreat are charismatic. The special ones wear beatific smiles proclaiming an inner peace and harmony with God; welcome to our community and share peace, love and spiritual fulfillment they say without mouthing a word. A clever friar takes us through the Ten Commandments pointing out how likely we fail with each and intimating all have. Offering respite from our alleged failures, when he comes to the fifth, "*Thou shalt not kill,*" he says with a forgiving tone, "There you go!" We all laugh; murderers are unlikely at this venue.

Yet frequently, all is not well with the world and the devil and his minions will corrupt all of mankind if the men of the Church do not cast out Satan with the help of the Holy Spirit. On that final Monday morning, arising before dawn as usual and treading under the stars, our senses are once again assaulted by the pungent pine needles. We sit for a hearty breakfast. Immediately following, all those judged as acceptable candidates for the priesthood are to come together for the first time.

The room is neither large nor small, neither dark nor bright. It suggests disciplined comfort. A polished wood wainscot is surmounted by cream colored plaster walls and a vaulted ceiling. A few supporting, wreathed columns add some style and warmth. Understated elegance comes to mind. There are rows of wooden chairs facing forward toward a low platform with three, more substantial high backed chairs on it and facing in the opposite direction. A few of the potential seminarians up front are more animated and vocal than the rest of us; obviously they see their ambitions moving closer to fruition.

A triumvirate wearing black, hooded robes enters from the front and stands in front of the three chairs. Their hoods are resting against the backs of their necks; their attentive heads fully exposed. Black leather straps circle their waists and extend down the front/left sides of their bodies almost to their black shoes. The rest of us take heed and orderly positions in front of our chairs. Mine is off to the side and next to a pillar which partially obstructs my view but that is fine with me; I find that my retention is usually enhanced when I close my eyes and concentrate on listening.

"In the name of the Father, Son and Holy Spirit," the one in the center says as he makes the sign of the cross. All take his lead and repeat the words in quiet reverence. "May the Holy Spirit be with us this morning," he continues.

"Amen," is the response.

"Gentlemen, if I may take the liberty to call you such." We all chuckle and the two priests on either side take their seats. There is a nervous energy in the room and I think that we would have laughed at anything bordering on humor. "I'm Father Bartholomew, Father Bart, as some like to say. I am the prior provincial of the Order of St. Augustine. Impressive, huh!" More laughter. "I'm here so that you can look me over." Now a titter, the group is loosening up. "In fact, let's look each other over." Father Bart goes into the audience and gawks individually at the neophytes with exaggerated gestures. A "tsk tsk" here. "He might do," there. "Questionable potential with this one," gesturing to another but he pats him on the shoulder. "Had any experience with women?" he asks still another. Taken aback the embarrassed young man stammers an inaudible reply. "Now, now, young man, I simply mean have you had dealings with them." Any tension that still exists evaporates into belly laughs. "Father Michael!" he shouts abruptly as he turns towards the dais. "Am I at the right gathering? Slim pickings here." The prior provincial is a hit and a familiarity begins to take hold.

"As you can tell, my deprecations are in jest. But I must warn you, becoming an Augustinian is not for the faint hearted. Discipline and obedience will dominate your existence. You will be tested physically and mentally. If you succeed, you will live as one, brother helping brother. You will be an Augustinian, a soldier of God in the struggle against ignorance and sin. May God bless you all. I must take my leave now. I am off to a resort town on the Adriatic, as a matter of fact... one of the perks of the order." Raucous laughter. "Thanks so much for putting up with my quips. You are in good hands with Father Michael now." With a hand wave to acknowledge the cheers, he turns on his heels and departs the way that he had come. We take our seats. Father Michael stands.

"Gentlemen, your training as Augustinians starts now, as of this minute. You will not return to your homes before the spring break. You need not send for anything; everything that you need will be provided. This morning you will write to your families to say that you have been called to God. Any questions?" The mood goes from joy to shock. Murmurings roll across the room like an incoming tide across a sandbar.

"But this is so sudden. I came here to inquire into the priesthood; I wasn't prepared to commit right now. I've made no arrangements," one volunteers.

"God has priority over all. We act not at our convenience but at His. Is God your first priority?"

There is a pause. "I say again, do you choose to live your life at your convenience or at God's?"

"Well... at God's, of course," one volunteers.

"Does anyone else have any questions?" Father Michael challenges. Another pause. "Father Bartholomew warned that becoming an Augustinian would be tough." He looks about gauging our reactions to adversity. "We need tough, disciplined, flexible men." Then another challenge. "It is today or never, gentlemen. I am going to walk through that door," he says pointing to the one behind him. "Follow me, otherwise, maybe the Dominicans will have you."

As Father Michael exits, the other priest stands in silence. His role is passive confrontation. Seven sheepishly leave. The others, including myself, follow Father Michael through the door. *What of Elsa*, I think. *I must give this a try to be true to myself. We aren't ready to get married yet anyway.*

The first ten through the door are immediately led off by a seminarian, only to be followed by the next ten, etc. I am in the trailing group commanded by a muscular young fellow with arms the size of most people's necks, carbon black hair, and a chilly demeanor. Hereafter I refer to him as Biceps. After a final stop at the supply room to get apparel more appropriate for seminarians, our group is marched to a nearby two story dormitory while we balance the items across our arms. I am assigned to the second floor.

At one end of the first floor there is a bath house having long, broad shelves with holes cut in them to receive a series of glazed, clay bowls. These are tended by teams who carry buckets of warm water from a stone utility building to the bath house each morning so that the candidates can freshen themselves and shave; all candidates are required to shave. Afterwards, each must take his bowl of dirty water and pour it into a trough, which empties into a trench outside. We soon learn that the teams will consist of us; many have already been whisked away to perform sundry chores.

We are ordered to change into the attire just supplied to us and proceed to the library. On the tables are bottles of ink, quills, sheets of paper, envelopes and sealing wax. Each of us is allocated three sheets of paper and one envelope. We are told to write well and carefully as no more stationery will be available to us. Restricted to one letter, priority has to be to my parents. But I quickly decide to use one sheet for Elsa and direct Mother to pass it on to her. I know that Mother will be elated that I have entered the seminary. Dad, on the other hand, not so.

I linger on the letter to Elsa. It must be short out of necessity and because it is best. I tell her how wonderful she is, that I miss her already, and that my heart belongs to her. I explain that this is an intellectual quest and it probably won't last more than the school year, then *Love always, Rafer*. I fold the letter into a tri-fold, apply her name and some sealing wax, and include it with that to my parents. When I hand the envelope to the cadre, it is with a profound feeling of angst.

By 9:00 p.m., we climb into our bunks. All, that is, but those assigned tasks such as the fire watch, which is part for safety and part discipline; one man would stay up for two hours and make sure that all was secure. He would then wake another, identified by a towel tied over the end of his bunk, who would in turn take the next two hour stint. So it goes throughout the night. Clergy having accompanied the military for centuries, I suspect that this was part of military bunk house custom.

I am fortunate to get the first shift. I say fortunate in the sense that, if you have the duty at all, going first is better than being wakened in the middle of the night. A half hour has passed when I decide to visit the latrine outside. The night air is refreshing. Dark, puffy clouds glide by in quick succession and moonlight races through any break in them. A sudden breeze causes some leaves to tumble across the lawn and spiral up toward the sky. It is a grand sight so I don't go back inside right away.

I see a candle flicker from the private corner room on the second floor. From the silhouette behind the glass I make out the figure of Biceps, who will rule our lives for how long we just don't know. He walks ramrod straight, shoulders always pulled back and with an attentive strut as if ever on guard against physical assault. Whether he does this to be assertive or as affectation, I have yet to decide. A few minutes later, the candle is snuffed. He turns in for the night, I presume.

I am about to return to quarters when I hear footsteps and then voices on the other side of some bushes. As the interlopers near the building they grow quiet and then pass silently through the doorway. I follow discretely only to discover that they have taken refuge in the bath house. Their voices are muffled so I strain to hear.

"These stinking chores, distasteful, never in my life," says one.

"A lesson in humility, I'm afraid."

"Do you think you will see this through?"

"I'll do what I have to do," says the other.

Only featureless shapes are discernable. I have waited for this moment since Father Bart's orientation. "You sorry bunch of wimps," I say. "That will be one demerit each. Nine more and you're gone."

"Who's that?" comes the rapid retort.

"Who's that, sir. You dare to question your superiors?"

"No sir."

"A few restrictions and some unpleasant chores and you whine. What are you going to do if you are given missionary work?"

"We will accept anything, if it is God's wish."

"You will accept anything. So you say. So you say. Will you accept responsibility for not reporting a sabbat in your own community?"

Silence reigns as familiarity struggles with disbelief. The larger shape comes forth with a tentative interrogative. "Rafer?"

I strike a sulphur stick on the rough stone wall and hold it above my head. "And you guys make a life change without telling me. Fine friends you are."

"Well, blessed be to God" Johann Carberry says with relieved delight.

"Rafer! Wunderbar! I don't believe it. This is too good to be true," Franz responds with equal fervor.

As if part of a planned celebration, moonlight suddenly bursts through the windows. Each of us rushes to tell the others our stories. It is serendipity as we catch up on the circumstances that got us here. As close as we are, none of us had an inkling that the others were contemplating the priesthood and certainly didn't think that we would have already embarked on the journey.

⁊

After morning Mass, we break our fast. The balance of our day and the following weeks are largely devoted to bible study, liturgy, and various classes in language proficiency. Theological discussion, my primary reason for being here, is not part of this indoctrination period. I persevere. Intramural sports or other extra-curricular activities such as choir practice or setting movable type in the seminary print shop are phased into the curriculum. Each day is concluded by a two hour study period capped by vespers and the evening meal.

As Christmas arrives, any hope of visits from family is for naught. I receive notice that my father was called to Rome at the behest of Pope Paul III and mother wouldn't travel without him. Johann has no family in Austria. Franz's family is consumed with a troubling financial crisis which has totally preoccupied them but they are looking forward to seeing him at the spring break.

At the start of the second semester, I am ecstatic. A visiting young instructor by the name of Father Hans Dietrich arrives on campus to teach a course called *Introductory to Theology*. Father Dietrich is a Dominican on loan from his order, a payback for some other service rendered by the Augustinians to the Dominicans. The course emphasis is on defining the Christian religion and defending it against its detractors. I think of the Greek word apologia meaning defense and for the sake of brevity will henceforth refer to this course or subject matter as apologetics. Otherwise, what spare time I have had, I spent in the library devouring any scientific or theological publication that I came across. I can't wait for class to begin. It doesn't take me long to run afoul of the visiting priest.

"If you take just one thing away from what I say here today, just remember that underlying everything, God loves you," Father Dietrich begins.

"By *"you,"* Father, do you mean those of us associated with this seminary or do you mean everyone in the world?" I ask.

"Why, everyone in the world."

"Then why does the Church go about burning heretics at the stake? Is this how one deals with those God loves?"

"God loves the sinner but detests the sin."

"Then condemn the sin but leave vengeance to God. Is it appropriate for the Church to be advocating the taking of life let alone by such cruel methods?"

"If one is only suspected of heresy, and assuming there is no second admonition of heresy, one is given a year to make suitable atonement before being condemned as a heretic. He or she has the opportunity to repent. All is done according to canon law."

"Still, contradiction lingers. What knowledge can you share with us Father that will justify this?"

"*Deuteronomy* deals with this, Chapter 13 as I recall. False prophets are to be put to death."

"Deuteronomy speaks of false prophets. What of someone who just has trouble accepting revealed truth as defined by Church dogma? Technically he is a heretic. Canon law demands that he be put to death?"

"For your information young man, no cleric may promote a sentence of death, or execute such a sentence, or be present at its execution. No sub-deacon, deacon, or priest shall practice that part of surgery involving burning or cutting. So states Canon 18 of the *Twelfth Ecumenical Council*, Lateran IV, in 1215, held under Pope Innocent III."

"I happen to be quite familiar with that canon. And Ecumenical Councils are the *sensus ecclesiae*, the mind of the Church in action, positioning themselves to take on the cloak of dogma and authoritative pronouncements. But you don't mean to imply that the Apostolic See is not responsible for these executions, do you? Canon 3 of the same council states that the Church will excommunicate and anathematize every heresy, condemning all heretics under whatever names they may be known. Secular authorities, whatever office they may hold, shall be admonished and induced and if necessary compelled by ecclesiastical censure to exterminate in the territories subject to their jurisdiction all heretics pointed out by the Church. If a temporal ruler, after being admonished by the Church, neglects to cleanse his territory of heretical foulness, he is to be excommunicated and the pontiff may declare the ruler's vassals absolved from their allegiance and may offer the territory to be ruled by Catholics, who on the extermination of the heretics, may possess it without hindrance. This Apostolic decree has been in effect for over 300 years. Even St. Thomas Aquinas in his *Summa Theologica,* Second Part of the Second Part, Treatise on The Theological Virtues, Of Heresy, maintains that unrepentant heretics are to be delivered to the secular authorities to be put to death because the Church must look to the salvation of others. Such God forsaken punishment doesn't square with a loving God regardless of what rationale is given."

"What is your name young man?"

"Rafer Schilling, Father."

"Herr Schilling, I find it extraordinary that you, a first year seminarian, are challenging doctrine and your superiors," he says testily.

"I am not challenging my superiors, Father. I am inquiring of my superiors. God has given us the capacity to reason. I would think it to be one's obligation to utilize that capacity to reconcile perceived inconsistencies. Also, according to St. Thomas, '*the will firmly pursues what is firmly believed by reason, and that it cannot abstain from what reason prescribes; this necessity, however, is not coercion, but the nature of the will.*' "

"Herr Schilling, '*perceived*' is the operative word here. You are here to learn, not question." His words are wrapped in contempt.

"But my understanding is that the intent of this course is to explore Christian theology. I for one have what I believe to be reasonable questions."

"I have a lesson plan to adhere to, Herr Schilling, and I will proceed with it now," slamming the door to further questions and supposed impertinence. The wind stirs with new found echoes, seeming to underscore the tension.

If the other students have doubts, they are not letting on. But I will not be deterred. Other skirmishes with Fr. Dietrich arise as the semester progresses.

"Father Dietrich, when various theologians are arguing opposite positions on certain theological questions, isn't it possible that the credibility of the Church is put at risk when the hierarchy proclaims one view or the other to be official Church doctrine? It seems that whichever faction holds sway in Rome at a given time is the one which determines Church dogma."

Dietrich braces once more with poorly controlled indignation. "These decisions are made with much consideration and with prayer for divine guidance, Herr Schilling," his words dripping with sarcasm as if any fool would know this.

"But is much consideration enough? Unless a position can be stated unequivocally, with virtually no opposition, isn't the Church boxing itself in?"

"Where are you going with this Herr Schilling?"

"It has come to pass that each pope is bound by the promulgations of his predecessors. This makes each papal pronouncement momentous. The Church becomes so irretrievably bound to the past that it precludes the future."

"How so?" He looks to the ceiling, possibly self-control may be found there.

"Science and discovery reveal things not contemplated by past generations. It is easy for us, through bias or false premises, to conclude things to be true that in reality are not. Things that can influence doctrine."

"I refer you to tradition and the living, and I emphasize living, teaching authority of the Church."

His eyes slowly descend from the ceiling to the floor, self-control has migrated.

"How does the Church of future generations distinguish prevailing tradition from dead traditionalism? The Church's position is that Earth is the center of the universe. Yet an astronomer, mathematician, and doctor of canon law no less, Nicolaus Copernicus, has proposed a heliocentric model, placing the sun rather than the earth at the center of the universe. The Dominican, Bartolomeo Spina, the Church's chief censor, has expressed a desire to stamp out the Copernican doctrine. What if Copernicus is right?" My classmates shoot puzzled glances at each other.

"As you say, this is just another theory. What makes you favor Copernicus over the Church's long held position?"

"I didn't say that I favor it, Father. He will be proven right or wrong when the scientific community explores the theory in depth."

"Well, let's wait and see, Herr Schilling, let's wait and see. I have no doubt as to the outcome," his condescension hanging in the air. An embarrassed silence permeates the classroom.

℘

My ecclesiastical journey takes another hit at the conclusion of quarterly exams. Fr. Dietrich is handing out the test results and a classmate asks about the correct response to a question concerning the Church's primary function.

"The propagation of the faith and maintaining its integrity," is Dietrich's reply.

"The Church's primary role is to promote peace, charity, and moral leadership as exemplified by Jesus. Man has to deal with enough misery in this world without others adding to it," I volunteer.

"Of what misery do you speak?" Dietrich fires back.

"The Black Death has wiped out 75% of the population in some parts of Europe. Then we have leprosy, smallpox... all indifferent to man, woman or child. War, the sport of kings, is incessant. Storms, floods and famine regularly devastate cities and towns. If God can abide these horrors besieging those whom He created in his own image, He can abide a few heretics."

"Herr Schilling, get out of my sight!"

℘

The next morning, our troika is gathered in high spirits. I am still packing to go home on spring break and trying to convince Johann to come and stay with me but he wants to remain at the seminary and help with a construction project.

"Rafer," yells a classmate as he steps onto the 2nd floor of our dormitory.

"Ja," I reply.

"The prefect wants to see you in his office."

Johann and Franz look at me ominously. I acknowledge their stares and just as quickly look down to finish my packing. Putting my bag at the end of my bunk, I say, "This shouldn't take long. Franz, we'll head out as soon as I get back."

Gazing out his office window, hands folded behind his back, it strikes me right away that his head is too big for his body. I cough to announce my presence. He turns on the heels of his purple, suede slippers and invites me to sit down opposite his large desk inlaid with ivory. The Oriental rug, massive bookcases and elegantly draped windows underscore his stature. He is cordial but serious.

"Herr Schilling, I presume?" I nod. "I am told by a certain faculty member that you are troubled by certain Church doctrine."

This is a slippery slope. "I have difficulty reconciling certain things, Father. So I inquire."

"Inquiry is expected here. But so is acceptance and obedience. As I understand it, you have trouble with acceptance."

"I have trouble with the correctness of the responses of a certain, relatively young, faculty member in particular. Perhaps a more learned and wiser professor would be better equipped for apologetic discourse."

"My, my! That's a bit presumptuous!" His eyebrows flare up.

"That is not my intention, Father. But I must be frank."

"I also will be candid, Herr Schilling. Fr. Dietrich is an exceptional scholar and accredited teacher of theology. As I understand it, you challenge fundamental Christian doctrine."

"As I understand it, Father, there are certain theologians who have questions similar to mine."

"Being a theologian doesn't give one infallibility. To be blunt, theologians have been excommunicated because of their vainglorious positions." I do not respond. "Herr Schilling, it is my job to ascertain whether or not you should remain as a student at this seminary. Your academic record is superior. By all reports you have an exceptional mind and are a born leader. The question is, and this is a big question, how strong is your faith?"

"I wish to be candid with you, Father. I believe that one should follow truth wherever it leads, more so the Church, whose main premise is righteousness."

"Well said. But your independence of thought troubles me Herr Schilling. And I'm not sure if we are dealing with tenacity or hubris."

"I am not aware that my fellow seminarians deem me arrogant."

"They don't, from what I hear." He purses his lips and seems to lose himself in thought. He turns back to the window and assumes his original pose. "I'm going to defer my decision until after the break. I want you to reassess your commitment to the Church in the meantime. Meet with me here immediately upon your return. If you can assure me at that time that you will obey your superiors, that you will accept the Church's teachings, I will see that you will continue at this seminary. If you are not prepared to do so, do not return. Do I make myself clear?"

"I do, Father."

The prefect slowly turns his head just enough to look over his left shoulder and make eye contact.

"Then God be with you."

I return to the dormitory where Johann and Franz are waiting. Their stares plead for information.

"I'm not coming back," I say.

CHAPTER 5

THE TRADITION CONTINUES

I had undertaken a journey not sure where I would end up - a lifetime of service in the priesthood, a devout, married parishioner or a disillusioned heretic. Right or wrong, my beliefs are starting to harden.

Not wanting to spoil my first evening home with such ponderous news, I make no reference to it and try to just rejoice at being back in Innsbruck with my family; luckily, Dad was not traveling. Every time Mother brings up the seminary, I become vague, somewhat to her consternation. After a hearty meal we adjourn to the main room and Dad serves schnapps all around. They bring me up to-date with the town happenings with one notable exception, not that it would be on their minds.

It is good to be home. All are in good spirits. After a while they notice me struggling to stay awake. It had been a tiring journey burdened by my disappointment. Mother declares that there has been enough talk for one night and insists that I proceed to bed. Kind to a fault, she had affectionately turned down the covers; I am asleep within minutes.

The next morning I awake with the scent of hot tea in my nostrils; Mother has just left a cup on the night stand. I catch her middle age, slightly plump silhouette, topped with graying hair tied in a bun, stealing back towards the kitchen. Five minutes later she returns with Fruhstuck, consisting of more tea, a roll, butter, jam and a knife to spread them. I nibble while shaving and freshening up.

Upon entering the kitchen I am greeted by two robust Good Mornings. Mother comes over and gives me a big hug followed by Dad doing the same, his dark complexion contrary to hers.

"You men go sit down, I have Gabelfruhstuck ready," Mother insists. The fork breakfast starts with Zwetschkenknodel, plum dumplings under mounds of buttery bread crumbs and honey. A cold glass of Sekt is there to wash them down.

"Well," I say, "there is a reason clichés become clichés. It's still true, there's no place like home."

"It's wonderful to have you back for a while," says Mother. "The place hasn't been the same without you; isn't that so Erich?"

"Well, I suspect that we can expect the unexpected again," Dad replies.

"Erich, what's that supposed to mean? Tsk. Tsk."

We laugh at her reaction. Mother joins us at the table and starts chatting about her flower boxes, which she watered a bit ago, and how the insects are such a problem already. She just loves puttering around with them and takes great pride in the color and beauty they bring to the chalet. The vases in the house always have something in them, roses and tulips are a favorite. She tells Dad not to forget that he had promised to take the wagon to town today to pick-up some top soil. And so our conversation goes, mostly happy talk initially, as we focus on downing the tasty meal.

"If your father is still here when you go back," she says, changing direction, "I would like us to accompany you. I'd love to see the seminary and meet some of your professors. I'm sure you did well academically as usual?" I knew that she was going to bring the conversation back to the seminary as soon as she could.

"Dean's List, right Rafer?" Dad says.

"Every quarter," I affirm.

"I'm so proud of you, Rafer. Imagine, having a priest in the family. And to think Johann and Franz will be priests too," Mother continues.

"Well..."

"Oh, that reminds me. Remember that pretty young girl that you used to date?" says Mother as she studies my face for a reaction.

"Elsa," I reply. "I plan to stop over and surprise her today."

"Then you don't know?"

"Don't know what?"

"I suppose you wouldn't know, sequestered as you were in the seminary. I suppose Franz just found out yesterday himself. His family wasn't thrilled about it. Happened so fast and all."

"Found out what?"

"Well she got married a couple of months ago. And they think that she's pregnant already, morning sickness. Not that she had to, mind you. Get married, that is. Still, it was rather sudden. The bans were announced one week and the next she was married. Shortest engagement I can remember."

I am stunned. "Are you sure it's the same person? Elsa Obernesser?"

"Of course I'm sure. I wouldn't have said it if I wasn't. Yes, Elsa Obernesser is her name. Was her name."

"Who did she marry?"

"Franz's older brother, Willem von Clausen."

"Willem? Willem?"

"Yes, Willem."

"He must be a dozen or so years older than Elsa."

"That's not so unusual," Mother says as she takes the dishes to the kitchen sink

"This is crazy. I don't believe it. I can't believe it," is the only exasperated reply I can muster. I am devastated.

"It was the talk of the town. He literally bumped into her, knocking her over, as Christmas decorations were going up in front of the Golden Dachl. Being a gentleman, he apologized profusely. Bought some flowers for her from a street vendor right then and there. Fell in love on the spot. She refused to date him at first, I heard, but he persisted. Showered her with gifts. The next thing they are engaged. His parents thought he was rushing things but he wouldn't hear of it. She did well for herself, marrying into the best family in Innsbruck."

"What's your definition of best?" Dad asks half seriously.

"Oh, hush! You know what I mean."

"No I don't," replies Dad.

I push away from the table in obvious consternation and head outside. Head down, hands on my hips, I stare aimlessly at the ground. I then sit putting my face in my hands. I don't want to believe what I have been told. It doesn't make sense. How can this be? Life is tossing me around in an avalanche of uncertainty. Hurt and despair course through my veins.

When I return to the chalet I hear Mother crying in their bedroom. "Oh Erich, what have I done? I never delivered his letter to that nice girl. I was afraid that she might come between our son and the priesthood. And now I suspect that he isn't going back anyway. Oh Erich, I'm a selfish person."

"I'll go talk to him," I hear Dad say. He comes into the main room and sees me standing there. Taking me by the arm, he walks me outside again.

"You heard, I take it."

"I heard."

"Your mother just showed me the letter. You were asking her to wait for you. Elsa never knew. We thought, even the von Clausens, I understand, that you and Franz committed to the Church."

"Ja," I reply, lowering my head and closing my eyes, my breath leaves me.

"I'm so sorry. She must have thought that you moved on. Let's take a walk."

We walk and walk. He mentions that my letter to Mother and him never indicated that I was on a trial run. As far as they could tell, I had decided to accept the Order's challenge and commit to the priesthood. I respond that I didn't want them to think that I was on a lark; the priesthood was a possibility. But in my own mind it was just that, a possibility. I didn't think it necessary to be so explicit at the time. I wanted Mother, in particular, to believe that I was giving it my best shot.

"Your Mother never opened the letter to Elsa until just now. She didn't deliver it because she was afraid that Elsa might complicate things for you; she wanted you to be a priest so much. She now realizes that she had no right to take that upon herself. She is mortified and heartbroken."

"And I have lost the love of my life," I reply.

"And life has a way of getting in the way of love. I can't tell you how sorry I am that it has come to this. A life changing experience if ever there was one." We walk on without purpose, neither speaking now; I lost in my devastation and he unable to console. Finally, it is Dad who breaks the silence.

"Tell me about your time at the seminary."

"Martin Luther was right all along. The Church selling bogus indulgences to fill its coffers, misrepresenting scripture. But what bothers me most is its obsession with so-called dogma and its enforcement. To question its theological positions and/or practices is to sign your own death sentence. It is a place where conformity, not love, is most prized. Charitable works aside, it is responsible for great harm.

Mother endows it with qualities that are long lost. It has become obvious to me, and others, that I don't fit in."

"Others?"

On the way back to the chalet I tell Dad of my encounters with Father Dietrich and the Prefect. As we enter we find Mother sitting at the table still wiping tears away. She looks at me and starts to cry uncontrollably. I lift her to her feet and we embrace. My long walk has absorbed some of my melancholy.

"I had no idea how much she meant to you. I thought you had committed yourself to…"

"I've spent the better part of an academic year at the seminary, Mother, and… And I've discovered that I just don't have a vocation. I'm sorry. I know how much you wanted it to be."

"Then it is God's will… my biggest anxiety in all this is that I cost you your love. And I am a major disappointment to you. I've let you down. I've done irreparable harm." More tears and sobbing.

"After all the indiscretions for which you pardoned me. I certainly can let this pass."

"Oh, Rafer… I never pushed you into it. In fact, it took me by surprise."

"Nein. Nein. You didn't. And I didn't mean to imply such. It was strictly my idea."

"Then why? What makes you so sure that you have no vocation?" her voice trembling.

"You just know these things."

"It's God's will then. I won't bring it up again… Please forgive me. About Elsa, I mean. Can you ever forgive me?" Tears drench the sobs.

"Never have you intended to hurt me. There is nothing to forgive."

We hug a bit longer until she says, "I really must tend to my flower boxes. Erich, take Rafer to town with you to get that top soil.

You can discuss how the empire should be run on the way," and off she goes. Dad and I head to the barn to hitch up the wagon.

"What of your faith now?" Dad asks.

"I'm a disillusioned idealist."

"Care to expand on that?"

"Jesus simply moved among the people preaching good will towards men. He was about creating a community, a society, of righteous people. He didn't even seek a leadership role in the temple. The Church, on the other hand, has become a power enclave with bishops and cardinals marking their turf in a quest for wealth and power. What is one to make of the Church?"

"And where is the Holy Spirit?"

"Different factions in the course of Church history have vehemently argued what should or should not be included as scripture. They were not even certain themselves. Then somewhere along the line some things became canon. In spite of that ambiguity, the Church won't re-examine canon when called upon to do so. Religion has come to be a thing of understanding, the subject of learned treatment, its essence reduced to dogmas and precepts. It has ceased to be a spiritual element in which the heart has free scope."

"Things do get set in stone over time," Dad agrees.

"Frankly, I think too much is made of scripture."

"Did you raise these issues at the seminary?"

"Ja. I wanted to reconcile what I perceived to be questionable teaching and put nagging questions to rest. But instead of erasing my doubts, they were magnified."

"Doubt is the secret torment of all clergyman, Rafer. On that, I have no doubt. What of the Evangelicals, the Protestants? They have railed against Church abuses."

"The Protestant movement has its pluses but it hasn't deviated from the same punitive atrocities in the name of God."

"Once again, only last year, at the Church's instigation, the Anabaptist[1] leader Jakob Hutter was burned at the stake." There is a lull and then Dad continues. "Historically, at times, people didn't believe in God. At other times they believed in many gods. Now it is one God. Who got it right? People cling to religion because it promises eternal life and because they fear a wrathful God if they don't believe. Has anybody ever come back from the dead over these thousands, maybe millions of years?"

"Jesus supposedly did."

"Supposedly," Dad muses. "Supposedly Jesus made appearances after his entombment. The Resurrection is the claimed proof of his divinity, is it not? But to whom did he appear? His own cronies, we are told. Wouldn't it have been more credible if Jesus had walked the streets of Jerusalem after his crucifixion? That would have gotten everybody's attention. What better way to proclaim his divinity rather than leave it for biased sources to affirm? This isn't a criticism of Jesus, mind you. I love the essential humanity of Jesus, if only the hierarchy would emulate it."

"We are told that faith preempts reason."

"Faith preempts reason. I am familiar with that refrain. And the definition of faith is belief without proof. Is it so extraordinary, with an issue of this magnitude, that there not be incontrovertible rational evidence?"

I don't respond so he continues. "For Saint Bonaventure, faith is infused by the Holy Spirit whereas reason is innate. I say faith is

---

1   Anabaptists were members of a radical sect that believed in adult baptism. At the time, this was punishable by death. They believed that infant baptism was a blasphemous formality since infants did not have the capacity of reason.

learned. Yet he says that faith and reason must be united if they are ever to be brought to fulfillment. I don't see that happening. For him, all science is subservient to theology; one who has faith embraces truth more firmly than one who simply desires to know. An audacious hypothesis, I say. But the Church declared him a saint, so the congregation takes to heart everything he said."

"Erich, is that you in there?" comes a shout through the open door of the barn.

"Ja. Who's there? Come in!"

"It is I, Fritz," the brim of his hat casts a dark shadow on his face.

"Herr Freihofer!" I say. "So good to see you."

"Rafer! Are you ever going to stop growing," he says rhetorically. "Erich, he's certainly has come into his own."

"That he has, Fritz."

"This is wonderful. Home for a visit I presume?"

"More than a visit, I'm afraid. Apparently I'm not cut out for the priesthood. I'll be working for Dad carrying on the family tradition, if he will have me."

"Well I'm sure he will welcome that. Frankly, I was somewhat saddened to think that there would be no more Schillings showing travelers the way through these treacherous mountains."

"Fritz, you soft soap artist. Here, let me put your horse in a stall."

"I'm a bit extended; do you mind if I sit on this stool?" He takes his handkerchief to his brow.

"You do look like someone exiting a storm. Rafer, grab those other stools over there!"

"Erich, the Gautier party is two days overdue. Winter may be behind us but no one knows better than you the bitter temperatures that we can still get at night; the layered soft and packed snow on the mountain at this time of year ripe for avalanches. A rescue party is being put together and they want you to lead it. As usual for such things, you will be compensated from the town treasury."

"Who is their guide?"

"They didn't have one, I am told. It being spring they thought they could forge their own way. Some of them had been through here before."

"Just who are they and where were they coming from?"

A group of Frenchmen returning from a pilgrimage to the Holy Land. There were six of them on horseback."

"You're saying that they went to the Holy Land with the Ottomans running rampant there and almost on our doorstep?" Dad's shoulders lift high against his neck.

"It's part of the *Capitulations*. Suleiman and the King of France made an accommodation last year. French subjects are now permitted to travel and trade in the sultan's dominions."

"So I heard. But I'm surprised they were facilitated that quickly. Curious that Gautier didn't travel by sea, Marseille or Toulon. It would have been much more direct and easier. Where were they last seen?"

"Roughly twenty miles east of here. We know that they left Schwaz at daybreak two days ago."

"Rafer and I will leave within a half hour. Have the rescue party start as soon as they can. Bring two mule drawn wagons to carry the incapacitated, anyone really, blankets, water, food, ropes, etc. You know the drill. Have them rendezvous at Richter Tavern. Stay there until I contact them."

"Then you think that they are not far from Schwaz?"

"I don't know a better place to meet up. On your way out, tell the missus, she's about the chalet somewhere. Say we are about to set out on a rescue mission. She'll have provisions in our packs even before Rafer and I have our act together."

"Danke schon, Erich, Rafer. I'll be on my way."

"The foehn, Dad?"

"That dry, south wind wreaks havoc this time of year. It had to be on them even before they started out. You passed through the area coming from Rattenberg. What was your experience?"

"Well, fog was already on us when we were receiving the results of our quarterly exams. I don't think I could have gone from one building to the next if I hadn't known the way by rote. But yesterday it was manageable."

"The Gautier party didn't have the sense to stay put. They probably wandered off the main road. At best, they're lost, probably dehydrating... but I doubt that."

"If they were lost, even injured, some would probably have found their way out by now. Is that your train of thought?"

"I'm afraid so. Yusuf is probably in his room over the workshop, bring him up to speed. Three will give us more flexibility. I'll start saddling our horses!"

The temperature is well above freezing and it is sunny, weather conditions for a rescue couldn't be much better. We ride the bridle path alongside the road as it is in better condition than the road itself, the road primarily the way for carriages and wagons. In the open valley we travel at a fast pace.

"We'll see if anybody stopping in Solbad Hall came across them along the way. If we get lucky, it could narrow our search area considerably," Dad says.

They hadn't. We continue east keeping an eye out for signal smoke, reflections from mirrors, whistles, but nothing so demonstrative is detected. We focus on areas where the trail might fall off, where horses on their own lead would gravitate away from the main path. Miles are put behind us.

I note the curiosity in Dad's face as his eyes keep returning to three golden eagles circling a bit to the southeast. Not exactly an uncommon sight but it certainly has his attention. The landscape fans out again and seemingly without purpose; Dad leads our small party southward following its contour. Anything irregular is searched for. The wind gets stronger and the temperature colder as we trot through the narrow channels of the slate mountain walls. We go another mile or so and he stops, staring at the west face. I draw my horse alongside his.

"What do you see Rafer?" he asks.

"I see a narrow trail ahead tracing the side of the mountain. Brush and rocks are scattered about, obviously out of service for some time. Most likely gave access to an abandoned salt or mineral mine."

"Go on!"

"Everything else seems to be in order, nothing exceptional."

"Nothing exceptional?"

"I see no recent human or animal evidence about. No demonstrative physical signs."

"No demonstrative physical signs? Stop looking down, look up!"

"The eagles?"

"More pertinent than the eagles."

"Steep, high rock face partially covered in snow," I say, staring at the mountain, feeling stupid.

"Yusuf, give him a hint." Yusuf brings his horse alongside mine then pointedly gestures towards the rock face I just described. I scan it from near to far until I finally note the broad black band of mountainside that appears incongruously among the nooks and crannies draped in white.

"A landslide... I'd say about a quarter mile away."

"Let's go!"

Copper mines had weakened the rock formation which in turn produced cracks in the 55 degree slope. Rainwater and melting snow penetrated these fissures only to later freeze and expand causing the rock to fragment. Over the years, probably decades, the face became unstable and eventually broke free under its own weight. What are the chances that anyone would be off the beaten path just when such a thing occurred?

The carnage is immediately apparent as animal carcasses and human appendages protrude from the rubble, only the cold preventing decomposition. We gingerly clamber about looking and listening for signs of life. On the far side of the pile, to our amazement, part of the trail has been torn away creating an uninterrupted drop of 100 feet or so, testimony to the possible precariousness of our present perch. Four of the six we could account for. Apparently they had been in single file and had stayed close to the side of the mountain. But were the others completely buried or had they gone over the edge? Amidst the carnage, nestled in the grey shadows, is an unspoken quiet.

I hammer an eye spike into a rock fissure and pass through it a long, doubled rope. Dad in turn passes it through metal rings at the waist of his harness while making necessary adjustments to his customized equipment. With his feet on the edge of the precipice, he leans out and looks down as the daylight rapidly diminishes like the oncoming darkness of a lunar eclipse. Snow flurries begin to whirl in the air.

"There's an outcropping about 20 feet down. There is a dead horse on it with its legs and head jutting over the edge. Appears to be something alongside it. Hard to make out, scrub branches," he says.

"Any movement?"

"Nein."

"A makeshift cover?"

"Possibly."

Dad "walks" down to the outcropping while I guide the rope to reduce any abrasion. It is getting even colder and the wind has not abated. His first inclination is to look down from there; it is another 70 foot drop or so to the bottom. He moves to the dead horse and pulls away the branches leaning against it revealing a man. The horse he had been riding undoubtedly took the brunt of the fall. Dad lifts the man's chin and puts his fingers at the base of his throat and discovers a pulse. The victim's arms, legs and torso are cold to the touch despite his ample clothing. His peripheral circulation has shut down and his body core is no longer generating heat. Dad's mind races. *Hypothermia, don't rub his extremities, this will only divert blood and heat away from the core. I will have to wrap myself around him to provide an auxiliary source of heat. Two of us should encase him but it's not feasible.*

"I'll spend the night here. We can't risk moving him now. Send me down a sleeping bag and the tarp. Then you and Yusuf make camp. At the crack of dawn I want Yusuf on his way to Richter Tavern. Tell them that, with one exception, it's a recovery party and not a rescue party."

Bracing himself against the mountain side, Dad uses his legs to shove the horse's rump just enough to shift its weight and it plunges into the darkness. They now have an adequate platform for the night and there is enough room to fashion a lean-to. He drives short, thin, metal spikes through the top and bottom edges of the tarp with only partial success; he uses dirt and rocks from the slide to help.

It is an uncomfortable night with fitful sleep. Dad is happy to see dawn break and the wind subside. His nocturnal companion's internal furnace has been stoked. Dad starts a small fire on the outcropping and pours water from his canteen into the copious cup that it had been inserted into; adds a tea bag; and holds it over the fire by its folding handle. He re-enters the lean-to and pats the man's face with his hands.

"Mon ami, can you hear me?"

"My companions?" he whispers.

"Let's just talk about you right now. How about something to drink?" He nods. The tea is more warm than hot and he sips away after being propped up. Dad cuts a beef stick into bite size pieces and feeds it to him one by one. In short order, shivering and weak, he falls back.

"Je m'appelle Erich. Et vous?"

"Henri." He winces in pain. "My right leg."

"Your ankle is swollen. I'll wrap your leg and put a splint on it."

"Merci."

"Dad, everything all right down there?" I call.

"Did Yusuf leave for the tavern yet?"

"Ja, he is well on his way."

"Then everything's all right."

"Are you able to see anything below you?"

"Just rock and earth from the landslide scattered down a gradual slope. Pretty much spread out."

"I'll dig out the bodies while we're waiting for the recovery team."

"Be careful!"

In the process I'm able to account for the whole party. All but one of the bodies are fairly easy to extract; I'll wait for assistance from the recovery party for him. One has his fist rising out of the rubble like a defiant warrior. I lay the battered remains side by side further up the trail. As I'm walking back I'm besieged by a shower of rocks.

"Rafer, what's going on up there?" Dad yells.

"Apparently the landslide isn't quite over."

"Take cover!"

"No, I better pull you out now. The slope is shaking."

Dad puts his harness on Henri and uses one of the ropes to guide the ascent from below. Henri has cuts and bruises all over his body so it isn't just his injured ankle that torments him. He gasps as the full weight of his body presses against the harness. I have my horse move slowly along the trail, the rope passing through the eye spike before being attached to the horn of the saddle so that the ascent will be as vertical as possible. Suddenly the rope grows especially taught and Henri cries out in pain.

"Stop! Rafer. Stop! The harness is caught near the lip."

I tell the horse to stay, hoping that he won't be spooked, and walk to the edge disregarding tumbling rocks. Reaching down, I grab the top of Henri's coat and pull him to one side and over the edge. I gently pick him up and carry him a short distance, putting him in a sleeping bag under an overhang. He sees the cadavers nearby and sighs.

"Dad," I shout. "The harness is torn. I wouldn't trust it."

"Then I'll climb out of here. The rope will be my safety line."

Keeping his body as vertical as the mountain face will allow, he stretches from toehold to toehold, pushing himself slowly upward, his hands used for balance as much as anything else. I take up the slack as he rises and then scrambles over the edge. We make for the overhang. The new warmth of the sun gives both of us some comfort.

"Hello, over there," someone calls, "do you need assistance?" It is the rescue party. The two of us start laughing to ourselves at the incongruity of it all.

∽

Through a window in our chalet I could see a bright red glow about the sun warning of rain to come. If we were to do any fishing today, it is best that we do it early.

In short order our fly lines are flicking above the chill water searching for a fish that would accept the bogus meals that we are offering. In parts of the stream the water races across protruding rocks but in others still pools are the norm. The sport is finding the fish in the first place and then convincing him that something made of only thread and feathers is a fly or other insect. Feeding below the surface so as not to reveal himself to predators, one must cast about and tempt him out of this security.

A mayfly rises off the surface so I go to my fly assortment to match its color and size and then let it float about in a still pool. Dad uses a white streamer that looks like a shiner and lets it drift through the current giving it a twitch now and then. Our lines are purposely light weight to add to the challenge. An eighteen inch trout might take fifteen minutes to land so as not to overtax the line and to wait for him to tire.

But now the ground is brighter than the sky as we are being assaulted by onrushing dark clouds spilling over the mountain. A fierce wind accompanies the assault followed by a clap of thunder and a downpour.

"Collect the gear and let's go," Dad shouts.

Bent like hairpins, we plod back to the chalet; the rain being driven so hard that it feels like needles are being shot into our skin. We no sooner reach the front door when hail the size of beechnuts starts pelting us. The storm continues through the next day; the rain is torrential and the wind refuses to die. We know that the Inn and Sill Rivers will overflow, they were already high. At least our chalet is relatively safe on high ground and some distance away from both.

Finally the sun returns and the sky is a gorgeous tint of blue, not a cloud in sight; the weather has gone from frightening to glorious. We journey towards town to survey the damage. Fruit trees are broken; vineyards torn apart; newly planted fields sodden; the destruction is shocking.

In town, roofs have been torn off and the sides of some homes have been ripped open. Looking into them is like looking at the set of a play except there are no actors to be seen. A bed is floating in a street. Exterior lamp fixtures are twisted into extraordinary shapes. Chimneys have been toppled.

People mill around looking like sleepwalkers as they pick up this or that, examine it, then put it aside. Fears are expressed about the welfare of relatives and friends. One family of five is known to have been crushed when part of their building collapsed; three of them young children. Eight or nine others, no one is sure, were seen being swept away by the flood. A mother trying to move to safety in swirling, waist deep water, holding her two year old in her arms and eight year old by his hand, felt her strength slip away as the current tugged at her. She desperately concluded that she could hold only one; she let the eight year old go. When later found to be safe and when he was reunited with his mother he stared at her incomprehensively.

An emergency center has been established at the Town Hall to house the homeless and to coordinate information. Patrol parties have been dispatched to protect against looters. Cardinal Wolfgang Gerhardt, his long face in somber countenance, and a retinue of priests, move about the people giving them their blessings. Some people are asking if it is a punishment from God. Disasters on this scale, they fear, mean that the community has strayed from righteousness and is guilty of moral turpitude.

"What is the link that connects a natural phenomenon to the wrath of God," Dad whispers to me.

"It is the faith that they embrace; they connect biblical disasters to their own misfortune," I say.

"During my travels I've learned of hundreds of people… children, the elderly, all ages, being wiped out by a single catastrophe. Earthquakes.

Entire coastal areas destroyed by huge surges of ocean water that seem to come out of nowhere. Villages that get smashed by violent winds and rain virtually every year. Many other places never get touched; do people think that those places are only inhabited by saints?"

"It is part of their indoctrination growing up, I'm afraid."

"If God created the world, he certainly had the power to make it a safe world. If there is a God, I say that he stopped caring about mankind long ago."

Practical matters interrupt our deliberations as an acquaintance happens by. "Erich! Rafer! At the Town Hall, they're looking for you"

"We're heading there now," Dad answers.

CHAPTER 6

KARL

My transition to mountain guide had commenced with three misfortunes, human error played a role in two. Mother Nature claimed the most victims.

So far my training has been mostly academic. Dad constantly drives home the point that catastrophes lurk everywhere in these mountains and a big part of our job is to anticipate danger and shield our charges from injury and even death. At our chalet he holds *"classroom"* sessions. We pour over maps; recount seasonal hazards; distinguish required vs. optional gear according to the circumstances; make lists of provisions to be carried when and where; sort out transport, security and medical requirements. He peppers me with questions at the most unlikely moments and demands rapid and correct responses, ones that are reflexive, not pensive. Emergencies leave no time to ponder.

Fundamental to my training is learning the routes and alternate routes through the crossroads of Central Europe, knowing the distances and travel times from place to place, knowing what to expect during a given season, knowing when to move on and when to stay put, knowing where, when and how to make camp. Dad calls these the mechanics and the currency of our trade, having been passed from Schilling to Schilling, from generation to generation. But the hardest thing to impart, he emphasizes, is wisdom. "There is a right way and many wrong ways, for lack of a better way of putting it, in managing people and the situation at hand," he insists. Our clients typically are strong willed, capable people and you can't let them tell you your job. "In addition," he is very pointed about this, "a misplaced word during this religious upheaval can get you killed as surely as falling into a chasm, just slower."

My indoctrination takes place in the wake of the great age of exploration. Historic personages have emerged such as Columbus, da Gama, Cabot, Vespucci, de Leon, Balboa, Magellan and Cortes, adventurers expanding the world beyond our comprehension. It is a New World and kings salivate to gain riches from exploitation and trade. Gold, pearls, spices and slaves are prime commodities sovereigns lust after across the turbulent oceans as well as territory to plant their flags of empire.

A young, Flemish cartographer named Gerardus Mercator begins constructing terrestrial and celestial globes based on these great discoveries, as well as mathematical instruments. A few years from now, because of his Protestant sympathies, he is caught in the net of the Inquisition and jailed as a heretic for many months. But Gerardus has friends in high places, however, and he is eventually released. He would go on to develop the famous Mercator projection, greatly simplifying navigation and a boon to the captains of the high seas. His maps and navigational aids bring him great renown. Fortunately for the world, his talents have not been extinguished by religious interpretation.

While the tales of navigational feats and conquests stir our imaginations, most of the peoples of Europe are preoccupied with the trials and tribulations of their day-to-day existence.

After the great storm of 1537, as the locals call it, Innsbruck is put back together in some instances better than it was before. Merchants and other travelers passing through continue to energize the economy and fill the coffers of the Schilling family.

Johann and Franz had returned to the seminary several months ago. Unlike me, their faith remains unbent. Clergymen may err but the Holy Spirit will protect the integrity of the faith they maintain. Johann carried my letter of withdrawal to the prefect for me but not before Dad insisted on rewording it. Initially I simply wrote, *Regrettably, I am unable to return due to a personal crisis.* I wanted to be truthful, brief and vague; I figured the less said the better. Dad agreed but under the circumstances of my departure he felt that a doctrinaire cleric might insist that *personal crisis* is code for a crisis of faith, which it is, and label me a suspect heretic. He insisted that I shift the responsibility for my not returning to him and to express more regret:

> *Due to a crisis within the family, which will apparently linger for a prolonged period, my father feels it best that I remain at his side. I wholeheartedly regret that I will be unable to resume my studies at this time and be a total and devoted servant to our Holy Mother, the Church.*

For the most part, this is true. But straight forward or not, I was okay with it.

So too, I would have to be circumspect in dealing with our charges. "Don't ever be taken in by the direction of someone's conversation, no matter how innocent that it may appear," Dad cautioned. "He could be duping you. Speak to the subject, if you must, but don't personalize it. Then again, your clients may say infuriating things. You, on the other hand must be disciplined." Dad was adamant about this. "Also, listen, observe and remember. Information is part of our commerce to use, to give or withhold."

It is still early in my apprenticeship when he begins telling me about Karl. It was March, 1517, months before I was born, when Karl joined a party of silver merchants that Dad was escorting to the Brenner Pass and from there into various regions of the Italian peninsula. He was a cheerful young man, about 19 or 20, and very learned. He was tight lipped about himself, inferring at most that he was something of a traveler. His intelligence and aplomb, however, marked him as someone special and undoubtedly someday he would rise to a position of prominence. Dad mentions in particular the theological discussions that Karl got into with the group yet, to this day, Dad is not certain of Karl's true convictions.

They passed through the erosion marked Italian Alps in the northeastern part of The Boot, as he likes to call the peninsula. Their jagged, saw-toothed crags of tinted sedimentary rock sometimes deposit limestone detritus along the trails and warn of possible trouble. Bolzano was the first town of note where they stopped. Even if one had to sleep on a crowded wooden floor of an inn there, it was much preferred to the stones and dirt surface of a tent pitched in the wilderness. Accommodations offered travelers at the Dominican monastery were often better but an ongoing Inquisition tempered the desire of some to mingle with the Black Friars. Peaks surround Bolzano on three sides and protect it from the frigid north winds. The town opens to the confluence of two tributaries to the south which become the headwaters of the Adige River.

Karl's paid fare only entitled him to be taken this far. Dad had been hired by some of the silver merchants to take them to Bologna, much farther to the south. Karl by now concluded that he was better off staying with the group but he had to be frugal with the money he had left. He knew that Yusuf and Dad had all things under control but he offered to lighten their load by assisting with the animals as compensation to continue to Bologna. Dad readily agreed and Karl was taken by his munificence. What he didn't know was that Dad was taken by Karl as someone who would be in a position of influence someday. People of influence often travel considerably so he thought it likely that they would meet again.

The Adige flows southward along the east side of the Apennines, the series of mountain ranges that form the topographical backbone of The Boot, and it set the course for much of the remaining trip. They passed through the ancient walls of Trent, which were built by the Romans fifteen centuries before. Almost three decades hence it would be the site of perhaps the most significant council of the Roman Catholic Church.

In Verona[1] they passed under a Roman gateway also dating to the 1st century AD and paused to view the white and pink limestone remains of a colossal Roman amphitheater which held 30,000 spectators in its day. As in Rome, gladiators occasionally fought to the death.

The ancient Via Aemilia took them to Bologna, which sprang from a Roman colony and was only incorporated into the Papal States the previous decade. Meandering through the arcaded streets they came to their final stop, the Visconti Inn, where Dad treated all to a hearty pasta meal and bottomless glasses of Valpolicella wine. The inn also served as a travelers' exchange. Here, if necessary, one could engage the services of other guides going towards all points of the compass. Just as important, it was a news center embracing travel conditions, politics, military actions, religious upheavals and gossip. Invariably, after a brief layover, if not continuing on, Dad would pick-up another party, often heading back north.

ᴄ⌀

---

1   At the end of the 16th Century, William Shakespeare wrote the famous tale of star-crossed lovers, Romeo Montague and Juliet Capulet, members of two implacable families of Verona. Reportedly, the original version was set in Siena but Verona is the locale known to all soon after.

The pope at this time is Leo X. On March 16, 1517, he calls an end to the *5th Lateran Council* which had been convened five years earlier by Pope Julius II to counter the conciliar movement by nine rebellious cardinals. *These cardinals were following the example of the Councils of Constance and of Basel of the previous century, which declared that Church general councils were superior to the pope.* It made me think of the great Schism of 1054, when the eastern Greek Orthodox churches refused to accept the supremacy of the bishop of Rome, otherwise known as the pope. So once again not all the hierarchy within the Roman Catholic Church itself was convinced of such supremacy.

The cardinals dismissed by Leo were returning from Rome directly or indirectly to their respective archdioceses. Karl, now alone, headed west. From Bologna, there are two passes through the Apennines, which one he took we are not sure and not that it really matters. We know he joined up shortly with a small party who knew the way well enough not to need a guide. They then turned south by southwest for Florence.

The group reportedly attended a service at the Duomo, the cathedral Santa Maria del Fiore, signaling that he had arrived safely in Florence. Brunelleschi's dome atop the cathedral is massive; its diameter far eclipses any dome erected before it and remains the architectural wonder of the day. Governmental administration takes place at the Palazzo della Signoria where the already fabled sculpture of *David* by Michelangelo stands. Karl has stepped into the nascent city of what I might call a high point of the Renaissance.

The narrow streets are made of stones placed there centuries before. Coursing westerly through the town is the Arno River; embraced by rolling hills, it is at once a source of practical beauty and potential menace as its waters occasionally rush over its banks dispensing hardship and heartache. The old bridge, the *Ponte Vecchio*, completed in

1345 under the direction of Taddeo Gaddi, has become famous in its own right. A segmental arch bridge requiring fewer piers than more ancient designs, it allows freer passage of raging flood waters. Small shops line each side of the bridge with a break in the middle to permit fishmongers and butchers to throw their waste into the river. The clop of hooves and rumbling wagon wheels among the clamor of vendors are part of the ambiance.

Karl's traveling companions find him some work setting up and tearing down vendor stalls in the piazzas. In his off hours he takes in Raphael's paintings of the Madonna, which bear a serene countenance. Leonardo da Vinci's unfinished *Battle of Anghiari* is an immense mural in the town's council hall. No one is sure why he hasn't completed it but some say that there were problems with the paint that he was experimenting with. As with the Florentines themselves, Karl is particularly taken by Leonardo's oil on wood, *Virgin and Child with St. Anne*, and its extraordinarily vital and three dimensional effect. His reputation as a universal genius continues to grow. His friendship with the influential Medici family is expedient, nevertheless his presumed homosexuality could have resulted in the premature demise of this unparalleled talent had he been caught in the web of an Inquisition.

Returning to the Duomo, as Karl is looking about, he hears voices coming from the sacristy. He decides to proceed there and is about to announce himself when he hears one say...

"The pope's physician is an ally of mine. He'll take care of the ingrate."

"You're talking about poisoning him?"

"Look, we got him elected and then he denies us our benefices. He's played us for fools. Just like he's playing France, Spain and the Emperor against each other. Politics is one thing but don't double cross your friends. He even had my brother removed from the government of Siena. My own brother, mind you. In my very own see. Can you imagine how humiliating that is? I'll never forgive him for that."

"Alphonso, we have been greatly wronged. But are you sure that you want to go forward with this? This is drastic and dangerous."

"Soderini, Sauli and Castellesi are supporting me."

"Supporting you or not opposing you? There's a difference."

"Are you with us or not?"

"Do what you will. I won't interfere."

Karl sees the adornments of two cardinals and quickly retreats. Upon making inquiries he discovers their identities and that they are visiting Florence before returning to their sees of Siena and Pisa. In fact, the pope is also in Florence to see what progress Michelangelo is making on the marble facade of the church of San Lorenzo and, also, to visit members of his own family. In many ways, he prefers Florence to Rome.

Pope Leo X is the second son of Lorenzo the Magnificent, a previous ruler of the Florentine republic, and a scion of the powerful Medici family. Being the second son, according to custom, Giovanni de' Medici was destined for the clergy. At age six he received tonsure and shortly thereafter preferment and rich benefices. At thirteen he was made cardinal deacon but not admitted to the Sacred College of Cardinals, the body that elects a new pope, until he reached seventeen. While still Cardinal de' Medici and upon the deaths of his father and older brother, he had become head of the Medici family and temporal ruler of the Florentine republic. Not a cardinal priest when elected pope, he was ordained and then consecrated a bishop.

As the great preponderance of Italian popes testifies, the election of the *"successor to St. Peter"* is dominated by the political machine of the cardinal deacons, cardinal priests and cardinal bishops of the sees (jurisdictions) proximate to Rome; simony and nepotism being the currency of attaining and maintaining ecclesiastical power. My father asks once again, where is the Holy Spirit while all this is going on? *Cardinal Deacons* typically reside in the Roman Curia and are the lowermost of the three classes of cardinals. The Roman Curia consists of various Vatican bureaus that assist the pope in administering the affairs of the Church. *Cardinal Priests*, the most numerous of the three classes, are the ordinaries of the dioceses and archdioceses. *Cardinal Bishops* are the highest ranking and are bishops of the seven sees surrounding Rome;

Karl was quite familiar with the papacy of Alexander VI, who held the chair of St. Peter at the time of Karl's birth. Of the powerful Borgia family, prior to becoming pope there were reports that he had his perceived enemies poisoned; reputedly he was only twelve years of age when his first victim was murdered. He was in his mid-twenties when his uncle, Pope Calixtus III, made him a cardinal and then vice chancellor of the Vatican from which he accumulated great personal wealth. Over the years, with multiple mistresses, he fathered ten known children including the infamous Cesare and Lucrezia Borgia. As pope, he made Cesare, still a teenager, a cardinal. As pope his immoral life persisted, even indulging in orgies.

Pope Alexander was likened to his immediate predecessor, Pope Innocent VIII, who in his youth sired two children out of wedlock. When Innocent's children came of age, he conducted the marriage ceremonies of his offspring in the Vatican.

Consequently, as to moral standards, Karl sees little difference between prince of the realm and prince of the Church; money and power are supreme. Having devoured anything written by Niccolo Machiavelli, an advocate of practical success even by unsavory methods if necessary, crystalizes Karl's modus operandi. Karl's family has prospered managing artisans in the building trades but laboring in one, often in adverse weather, isn't within his temperament. This had led to a falling out with his father, who accused him of being lazy, and sped his departure from home. He decided that becoming a prelate would be his passage to prominence, prosperity and pleasure. He would make his mark in Rome, the center of ecclesiastical power. Perhaps he too can be named pope someday with the right allegiances.

Karl is quick to realize that imparting his knowledge of the plot could ingratiate himself with the powerful pope and the Medici family. But how does one get an audience with the pope. And he certainly can't trust the information to papal subordinates not knowing which side they are on.

❦

An old man, his coat buttoned to the collar, is dozing by a fountain; the few stray hairs he has left flutter in the breeze. Karl watches him instinctively jerk upright so as not to topple over. Two others in tattered caps sit at a table studying their chess pieces as if transported to another dimension, white eyebrows betraying their lost youth. A grey and white cat slumbers between the scuffed, brown shoes of the players. Karl turns to a street vendor to buy an apple when someone calls his name.

Like a chance meeting of old soldiers who survived a war, there is an explosion of camaraderie. Vito and Karl know they are birds of a feather. Taking a table near the chess players, they reminisce over lentil soup poured over stale bread and glasses of red Tuscany wine. Karl can't believe his luck, finally...

"Vito, I would very much like to meet the pope. I understand that you are a Medici. Could you arrange an audience with him for me? Perhaps I could be included with a small party already scheduled."

"Well, I might not have to. If you attend the first Mass at the Duomo tomorrow, Giovanni will be there. He is keeping it low key; it is unannounced. But he always pauses to greet some of the parishioners afterwards. If unsuccessful you can usually find me at the

Medici palazzo." His right shoulder shrugs front to back almost involuntarily as if essential to his existence.

∽

Karl arrives at the cathedral a bit early. The Baptistery is across from the main entrance and he pauses to admire the pairs of bronze doors inset with sculptured figures. The workmanship is extraordinary.

"I'm especially fond of this pair here," says a man just a few steps away. "By Lorenzo Ghiberti." Karl looks at him and then at the doors. "They are about a hundred years old. I hope I look this good when I'm a hundred." They both laugh. Karl estimates his age at forty, about twice his own.

"Si, they are extraordinary. Then again, I find everything about this city to be extraordinary," replies Karl.

"You are new to Florence?"

"Si."

"Did you know that at one time baptisms were only performed on the Epiphany, Easter, and Pentecost? Baptisteries had to be big then."

"I had heard something to that effect."

"Many churches today just have a font near the entrance. Placed there to signify the beginning of one's Christian life."

"There is much symbolism in the Church."

"Are you familiar with Ghiberti's work?" the man asks.

"Non. Non."

"Ghiberti was trained as a goldsmith but he was quite versatile. Sculptor. Architect. Designer. A truly great artist. These doors, however, are my favorite. *Gates of Paradise* is how I describe them."

"Si, they are magnificent," says Karl. Just then the bells in the church tower ring.

"I must be off. Enjoy Florence." the stranger says.

"It's been a pleasure speaking with you. You have been very informative."

"Grazie. Arrivederci."

"Arrivederci." Karl turns and proceeds to the cathedral.

An usher greets Karl at the entrance. "You are a friend of Signor Buonarroti?" he gestures at the departing figure.

"Signor Buonarroti?"

"Why yes. Michelangelo Buonarroti." Karl stares back in awe as the door is held open for him.

Relatively few parishioners are in the pews. Pope Leo enters from the sacristy attended by his cousin, Cardinal Giulio de Medici, two priests and two deacons. The Mass passes quickly. An announcement had been made at the homily that His Holiness would greet the parishioners at the altar rail at the conclusion of the Mass. As Karl does so he presses his note into the surprised pope's hand who quickly slips it under his surplice and into his cassock pocket. Unlike the other parishioners, Karl returns to his front row pew. In short order he is approached by one of the deacons and is told to proceed at once to the Palazzo Medici.

Vito is surprised to see his comrade so soon and more so that he is there at the invitation of the pope. Like a caring friend seeing his companion to his door after a night of revelry, Vito escorts him to the pope's chambers.

It is subsequently discovered that Cardinal Alphonso Petrucci, while staying in Lazio, sent letters to his secretary, Domenico de' Nini, in Siena, which alluded to his assassination plans. The secretary, the malevolent physician, and the cardinals with close connections to Petrucci, immediately come under intense investigation. Any hope of moderation quickly vanishes. The felonious cardinals are unceremoniously dragged from their palaces as they are taken into custody. Most are bewildered by the inexplicable exposure of the duplicity and suddenness of the arrests. All are unnerved, while one, the ringleader, Petrucci, smirks in defiance. During his incarceration he is strangled. Cardinals Sauli, Riario, Soderini, and Castellisi, guilty of at least of being aware of the plot, are fined with Cardinal Riario of Pisa having to pay the huge sum of 150,000 ducats, tantamount to a king's ransom.

On the 1st of July Pope Leo takes advantage of the turmoil to pack the college with thirty one new cardinals who are acquiescent to him and willing to pay handsomely for their positions. Karl, now a confidante of the pope, achieves a primary goal, an appointment to the Roman Curia and the title of Cardinal Deacon. Events have moved quicker than his most ambitious dreams.

☙

On October 31st of that same year, 1517, Martin Luther, a Roman Catholic pastor and professor at the University of Wittenburg, Germany, explodes in frustration at the long ensconced perfidy in Rome. In his *Ninety-five Theses*, he declares, among other things, that the selling of indulgences is not within the purview of the pope and by one simply purchasing indulgences from the Church does not remit one's sins.

It was only a few years before that Albert of Brandenburg, Archbishop of Magdeburg, was also given the Archbishopric of Mainz and the Bishopric of Hallerstadt in exchange for monetary payments to Rome to rebuild St. Peter's Basilica. To offset this expenditure, Albert was allowed to promise plenary indulgences to those who contributed to the new edifice and retain half of such revenues. This did not sit well with the German people and Leo had no sense of the extent of their discontent. Luther also rails against the notion that one can remain in the state of divine grace through good works;

he says remaining in the state of divine grace depends on one's faith.

Having grossly underestimated the resentment of Church policies in Germany and the strength of support that had gravitated to this young Augustinian, Leo primarily remains focused on influencing battles among Italian Papal States and his own insatiable fondness for the arts, revelry, and extravagant entertainments. The Reformation is at hand yet Pope Leo X is oblivious to it, a ponderous miscalculation. His political problems are real, however, as his policies of subterfuge and shifting loyalties with the warring Holy Roman Emperor, Maximilian I, and the King of France, Francis I, manage to alienate both. Leo becomes isolated when these two adversaries come to terms and agree to the partition of Central and Northern Italy in the 1517 *Alliance of Cambrai*. In 1518 Leo espouses a Crusade against the Turks but it lacks momentum, the German people think it just another scheme to raise money for the Church.

But the question as to who will succeed Maximilian as Emperor now comes into play. Maximilian advocates his grandson, Charles of Spain, to be his successor. Francis I wants it for himself. Leo wants neither and supports another German electoral prince.

Maximilian dies in January, 1519, and his grandson ultimately becomes the Holy Roman Emperor, Charles V, chiefly by obtaining money from the Fugger banking family and buying German electoral votes held by a handful of privileged personages of the Electoral College. Death also takes one of Leo's greatest artists, Leonardo da Vinci, at age 67. The year isn't going well for the pope.

CHAPTER 7

THE MUSLIM TIDE

In September, *1520*, as I am approaching my 3rd birthday, Suleiman the Magnificent, as he eventually would be known in the West, comes to power; destined to be the most renowned sultan of the Ottoman Empire. One wonders why those, who are transgressed by an invader, refer to him as magnificent; is it out of respect for his successes? Perhaps it stems from the Italian practice of giving anyone of importance the title *magnifico*. To the Turks, however, he is Suleiman the Lawgiver, for he solidified the legal code for situations not addressed directly by the Shari'ah laws, those of the Qur'an itself.

Suleiman's authority is unchallenged from within since he has control over the Turkish nobility as well as the D*evsirme*, a powerful class developed during the previous century to counter balance the influence of the Turkish elite. They arose from captured Christian youths who were then converted to Islam and servitude to the sultans; the *Janissaries* are the military arm of this class. The power of indoctrination, especially of the very young, is evident again. If raised in a given religion, then one is predisposed to adhere to it to the exclusion of others. *The Muslims believe that the Jews and Christians broke their covenants with God and incurred His disdain*; so states Chapter 5, Verses 12, 13 and 14 of the Qur'an. *The Christians have similar feelings about the Jews*. On the other hand, *Christians and Jews* *don't recognize Muhammad as a prophet and therefore the legitimacy of Islam.* So goes the myopic world and its consequences. Whom do you say is correct? What is your basis?

Financed by the wealth accumulated from the conquests of Selim, his now deceased father, Suleiman has rejuvenated the clash of Islamic and Christian cultures. Fear has crept into the European landscape. To make matters worse, parts of Europe are divided by the religious schism that is so deep felt that it teeters on civil war. This works to the advantage of this powerful ruler who refers to himself as the *"Deputy of God on Earth"* and the *"Shadow of God over All Nations,"* who views himself as the *"Enforcer of the Commands of the Qur'an."* The world itself is a gift to him from God; he claims. I ask, why is it that God never takes it upon Himself to announce such appointments?

Muslim threat or not, the schism is not to be denied. In June, 1520, Pope Leo X issues a papal bull condemning Martin Luther on 41 counts of heresy and orders him to submit to the authority of Rome. Luther, now with influential friends, openly defies the pope. And, as in the previous year, Leo had another setback, a loss to the arts which he so loves; Raphael, another giant of the Renaissance, dies on his own birthday at the age of 37.

In January, 1521, the pope issues another papal bull, this time excommunicating Luther. He then enlists the aid of Charles V, the 21 year old emperor, in bringing Luther to account. On April 17, Luther is called before the imperial *Diet at Worms* to defend his theses. Though granted a safe conduct pass, to the consternation of his adversaries he enters the town with a retinue of German knights and vocal supporters. The streets are mobbed in anticipation of the showdown.

The proceedings begin by Charles having his own confession of faith read aloud, leaving no doubt as to which side of the issue he is on. His demeanor is unequivocal, cold and menacing.

Then Luther is confronted with his own writings and he is asked to affirm or refute them. Instead, Luther asks for a day's grace to consider the matter. Catching his opponents off balance with this request, they reluctantly decide that it would be judicious to accede. The clash stalled, the tension becomes even more palpable.

The next afternoon, defying the emperor and the pope, Luther stubbornly refuses to back away from his theses and disputes the assertions thrown at him by the theologian Johann Eck. Demanding that he answer directly the question, *will he or will he not retract his heretical statements?* Luther replies that he would do so only if the council can disprove his teachings through reason or scripture; he will not go against his conscience. A shouting match ensues and the proceedings are cut short. Luther pushes through his accusers to the embrace of his friends and raises a clenched fist in defiance.

Luther departs the town under his safe-conduct. His local sovereign and protector, Frederick, Elector of Saxony, fearing for Luther's life, has him *"kidnapped"* and hides him in the Wartburg castle overlooking Eisenach. Charles publicly rejects Luther's doctrines and the evangelicals. *The ensuing Edict of Worms condemns Luther as a heretic and outlaw and calls for his arrest.* This makes him a fugitive within the empire and severely curtails his activities for the rest of his years.

☙

Suleiman, meanwhile, is intent upon destabilizing Europe and annexing territory; in part to offset Portuguese expansionism in east Africa and Russian expansionism in central Asia; in part to add wealth and more land to his own empire; and in part to spread Islam. Suleiman designates himself as the universal Caliph of Islam.

The notion cherished by the pacifists, that the words of the very

Qur'an itself will deter Muslims from initiating war, may be wishful thinking. They point to certain verses and ignore others. Decide for yourself:

> *"Allah does not forbid you respecting those who have not made war against you on account of (your) religion, and have not driven you forth from your homes, that you show them kindness and deal with them justly; surely Allah loves the doers of justice."*

Chapter 60, Verse 8

Based on other text in the Qur'an, do the words kindness and justice simply mean giving others the opportunity to convert to Islam?

> *"So when the sacred months (Ramadan) have passed away, then slay the idolaters wherever you find them, and take them captives and besiege them and lie in wait for them in every ambush, then if they repent and keep up prayer and pay the poor rate, leave their way free for them; surely Allah is Forgiving, Merciful."*

Chapter 9, Verse 5

More specifically, who is an idolater? With respect to the Qur'an, one is an idolater *who imputes a shared union with Allah, such as the Holy Trinity, or others who share attributes of God.*

Chapter 5, Verses 72, 73

Would you say the Qur'an holds Christians and Jews in disdain?

> *"Oh you who believe! do not take the Jews and the Christians for friends; they are friends of each other; and who-*

*ever amongst you takes them for a friend, then surely he is
one of them; surely Allah does not guide the unjust people."*

Chapter 5, Verse 51

*"Oh you who believe! do not make friends with a people
with whom Allah is wroth..."*

Chapter 60, Verse 13

*"Let not the believers take the unbelievers for friends...
and whoever does this, he shall have nothing of (the
guardianship of) Allah..."*

Chapter 3, Verse 28

*"And the Jews will not be pleased with you, nor the
Christians until you follow their religion. Say: Surely Allah's guidance, that is the (true) guidance. And if you
follow their desires after the knowledge that has come
to you, you shall have no guardian from Allah, nor say
helper."* [Christians for centuries spoke of the loss of
God's favor if one rejects Christianity after the knowledge that has come to you.]

Chapter 2, Verse 120

Must Muslims accept every word of the Qur'an?

*"Do you believe in part of the Book (Qur'an) and disbe-
lieve in the other? What then is the reward of such among
you as do this but disgrace in the life of this world, and
on the day of resurrection they shall be sent back to the*

most grievous chastisement, and Allah is not at all heed-
less of what you do."

Chapter 2, Verse 85

Christians and Jews, however, fall into a special category because they are of the New and Old Testaments respectively, which the Muslims recognize. The Bible provides a foundation for the Qur'an. Because of this, Christians and Jews are considered "*People of the Book.*" Their fate is slavery or, depending on what circumstances will allow, the payment of special taxes and/or assessments. Pagans must convert to Islam or die.

According to the Qur'an, Allah condones slavery and tolerates prostitution (as long as it is not forced).

"And marry those among you who are single and those
who are fit among your male slaves and among your fe-
male slaves..."

Chapter 24, Verse 32

"...and do not compel your slave girls to prostitution,
when they desire to keep chaste, in order to seek the frail
good of this world's life..."

Chapter 24, Verse 33

While most Muslims may be tolerant, even friendly to others and just want to get on with their lives, radicals rigidly adhere to every precept of the Qur'an and consider those who don't heretics. In so doing, these radicals bar themselves from assimilation into the world community. It is these zealots, when in power, who render the desires of the submissive, peaceful majority irrelevant, as they pursue a world caliphate with ruthlessness. Still others reference the Qur'an as a pretense to disguise their lust for power and control.

Islam means surrender to the will of God. A Muslim is one who has surrendered to the will of God. The Holy Qur'an is deemed the speech of the Almighty and the final conclusion of all divine revelations beginning with the first five books of the Old Testament as revealed to Moses and the psalms and the gospels of the New Testament, pertinent to the prophet Jesus. Christians and Jews are to forsake their religions, which were established by God, and adopt this newer religion established by God. This begs the question, why would God cast aside a religion, two in this case, that He established rather than just castigate those followers who had gone astray? One might ask if much of the Muslim world has broken its covenant with Allah since they accuse one another of not following the Qur'an as written; they don't accept each other's particular version as to the legitimate succession of caliphs, and they war with each other. It may be helpful to mention how Islam came to be.

According to Chapter 33, Verse 40, of the Qur'an, "*Muhammad... is the Apostle of Allah and the Last of the prophets...*" Muslims believe that, when Muhammad was on a retreat in a cave in the Jabal-an-Nur Mountain during Ramadan, the 9th month of the Islamic lunar calendar, about A.D. 610, he was visited by a magnificent presence during his sleep, later identified as the angel Gabriel, who made known to him that he was chosen to be a messenger of God. When his retreat ended and being somewhat shaken, he told his wife Khadijah of his experience and his concern that he might have been the victim of evil spirits. She comforted him and pointed out that he was a kind man of character, honest, compassionate, charitable, benevolent, and without malice. God would surely favor him and shield him from diabolical powers. This 40 year old merchant would not experience another revelation for three more years. During this pause he became more prayerful and spoke of his vision. The situation was ripe for ridicule and he suffered indignities.

Many idols, believed to be able to intercede with the One God, were common in the land at the time. The Ka'bah, the ancient shrine in Mecca that most believed dated back thousands of years to Abraham, was considered a sanctuary. But pilgrimages to this holy site had become largely a commercial endeavor diminishing the sanctity of the place. Also, unlike what Muhammad would come to espouse, the people did not believe in an afterlife. Muhammad maintained that there was only one God and that all mankind would be resurrected to face a Last Judgment. The New Testament, 2 Peter 3:7 and Matthew 25:31, 32, 33, 34, 41 & 46, which preceded the Qur'an by hundreds of years, refers to this day of judgment.

After the hiatus, Muhammad related receiving revelations at recurrent interludes but now they occurred during wakefulness and there were no visions or voices involved; he might hear a sound or break into a sweat for no apparent reason and at the same time discover messages formulated in his mind. This continued until his death. Khadijah's Christian cousin, Waraqah, aided Muhammad in comprehending the revelations and maintained that they were comparable to those messages given Christian and Jewish prophets. All this confirmed Muhammad's notion that he was God's messenger. It is upon these suppositions that the foundation of Islam rests.

Muhammad's followers grew in numbers very slowly. By and large, his preaching was met with great resistance and scorn for years to come; the fact that it was critical of the comportment and practices of the affluent merchants of Mecca didn't help. In 616, the chief clans of Mecca boycotted Muhammad and his clan even though most of the latter were not Muslims. This caused terrible hardship and deprivations for three years but it eventually lost momentum and was lifted. Muhammad's most steadfast supporter, his wife Khadijah, died not long after.

A while later, Muhammad asserted that he envisioned his ascension to heaven and exchanged greetings with God, those words are now part of Muslim services, and received the divine blessing. This assertion riled his enemies even more and his disfavor persisted. He and his adherents were abused to the point that they vacated Mecca in 622 and retreated further north to the more hospitable town of Medina, this marks the beginning of the Islamic calendar. Unlike the harsh landscape of Mecca, Medina has an oasis and arable land suitable for agriculture which the Arabs shared with Jewish clans. The Arab clans, however, had engaged in blood feuds among themselves a few years before and animosities still lingered. Muhammad brokered a peace among these clans and a confederation of all clans, Arab and non-Arab alike. If any significant controversies should arise, they were to be referred to him for mediation. Revelations at this time largely pertained to rules of jurisprudence. Did circumstances dictate the course of his thoughts?

Once settled in Medina he took several wives to promote internal cohesion and established alliances with nomadic tribes for increased security. He initiated a campaign to assert economic pressure on the Meccan clans which had appropriated the property of his followers or otherwise caused them harm. Muhammad authorized raids on their caravans passing near Medina on the way to Syria and led three of them himself but none were successful. As one anointed by God, one wonders why not? But success did come when a more clandestine raid was made on a caravan from Yemen near Mecca itself. That in turn animated the Meccans and large supporting forces then began accompanying the caravans.

In March, 624, a major clash occurred near Badr. The Muslims prevailed and were elated by their victory and Muhammad took it as confirmation of his prophethood. Again, using the same logic, one would think that military losses would indicate the opposite. This euphoria carried over to the assassination of some opponents within Medina itself and the expulsion of the Jewish clan which ran the market there. Difficulties with that clan and the Jewish refusal to recognize Muhammad as a prophet led to Islam becoming less accommodating. Respect of the *People of the Book* was diminishing. Muhammad now ordered his followers to face Mecca when they prayed rather than Jerusalem.

The Meccans spent the following months raising a force of three thousand men and then advanced on Medina in March of 625. The Muslims, outnumbered three to one, took positions on the hill of Uhud and inflicted serious casualties. The Muslims were then outflanked by the Meccan cavalry but regrouped and held their positions. All in all the battle was indecisive but the Meccans did withdraw. Both sides knew that their differences hadn't ended and another showdown was inevitable. It came two years later.

The Muslims dug a trench around much of the oasis to stymie the Meccan cavalry and when their forces, about ten thousand strong, returned in April of 627, it did just that. The siege lasted about two weeks. The Meccan supplies dwindling and their mercenaries disheartened by their lack of progress, the army faded from the landscape. Believing that the Qurayzah Jewish clan had plotted against him, Muhammad's forces attacked and subdued it. Following its capitulation, Muhammad had all the men killed and enslaved the women and children. As his hegemony continued to expand, more converts came to Islam.

In March, 628, Muhammad and the Meccans made a treaty to end their conflicts. But the treaty was breached in November, 629, when some Meccan elements attacked supporters of Muhammad. This caused Muhammad to covertly raise ten thousand troops and move on Mecca in January, 630. Caught by surprise, the town submitted with little resistance. Amnesty was granted to almost all, gaining the allegiance of many by doing so and forging a unification that otherwise might have been elusive. The city of Ta'if, about sixty miles southeast of Mecca, continued its confrontation but that was quickly quelled.

People of the Persian Gulf now looked to him for protection; the Persians having been defeated by the Byzantine Christians in 627-628. Muhammad then marched on Syria late in 630, at the outset with thirty thousand men, and with military success. Treaties were negotiated but the loyalty of certain Christian tribes to the Byzantines induced him to be less accepting of Christians than he had been. Nevertheless, a new champion was now on the scene and conversions to Islam swelled.

Muhammad died in Medina on June 8, 632. In short order, the seeds of schism were sown. Abu Bakr, a father-in-law of Muhammad, was chosen caliph (successor of Muhammad as temporal and spiritual head of Islam). Many claimed that Ali, who was raised by Muhammad and became a son-in-law, was explicitly designated by Muhammad to be his successor as he was returning from his last pilgrimage to Mecca. Ali did not recognize Abu Bakr's election but did not contest it. Ali is celebrated by the Shi'ah as the true first caliph, not Abu Bakr, and his descendants the real successors of Muhammad. The Shi'ah and Sunnah branches of Islam were thus born.

With the murder of Uthman, another son-in-law of Muhammad and the third caliph, Ali was chosen to become his successor in 656. He immediately set out to restore the fundamental Islamic precepts of equality and righteousness, which were being ignored by those Muslims of wealth and influence, nor did he accede to their demands. This made him unpopular with powerful elements of Mecca and he had to quell several rebellions. Eventually he lost control of Egypt and the Hejaz, a long mountainous area running along the eastern coast of the Red Sea. In 661, he was murdered while praying in a mosque in Iraq. Hasan ibn Ali, his son, succeeded him but he abdicated in a matter of months causing a quick break in that line of succession.

What does one make of this flawed start to Islam? And what of Judaism and Christianity? *Men penned scripture. Men have decided what scripture is and what is not. Men interpret scripture.* Common agreement has not been attainable so Jews and Christians have split off into numerous sects within their own creeds. How can these religions justifiably maintain that their dogma is not subject to challenge? Isn't it without question that *all religions are man-made*?

Religion is behind great charitable endeavors and at the same time it has been used as an excuse to unleash harsh punishments, ethnic oppression and war. Didn't Jesus preach good will and brotherhood? And virtually every chapter of the Qur'an begins, "*In the name of Allah, the Beneficent, the Merciful.*" Does a beneficent and merciful God really want His congregation established through force?

Islam accepts predestination in common with elements of Christianity. Apparently, it is not up to us as to whether we are saved or not, God inclines us one way or the other:

> "*Allah guides whom He pleases to the right path.*"
>
> Chapter 2, Verse 213

> "*And we did not send any apostle but with the language of his people, so that he might explain to them clearly; then Allah makes whom He pleases err and He guides whom He pleases, and He is the Mighty, the Wise.*"
>
> Chapter 14, Verse 4

The Qur'an, the word of God according to Islam, tells us over and over again that God is Just, Merciful. It seems a great contradiction, that regardless of how good a life one leads, one may still not attain Paradise. Martin Luther's message is the same. Man is saved by God's grace alone, not as a reward for human merit. And most of us, he maintains, are not going to see Paradise, regardless of leading a good life because, unaccountably, we are not being favored with God's grace. This doesn't square, of course, with those clergy who insist that God loves us. And what of those who say some may be condemned to the fires of hell? Just? Merciful? Love?

Ↄↄ

Muslim incursions into Europe happened over and over again. In August, 1521, Suleiman captures Belgrade. The independent kingdom of Hungary is in jeopardy. The Hungarian king, Louis II, is burdened with the Reformation setting one sect against another; the feudal system is in turmoil and peasant anarchy is rampant. The nobles are divided about asking for much needed military assistance from a Habsburg, namely Charles V, for surely Hungary would be added to his so called Holy Roman Empire, if he does prevail. Adding to the confusion, Pope Leo X dies on December 1, 1521, of malaria. His successor, Adrian VI, attempts to reform the Curia but accomplishes little in the face of obstinate Italian cardinals, the schism in Germany, and Ottoman military expeditions including Suleiman expelling the Christian Knights of Rhodes from Rhodes itself. Fortunately for Hungary at this point, it doesn't have Suleiman's full attention as he is also strengthening his position in the Mediterranean.

It is remarkable to note a written statement by Adrian that a pope *may err in a decree on matters of faith.* When a pope speaks ex cathedra (infallibly), the Church maintains that such error is not possible. Adrian's assertion is dismissed by the Church since he was not speaking ex cathedra at the time. Ex cathedra or not, it is clear that this pope rejected the infallibility hypothesis.

Upon Adrian's death, Giulio de' Medici, who was born out of wedlock a month after his father Giuliano de' Medici's death, becomes Pope Clement VII and will reign from 1523 until 1534. The Church maintains that Giulio's parents were betrothed *per sponsalia de presenti (a formal promise to marry being made)*, thus Giulio was deemed legitimate. He, however, is believed to have had a son born out of wedlock himself.

In August, 1526, Hungary loses its independence. With less than 20,000 men and not waiting for allied forces, King Louis II attacks more than 100,000 Ottoman Turks and is soundly defeated and killed at the Battle of Mohacs. Suleiman advances to Buda but pressing matters in his home territory, Anatolia[1], moves him to withdraw shortly thereafter taking tens of thousands of captives with him.

Ferdinand I, a Habsburg and the Archduke of Austria, at the invitation of a number of Hungarian nobleman, moves forces into northern Hungary. His brother, Charles V, depends on him to be a bulwark to Suleiman since Charles is preoccupied with the Reformation and the exploits of the king of France. John Zapolya, the prince of Transylvania and anti-Habsburg, establishes himself in southern Hungary as a vassal of Suleiman.

Ferdinand moves to control all of Hungary so Suleiman returns; drives him out of Hungary altogether and lays siege to Vienna in 1529. This siege is parried but he makes another thrust in 1532. His overextended supply lines and Austrian winters hamper further

---

1   Most of modern day Turkey, Asia Minor.

Ottoman incursion into Europe. For one thing, camels are Suleiman's prime vehicles of transport and are not suited for cold weather.

Suleiman's emphasis returns to the Mediterranean. Charles V had re-established the Knights of Rhodes on Malta in 1530. These knights raided Ottoman shipping and coastal towns extending to northwest Africa. The renowned Genoese admiral, Andrea Doria, was enlisted by the emperor and he severed the shipping lanes between Istanbul and Alexandria. Suleiman responded in 1533 by recruiting Barbarossa, the formidable Turkish captain of a pirate fleet, who proved to be an able adversary and bent on attacking European coastal towns to capture Christians for the Ottoman slave trade and general Muslim slave markets.

In 1534-35, Suleiman personally leads a campaign into Persia. He would do so again on two more occasions, the last being in 1554. This is indicative of his trials and tribulations. While he would attack and conquer, he has to revisit his conquests to retain control, just as he did in Hungary after the death of John Zapolya in 1540. Suleiman once again expels Ferdinand from encroaching into central Hungary and now puts that region under direct Ottoman rule for the first time.

Typically, the Turks don't permanently settle in occupied territories themselves. They exploit them for their commodities and impose oppressive taxes. They would herd the able bodied like livestock to slave markets, millions of others slaughtered.

Suleiman has brought the Ottoman Empire to its greatest expanse to-date. He controls not only Anatolia but the Balkans, Ukraine, Iraq, Syria, Israel, Egypt, much of the Arabian Peninsula and North Africa. And to say that the arts flourish under his regime is an understatement. He, himself, is recognized as a great poet. His architect is the incomparable Sinan, master of the impossible.

❧

The Reformation proceeds in spite of the Ottoman threat. Catholic and Evangelical princes are battling each other. The carnage is so bad that concessions are made to re-establish some normalcy. The *Diet of Speyer of 1526 suspends the Edict of Worms, which had outlawed Luther and condemned his Evangelicals.* The same year the disaffected Cardinal Pompeo Colonna and his forces raid the papal territories; shut the pope up in the Castle of Sant'Angelo, and plunder the Apostolic Palace.

The duplicity of Pope Clement VII, who at one point joined in a treaty with the king of France in opposition to the emperor, alienates Charles. In 1527, German mercenaries under the Duke of Bourbon march on Rome. During the siege the duke is killed. The troops, lacking a leader, provisions and unpaid, sack Rome committing untold atrocities and force the pope to again take refuge in Castle Sant'Angelo. This marks the end of the Renaissance.

Another diet is convened in Speyer in 1529 and with significant pressure from the Catholics the earlier concessions to the Evangelicals are rescinded. A widespread Evangelical protest of this reversal ensues and from that time on they are commonly referred to as Protestants.

While these realities of life are adding to the pages of history, Martin Luther is struggling with his own theological demons. According to his students and colleagues, Luther told them: *"That reason in no way contributes to faith... For reason is the greatest enemy that faith has; it never comes to the aid of spiritual things, but - more frequently than not - struggles against the Divine Word, treating with contempt all that emanates from God."*

For Luther, like theologians before him, reason must subordinate itself to Revelation. Could it be that the incompatible Revelation isn't really Revelation?

The Renaissance Humanist, Erasmus, who became the oracle of the enlightened, is a contemporary of Luther though 20 years his senior. He too is a monk but unwillingly so having been compelled to Holy Orders by his guardian. He is sought out by the elite because of his scholarship, intellect and wit. He denies Luther's contention that man would only be saved by the whim of God's grace. And to Erasmus, scripture conveys a message but he doesn't accept every saying, or every incident as fact, believing many are poetic stories and allegories. To him, *"almost all Christians [are] wretchedly enslaved by blindness and ignorance."*

Speaking of allegories makes the biblical story of Abraham come to my mind. Considered to live about 2,000 years B.C., this reputed devout man of faith is said to have been in periodic, direct contact with God. This *"loving"* God commanded him to slay his son in sacrifice as a test of faith, although the son was spared at the last moment. Was this cruel test necessary? We are told God know all things, even the future? Yet this story, found in Genesis, arising from primitive people in primitive times, containing still other bizarre twists, is celebrated by Judaism, Christianity and Islam as true. – Oddly, it will be another 600 or so years before God speaks to man again, Moses.

❧

Pope Clement VII dies from the bite of a spider in September, 1534. He is succeeded by the slender but charming and shrewd Pope Paul III of the influential Farnese family. Paul restores the pomp and ceremony that had languished since the sacking of Rome in 1527; promotes the resumption of festivals and other secular excesses; directly supports public works to stimulate the economy; and is a great patron of the arts breathing some life back into the Renaissance. He is heavily into nepotism, even appointing two of his teenage grandchildren cardinals. He confirms the new order of Jesuits, which plays a prominent role in the Counter Reformation.

Different factions want any proposed council to conform to their own parameters and agendas. Despite numerous obstacles posed by the emperor, other nobles and prelates, he perseveres for nine long years for the convocation of the *Council of Trent*, which convenes on December 13, 1545. Although just the beginning, this initial phase made great progress in definitively clarifying certain doctrine and promoting Church discipline. With multiple interruptions, it would not conclude until December, 1563, long after Paul's death in 1549.

In his youth, Paul was quite worldly. At the age of 24 he had been appointed treasurer of the Church and a year later, in 1493, made a cardinal deacon by Pope Alexander VI. His rapid advancement, according to gossip, was prompted by his sister Giulia's intimacy with the pope. Consequently, Cardinal Alessandro Farnese was referred to as the *"petticoat cardinal."* Receiving multiple benefices, his revenues increased substantially. He kept a wellborn Roman mistress by whom he fathered four children. As to his fornication, I mention two New Testament strictures:

1st Thessalonians 4:3

> *"For this is the will of God, your sanctification: That you should abstain from fornication."*

Jude 1:7

> *"As Sodom and Gomorrha and the neighboring cities, in like manner, having given themselves to fornication and going after other flesh, were made an example, suffering the punishment of eternal fire."*

In 1509, Paul was installed as the Bishop of Parma by Pope Julius II. Four years later, at age 45, he ended his relationship with his mistress. Finally, in June 1519, age 51, he was ordained a priest and said his first mass on Christmas Day.

Upon Paul's death, Pope Julius III reigns from February 7, 1550, until March 23, 1555; he, also, succumbs to nepotism excessiveness. Disparaging rumors about his relationship with an adopted nephew circulate. He is followed by Pope Marcellus II, who opposes nepotism and lavish expenditures. Unfortunately, Marcellus dies within a month of taking office.

It is about this time that the lives of Johann Carberry, Franz von Clausen and I come together again. Once more, Innsbruck is the unifying circumstance.

CHAPTER 8

THE ENCOUNTER

1555/1556

Pulling up my collar, I step rudely onto the street as a wintery twilight settles over Innsbruck. A faint, early moon is resting on the mountain hesitant to herald the advancing stars. Timeworn cobbled streets are tainted with an amber glow escaping from timeworn shop windows; Klaus the butcher peers out searching for a tardy customer. Occasional sparks accompany the smoke spiraling awkwardly from soiled, soot-choked chimneys while a delinquent gust rustles my uncombed hair. Indistinct, demoralized faces too troubled to look up follow their shoes disturbing the shadows in the nearby alley. If children are about, they are not to be heard. Contemplating what was and what is to come, I nudge my horse leisurely toward the dim lights dotting the valley and the path home, having abandoned an unusually restrained, forlorn Boar's Head Tavern.

I had been away from Innsbruck much of the time while honing my skills with Dad and Yusuf. Eventually I came into my own and escorted parties without their help. Max, a former blacksmith's apprentice, whom I met on a trip to Vienna, became my counterpart to Yusuf. He had joined me not to become my permanent right hand man but as a mountain guide in training. Max, like me, is an independent spirit with wanderlust in his veins.

Popes had come and gone, more often acting like Renaissance noblemen than spiritual leaders. I keep asking myself over and over again, where was *Divine Providence* when these scandalous "*successors to St. Peter*" were chosen? According to Catholic theology, "*as applied to God, Providence is God Himself considered in that act by which in His wisdom He so orders all events within the universe that the end for which it was created may be realized.*" Surely a schism in His Church can't be part of God's design and lend itself to the manifestation of his glory? On the other hand, possibly it is Divine Providence that the Roman Catholic Church not be allowed the mantle of "*the one true church*" that it claims to be. Perhaps a Bishop of Rome made a wrong turn along the way by declaring himself the Universal Priest, putting himself above all others.

After their ordination as priests, my friends, now Fr. Johann Carberry and Fr. Franz von Clausen, had been assigned to different parishes elsewhere in Austria. For two decades I only saw them on their occasional visits to family or friends in Innsbruck. We had avoided discussing religious issues and the armed conflicts between Catholics and Protestants during those visits because we knew we would not see eye to eye on some things and we also knew that minds would not be changed. Our friendships were still very important to us and in these troubled times, with brother opposed to brother, we didn't want our relationships to become another such casualty.

Having longed to return to the town of their births, and having the friendship of influential ecclesiastical superiors, Johann and Franz were eventually assigned to St. James' in Innsbruck only months apart. Mother would invite them to our chalet for dinner whether Dad and I were there or not. She always makes sure to put unsweetened knodl in Johann's soup, a touch that he relishes. For Franz, he can always count on his favorite stuffed cabbage in tomato sauce. Both are amused and pleased by her animated attacks on positions held by the Protestants while Dad and I just smile and indulge her.

On each occasion Johann flamboyantly insists on demonstrating a new trick. His bulging flanks, pudgy face and stutter step subsidize a comic flair. To my chagrin, at times I sense that Franz, neglected by humor, secretly begrudges Johann's charisma but I am just as certain that a deep underlying affection remains intact; he eyes him with an odd dependence in his expression. When they prepare to depart for the rectory, however, Mother always demands that both give us their blessings even when Johann's is a bit slurred because of his fondness for schnapps.

❧

In February, 1555, the *Diet of Augsburg* was convened by order of the emperor, Charles V, but his brother Ferdinand presided. *It stressed that any armed conflicts within the empire on religious grounds are prohibited. A given territory is to be either Lutheran or Roman Catholic by decree of the local prince and his decision is mandatory on his subjects;* if a subject doesn't like it, he and his family may move to another territory of his choice. The free and imperial cities, having no religious homogeny, are exempt from the diet's religious affiliation decree. Promulgated on September 25, 1555, this Peace of Augsburg effectively curtailed serious internal clashes within the Holy Roman Empire. The newly elected Pope Paul IV denounced it as a pact with heresy. All this wasn't to Charles' liking but he had to deal with realities. The same month Innsbruck suffered a devastating storm reminiscent of what it experienced decades before.

In mid-April of the next year, while Dad and I are away, Mother complains of headaches and weakness during a visit by Fr. Johann. Black clouds, so low that they seem at one with the earth, hover like evil spirits as the wind hurls rain impolitely against the windows. She takes to her bed. Johann sends for a physician and later arranges for Sister Mary Bernard, a gentle nun known for her selfless and skilled caring of the sick, to be with her.

As the days pass Mother's appetite diminishes and fever takes hold; too hot one moment, chilled the next, her body restless under the woven blanket. Her intake is reduced to hot chicken soup, warm bread and fluids, mostly tea and water. Her words acquire a dreamy quality, "Somewhere to the south lay the sea," she says inexplicably. "Erich, are you there? Rafer?" Heavy wheezing and coughing persist and specks of blood appear in her sputum. The doctor is summoned once again.

Johann and Franz are notified that her condition is deteriorating. Both arrive and make their way quietly along the corridor to her bedside. Dr. de Barton, a fastidious tense man, solemnly shakes his head. Her eyelids are heavy, her body noticeably fatigued, her chest heaves pleading for air. On the polished bedside table Johann unfolds his black leather kit containing the holy oil of Extreme Unction as Franz prays silently for her soul. Within hours of their vigil, Mother dies.

Dad and I had been leading parties from Vienna and Rome respectively during this crisis and were totally unaware. Tardy communication of events is the norm. Had we known, we would have pressed on and perhaps been there before she passed. I arrive home with the approaching dusk, surprised by the apparent activity. All eyes turn to me as I enter the chalet. Johann approaches. "Your mother had been sick, Rafer. This morning she went to Our Lord. All of us grieve in losing such a kind and special friend, Franz and I especially."

I sit at her side and take her hand. "I'm here, Mother." Sister

Bernard stays with me this night attending to any need or detail. Dad thankfully arrives the following afternoon. I see him approaching the chalet and go out to meet him. He gives me a hearty greeting but, when I don't return it and he sees my demeanor, he stops short. "Don't tell me it's your mother?" I nod. "Is she?" I nod again. He slowly shuffles to a stone wall to sit and goes pale. This captain of men buries his head in his large hands and weeps in strained silence. I tell him what I know.

"One more year, one more year, I have been saying for the last three years. I was selfish, Rafer. I had such a passion for my job. She dreamed of me retiring but she knew that I loved my work. She was so tolerant, loving." He pauses. "She was always late for everything," he laughs. "When we were leaving the premises, regardless of how late we were to something or other, she insisted on inspecting her flowers first; drove me nuts... still, she was a saint, better than that, too many counterfeits in that collection." He twists his gold ring, staring at it wistfully, only to swat aside an insect which threatens to obstruct his view.

Dad is never the same, losing some of his zest for life and retiring on the spot; mostly out of guilt, I suppose. No more foreign horizons to approach. No more commerce in human nature. She had always been there for him but he wasn't there at the time of her greatest need. It wasn't supposed to be this way. If anything, he would be killed on one of his trips, not the other way around. Now we only have each other. A repressed reflection now screams at me for recognition; *Rafer, is your life restricted to one dimension?* Extending the implication, I grudgingly admit to a masked mistrust of women, the residue of my searing disappointment in Elsa? How could she marry another so hastily? Fleeting dalliances certainly have not displaced my ambiguity.

St. James' church had just been rebuilt in 1551 and was never more picturesque, its spires and dome accentuate the town. The church had been of Romanesque design but there have been changes, more Gothic now. The splendid outer doors have been retained and their superb condition belies their age and gives testimony to the extraordinary care rendered by the men's and ladies' auxiliaries, of which Mother was a stalwart. Frescoes depict St. James as intercessor for Innsbruck and the Virgin Mary is even more prominently featured. There are assorted biblical scenes and side altars dedicated to various saints. Beautiful stained glass windows add a phalanx of colors.

Dad and I follow Mother's coffin down the center aisle and take our seats near the pulpit, which is a few yards in front of and to the left of the main altar. The whole congregation seems to be present, an empty pew is nowhere to be found. Out of esteem for Mother and Dad, Cardinal Wolfgang Gerhardt is on the altar. Father Johann Carberry will say the requiem Mass pursuant to our request; he is my oldest and closest friend. Father Franz von Clausen will also assist, at our request. Cardinal Gerhardt is still only a cardinal deacon and apparently, unlike others of my acquaintance, not inclined to higher ecclesiastical ambitions.

Johann bows to the altar and the service begins; the ritual repeated as it has been for centuries. The Latin hymns of the choir wrap their melodic arms around us. The moment comes to give the eulogy and Dad is motioned to the pulpit. He is unhurried and solemn as his eyes make random contact with friends and neighbors. A tear stumbles down his cheek. He waits for the sound of coughing to dwindle…

> "Maria Schilling, my dear wife and love, I will miss you
> so much. You were always there for a friend in need,
> for your Church, and especially for our son Rafer and
> me. You never took yourself too seriously. Your smiles

outdistanced your frowns. You were not given to criticism. You were flexible to a fault, pride never a stumbling block to reconciliation. You always found a way to express your disappointments or make your desires known without scolding the offending party. I know I was quite a challenge." There is subdued laughter. "We all need that special someone to love and to love us. Few people have been as privileged as I.

"Life doesn't proceed at our convenience. Our work is often demanding and critical to our well-being but it isn't primary. That position is reserved for our relationships. Fortunately, Maria and I realized early-on that gender differences themselves can be the source of disharmony in a marriage. Men and women think differently. They handle things differently. They have different priorities. The problem is that each expects the other to think and act the way they do. It is not going to happen. It goes against nature. We decided to go with the flow rather than get upset with each other over those differences and be grateful for the positive things. That's the way he is. That's the way she is. Let it go. When life's journey is all but over, when we take that final inventory, many realize to their lingering sorrow that their relationships were poorly dealt with.

"The job of a mountain guide causes one to be frequently away from home. I would like to think that some separation is like rain to the flowers. Maria, I missed you so much on those journeys, that hug on my return was a much longed for embrace. Oh how I am going to miss it." Dad struggles to keep his composure. "I will think of you always. I love you so much, my sweet, auf wiedersehen." A dry eye is not to be found; the Mass continues.

After the services, as we are leaving St. James', Elsa Obernesser, I should say Elsa von Clausen, approaches to offer her condolences. Except for a few fleeting glances, I hadn't seen her in twenty years but she is as beautiful as ever. Our voices choke momentarily in recognition of love lost. We hug each other and tears fall once more. Willem comes over and takes my hand. As they turn to leave, tears streaming down her face, she says, "Rafer, I'm so sorry." I feel that she means more than just the loss of my mother.

Interment is in the church cemetery. Franz leads us in a graveside prayer. Yusuf hands some roses to Dad and me to put on her coffin. He whispers that they are from Mother's garden. We both try to stem the tears but to no avail.

The clergy, our few relatives who had to travel some distance, and close friends had been invited to a reception at our chalet. The ladies' auxiliary brought and prepared food & beverages; at times like these they are indispensable. Dad personally thanks each member for their thoughtfulness and help and in due course will send a donation to their organization.

Fortunately the weather is warm and sunny, facilitating the mobility and comfort of everyone. Cardinal Gerhardt stays about a half hour and then excuses himself saying that he has some pressing matters to tend to back at the chancery; he insists that Franz come with him. After a while, after all the guests have left with the exception of Johann and some of the ladies who stay to clean up, Dad excuses himself and retires to his bedroom; he needs to be alone. Johann and

I grab some glasses, a bottle of white wine, and proceed outside to the terrace to regroup. Our chairs are in the shade but we can see the sun as it dips lower in the sky. Johann appears taciturn and uneasy, holding his glass like he is about to elevate the host; his hands tremble as he leans forward and swallows. He smiles sheepishly before taking a deep, almost sober breath.

"Rafer, I fear that all hell is about to break loose in Innsbruck. And Franz, he isn't the same person we knew as youngsters. I'm afraid he is aligning himself with the radicals. And I don't know what to do about it."

I look at him in amazement. The only word that I can muster is, "What?"

"In addition, Pope Paul, while I commend him for some reforms, is acrimonious and heavy-handed. Worse, he continues to sponsor and even amplify the Roman inquisition. You're just back from there, you must be aware of what is going on." Johann makes a conscious effort to sit erect.

"Ja, very much so. He blames the Jews in part for the schism. They must now live in a ghetto and wear yellow markers to identify themselves as such. A few had joined the party that I was just leading. Left possessions behind. Max will take them to Germany from here."

"Incredible, isn't it." Johann pours more wine into his glass, any notion of temperance continues to slide.

"But what does that have to do with Innsbruck and Franz?

"There are recent reports of witchcraft here... and... and it isn't being ignored, far from it. Franz has become a religious zealot... that's all I want to say for now. I want you to see for yourself. He will be saying the early Mass Sunday and will make an announcement to the congregation. The cardinal wants Franz to be the point man on this. I urge you to be there."

May 3, 1556 (Sunday)

Nearing the cathedral, I never fail to notice the basilisk sculpture adorning the exterior of the center apse. A basilisk, for the uninitiated, is a legendary reptile which, according to the tome Malleus Maleficarum, infects the atmosphere by darting lethal venom from its eyes. A man can save himself if he is alert enough to spot the basilisk first and reflect the venom back with a mirror and thereby kill the basilisk with his own poison. This image is a precursor of the insanity to come.

Someone walking in my direction catches my eye, a dark haired, well rounded beauty, who I guess to be in her late twenties. I stare at her trying not to be caught doing so and the closer she gets the more I sense that I have seen her before. She looks up as she is about to pass and right into my eyes. Her eyebrows lift as if I had been impertinent but she looks down just as quickly and continues walking along the square. I turn to watch her go when she stops and stares back. To my surprise she reverses course and approaches me.

"I think I know you. Did you try to disrobe a naive young girl by a swimming hole about twenty years ago?"

After a few seconds of disbelief, "Katarina?"

"Well, at least you got the name right this time. But you never did apologize," she laughs.

"Why should I apologize? I had the best of intentions," I chuckle.

"Rafer, it is so, so good to see you. Where have the years gone? You look terrific." I can't help but notice an engaging quality about her.

"Well so do you. And I have no trouble whatsoever telling your gender now." We both laugh.

"I heard about your mother passing; I'm so sorry. I heard so many speak of her; she was much loved. I wanted to go to the service but duties kept me away."

"Danke schoen, it's nice of you to say so. We were shocked; it was so sudden. The doctor said it was a respiratory infection, that's all we know."

"Speaking of a tragedy, did they ever find out who killed your friend Albert all those years ago? I've been meaning to ask his father but the time never seems right. Herr Freihofer is still rather sensitive about it, I'm told." She has a way of tilting her head when asking a question.

"No they haven't, I'm sorry to say. There is no guarantee of justice, I'm afraid. Then again, maybe it was an accident... you are living in Innsbruck now? You have talked with Fritz?"

"Not only that, I'm now his general manager; moved here a couple of weeks ago. I love it. I'm thrilled with the opportunity. Herr Freihofer is wonderful. Not many people would give a woman so much responsibility. I'm working myself to the bone, though. If there is a void, I fill it."

"I had heard that Fritz was looking for someone to lighten his load. If I remember correctly, you had an exceptional education at the convent. And from personal experience, you're smart."

"Danke schoen to you Mr. Schilling. You and Mrs. Schilling must ask for me, when you come for dinner. You will come to the Boar's Head, of course? Everyone does."

"I certainly will but there is no Mrs. Schilling. Mountain guides don't stand still long enough to get married."

"Well your mother managed to do it; was she a fast woman? Oops! I didn't mean it the way it sounded. I'm sorry." I smile back, knowingly.

"And you?"

"I'm afraid men find me too independent minded. And progressive. But enough about me. I'm anxious to see your old friends,

Johann and Franz. I've seen Snuff; he's outrageous. And his buddies
Harry and Basil. But Johann and Franz have escaped me, although I
understand they are priests, right here at St. James'."

"If you want to see Franz, he's saying the Mass starting in a few
minutes. Care to join me?"

"Let's go to church then."

"So you know, I've just been warned by none other than Johann that
Franz is bringing bad tidings and that he has become, let us say, strident."

"Oh my!"

We sit at the end of a pew on the center aisle; the pulpit is just
above and left of us. Franz enters from the sacristy preceded by two
altar boys; all rise at their entrance. Franz bows to the altar and begins
reciting a prayer in Latin. The altar boys, one kneeling on each side
of him, respond in kind. A methodical person, Franz proceeds in a
deliberate way, no rushing through the liturgy as Johann is inclined
to do. Then we come to his homily...

> "Reports have reached our ears, that there are doting
> parents in our diocese. Their infant has become sickly.
> She never gets enough milk to satisfy her even though
> her mother is abundant. She has become exceptional-
> ly heavy; yet does not seem to grow. These symptoms
> suggest that the child is a changeling." The assemblage
> gasps as one. "A child of the devil that in some cases
> are substituted by one means or another for one's own
> child." A rumble courses over the pews like a rogue
> wave rushing headlong towards a beach. Heads turn,
> eyes wide in astonishment. Katarina reaches for my
> hand. I get that certain feeling at her touch, a feeling
> which I thought was lost forever.

"A man impregnates a succubus devil through intercourse or with the semen obtained from a man's nocturnal pollution during sleep. While an incubus devil impregnates a woman with the semen obtained from some man other than her husband. Thus the child is not entirely of husband and wife. Or such a child has been switched for the child produced of their own union. The devil's treachery has no limits.

"In this case, initial reports do confirm that the mother is a superstitious woman and suggest that she has been seduced by an incubus." A roar goes up from the parishioners. After an eternal pause, Franz continues. "I quote Malleus Maleficarum, Part I, Question VI:

'Because women are the more credulous and because the chief aim of the devil is to corrupt the faith, he rather attacks them... for though the devil tempted Eve to sin, yet Eve seduced Adam. And as the sin of Eve would not have brought death to our soul and body unless the sin afterwards passed on to Adam, to which he was tempted by Eve, not by the devil, therefore she is more bitter than death. More bitter than death, again, because that is natural and destroys only the body; but the sin which arose from woman destroys the soul by depriving it of grace, and delivers the body up to the punishment for sin.'"

Franz then adds, "All punishment from God proceeds from our own sin or from that original sin to which we were all born. And those who grievously sin and do not repent are condemned eternally to the fires of hell and excruciating pain. We may ask why this loving God permits the devil and witches to afflict man with diseases, wreak devastation upon his crops and possessions and even smite him. It is fivefold. I cite Malleus Maleficarum, Part 1, Question 15:

'First, that God may be glorified. God is exalted when an affliction is removed.

Secondly, that merit may be acquired through patience and manifest to others.

Thirdly, that virtue may be preserved through castigation.

Fourthly, that eternal damnation should begin in this life that it might be in some way shown what will be suffered in hell.

Fifthly, that man may be purified, by the expulsion and obliteration of his guilt through scourges.' "

Franz pauses and gazes upon the congregation. "Pray! Do not dote on your children too much or God will take them from you or suffer them an affliction. Fear God! For the wrath of God escapes no man." Another pause. "Let us now offer sacrifice to the Lord."

Franz leaves the pulpit and proceeds to the altar. He begins the offertory. When Mass ends, admonitions and rumors are the commerce of the moment. People rush off to spread the news. We gladly detach ourselves from the troubled crowd. Katarina looks decidedly younger than her age. Our shoulders touch making me want to hold her close.

Being in-love is for teenagers, I admonish myself. *Only love is available for the mature.*

"Well, that was quite a sermon," I say.

"Franz said that *God is exalted when an affliction is removed.* It is like someone sets fire to a building so he can be a hero by rushing in to warn everybody to get out."

"And women come up short once again, I notice."

"To my ears, the word love has gotten lost. Franz's God is all about punishment and suffering."

"Martin Luther was tormented for years by the specter of the wrathful, punishing God. Such God could be feared but not loved, he ascertained. At one point he reportedly said that he not only didn't love God, he hated God."

"Did he ever come to terms with it?" Her head tilts again.

"Apparently so. He concluded from pondering the Gospel that the just man lives by the gift of God, that is to say, by faith. Salvation doesn't depend on human merit; it is achieved by faith alone."

"I wasn't aware he professed that."

"He said that he felt born again."

"If that is what God meant to convey through scripture, that faith alone is the centerpiece of salvation, why would scripture be so obscure about it? It took Luther how long to come to his epiphany?"

"He was about sixty two. The reconciliation came not many months before he died."

"And everything reverts back to interpretation of scripture."

"Most of the faithful just assume that if it is in the Bible it must be correct. They don't realize that much of scripture was contested and from dubious sources. They don't question authority."

"Can you blame them," Katarina volunteers, "if they do, breathing will no longer be an option... Rafer, I should have been at the inn an hour ago. However, I couldn't pass up this opportunity to visit with you and see Franz. Can you come over for the breakfast buffet?"

"Dad is expecting me back at the chalet. I'll be seeing you; you can count on that." Katarina leans in to kiss my cheek. I watch her walk briskly away.

CHAPTER 9

THE TAVERN

May 7, 1556 (Thursday)

In the countryside you will likely be greeted by larks and nightingales. In town, swallows and kestrels take refuge in the eaves of the shops and homes. But land-bound free spirits head for a side street off Herzog-Friedrich Strasse and the tavern entrance of the Boar's Head Inn. Inside the men tell tall tales, play cards and, if they can afford it, smoke their pipes, a new found luxury. The kitchen is just adjacent to the patron's area and against the back wall next to the alley.

Harry Schmidt, known affectionately as Horseshit Harry, is with three of his cronies at a corner table having a jolly old time between bites and gulps. A church bell, refusing to be ignored, marks midday. Looking hard at forty, tattered about the seams, big belly, double chin, bushy eyebrows, and favoring inebriation, his reddish complexion becomes more flushed as he assumes his most pedantic air. "I express to you, it is so. It is so."

"Eee's right," says Snuff, "go on Arry."

"As you will," replies Harry, "as you will. In the fourth century, and long before that, people were saying that through devilish arts men could be transmuted into brute animals. St. Augustine countered, if it happens at all, demons make it appear that men are changed into beasts. But in fact, they are not really changed."

"It all sounds dubious to me," says Basil, an angular man who has a resolve about him absent in the others.

"Cross me heart [1]. I read it's in his *De Civitate Dei*, Book 18, Chapter 18. It is. It is. The devil works on your mental images and transmutes them." Harry then adds, "They're called glamours."

"I told yah," says Snuff, who always speaks a bit louder than need be.

"Smacks of mythology," replies Basil,

"The Church says both happen," continues Harry, "in that witches not only can create illusions but they can actually do these things."

"Father Carberry doesn't believe in witchcraft," chimes in Bear, a huge and powerful but rather un-complex man with a fanciful memory. "He says it's all nonsense." Bear looks at the others and then says, "He told me not to let on that he said that." All laugh at his unwitting breach of trust.

"An witches kin make yur member disappear," adds Snuff almost triumphantly.

"I beg your pardon," says Basil, doing a double take. Unlike himself, who imbibes sparingly, the others decide to guzzle their beers in unison.

"Yur festoolis," Snuff clarifies.

"I know. I know," says Basil. "Now is this just an illusion or would I really lose it?" The others start laughing.

"An tink bout the poor wimin; does they knows if they'd been ad or naught?" The snickering gets even louder.

"What you don't see is what you don't get," says another. At this point anyone could say anything and they laugh.

"This is diabolical," says Basil, who decides to abandon reality and join in. "Do you realize that, if this is true, it is a threat to our very essence."

---

1   Crossing one's heart emphasizes that one is telling the absolute truth, as God is my witness. The cross is the cross of Crucifixion.

"Here! Here!" the others respond in solidarity, clinking their mugs together and taking another swig. Harry decides to swish his beer between his cheeks then suck it through his teeth.

"We must pursue this further," says Basil, "and Horseshit Harry is our man to do it."

"Here! Here!" comes the response and another excuse to imbibe, including Harry. They look to Basil to continue. He doesn't, just to goad them. They look at each other and then back to Basil.

"Harry is our man to do what?" demands Harry indignantly.

"Oh yeah!" says Basil as though he had just been awakened. His small, skeletal hand motions them to lean forward as he begins to whisper like a penitent to a priest.

Things are less jovial near the center of the tavern where another group of men are sitting. One named Heinz, a melancholy, ferret faced man with a bent for imagery and convinced that he is singularly well-informed in these matters, says that a werewolf has been seen at the Leutasch Gorge near Mittenwald. "French honeymooners had been out on Daredevil Walk on a romantic interlude. They were gingerly traversing the gorge and watching the water spew plumes of colored spray, so they intimated. Then, just downstream and near an outcropping of rocks, they spotted this loup-garou dragging an infant."

"A werewolf?" roars the one with a head as square as a block of wood.

"The husband, young and rugged, threw a rock towards it but it fell short. The werewolf dragged the wailing child into the brush. The husband told his bride to stay put and, with his walking stick and unsheathed knife from his belt, made his way down a path even though she pleaded with him not to go. He replied that he had to do something. When he was within ten yards of the spot the wife saw what she thought was a man nearby. Just as quickly, he disappeared.

The husband proceeded cautiously and found some blood on the ground but nothing more."

"You say that the wife saw a man appear; the husband didn't see him?"

"Apparently not."

"So what then?"

"That's all I know."

"No body parts or torn clothes? Nothing else?" another asks, sitting back and puffing on his pipe.

"Nein, as I said, nothing more."

"For all we know it was a brown bear dragging a wild piglet. This lycanthropy thing is all the rage in France these days, I hear," says the blockhead without sympathy. "And you know how dramatic the French can be."

"But the wife saw a man leave the scene. The werewolf changed back," insists Heinz.

"Bah! I doubt she saw anyone. Probably her husband's reflection. They said that there was a lot of mist in the air, and with the sunlight, whatever."

"Hard to believe... Fraulein! How about another round of beers?" the pipe smoker speaks up once more.

"Be right there boys," Katarina shouts from behind the swinging doors to the kitchen.

Recently moved to town from Igls, a village roosting in the Patscherkofel Mountains not far to the southeast but soaring a thousand feet higher than Innsbruck, Katarina von Hoffen is filling in for the barmaid who is out sick. She notices once again a beggar woman going through the trash in the alley behind the kitchen. Stuffing some marinated roast chicken and lettuce into a small loaf of bread, she opens the back door and hands it to her. Katarina's cat, Pussfuss, purrs for attention and similar treatment.

"Danke schön, beautiful lady," lisps the woman through her broken teeth and strings of oily hair across her face. She then saunters off to savor her treat. Katarina goes to the bar and pulls three steins of beer from an ice packed barrel, puts them on a tray and takes them to the men. Back outside, two unsavory chaps turn into the alley and lean against the wall.

"There he is now. My information was right."

"The guy in the cap?"

"Nein, over there, the bigger one with the hairy arms. The boss wants your blade in the son of a bitch before the day is out. Move back, don't let him see us."

Striding down Herzog-Friedrich Strasse is Walker Hess, a bloke with an unrivaled resume for abusive behavior and unsavory activities. Financially strapped, blackmail is his latest scheme but he is about to find out that the nobility is more adept when it comes to felony. As he passes, the two men follow.

Katarina is still at the table chatting with the men. Austrians, besides being warm and friendly, are curious and inquisitive to a fault. This newcomer especially has to be queried because she is shapely and feisty.

"Heinz here says that a werewolf was spotted out at Leutasch Gorge," the pipe smoker proffers. "What do you think of that, Katarina?"

"A hairy man, what's so unusual about that?" All but Heinz laugh.

Blockhead picks up on it. "Heinz thinks we should take this seriously. He says werewolves and witches are all about."

Katarina grabs a broom near the bar, puts it between her legs and swishes around the table cackling. Stopping next to Heinz, she leans over and says, "Want a ride?" Only Heinz, is not amused.

All heads turn as Walker Hess struts into the tavern with his trademark scowl. An imposing figure with tanned, muscular arms dangling from his sleeveless shirt; the word bully comes to mind at the sight of him. He proceeds to the center table and stops next to Katarina. Hess' gaze takes inventory of the men at the table and then surveys Katarina from top to bottom paying particular attention to her cleavage, her embroidered blouse doesn't mask her rounded figure. She returns the rude gesture taking particular note of his hirsute limbs. Turning to the seated men she quips, "Who says that there are no such things as werewolves?"

Hess, his self-image bruised, takes Katarina's face in his right hand, almost lifting her off the ground, "I don't know who you are bitch but don't you ever make fun of me again." Katarina twists free in a fury and thrusts the broom handle into his left cheek striking him just under the eye and causing him to stumble onto the floor.

"Don't you dare touch me again you schweinhund or I'll see your way to hell," she shouts, grabbing a mug of beer from the table and dumping it on him. She tosses her hair back and retreats to the kitchen. The men stand in alarm. Hess, at first clutching his eye, scrambles to his feet. He shoves one of the men aside and makes to go after Katerina but manages just a few steps when a mountain of man in the person of Bear, his huge forearms crossed, blocks his path. Harry, Snuff and Basil are right by him ready to assist.

"Better let Herr Doctor have a look at that eye my friend," Basil nods to the bar. Dr. Charles de Barton has been sitting alone at the bar having a mid-day snack with no intention of becoming involved in any of this but sometimes choice is not an option. Grabbing Hess' arm, Bear walks him to a stool next to the doctor and sits him down. De Barton perfunctorily examines the cheek and eye as the others stand by. The cook, a burly woman with cropped, gray hair, emerges from the kitchen with ice wrapped in a cloth and hands it to the doctor, who then holds it to the left side of Hess' face.

Returning to the kitchen, the cook tells Katarina, "Please keep an eye on the hearth for me. I going down the cellar to get some vinegar."

The beggar woman, having observed the confrontation through a side window, comes back around to the alley door and enters; her gait and manner is tentative. "Fraulein, I knows how to take care of the likes of 'im." She pauses as Katarina stands there still shaken. The woman then takes a pitcher of water and pours a little into a pan. Taking a ladle from a rack, she puts a small, brittle piece of lead into it and holds the ladle over the hearth. In short order she pours the molten lead in a measured way into the pan of water. Quickly the lead solidifies roughly into a human shape. She pours out the water and shuffles alongside Katarina, where she extracts the contents. "Thar he is, Fraulein, laying the '*man*' on the counter."

"There who is?" asks Katarina.

"That awrful fella, me pretty lady. At's him thar," pointing to the figure on the counter. "Or might as well be 'im. Now, whar do yah want to stab 'im?" she asks while holding a knife by the blade in front of her. Katarina decides to humor her. She takes the knife and stabs the leaden figure.

"Fraulein Katarina, what in the world?" the cook utters as she emerges from the cellar. The old woman beats a retreat through the alley door.

Hess' patience having worn thin, had gotten up from his stool and threw the ice pack on the floor. Gesturing towards the kitchen he bellowed, "you haven't seen the last of me wench," and stormed out.

Katarina, seeing that Hess has gone, returns to the customers to tend to their needs. The men involved, where the trouble had started, have decided that enough is enough and are preparing to leave.

"It's been a disturbing afternoon, hasn't it? Sorry to have been part of the problem," one says to Katarina.

"No, it wasn't your fault. Please come back soon,"

"We will." They all head for the door.

Katarina turns towards the corner table, where Snuff and his cronies are sitting still somewhat concerned. She walks behind Bear and puts her hands on his substantial shoulders. "I don't know your name but thanks so much for the help. No telling what he might have done. And that goes for the rest of you guys."

"We cull im Bear fur obvious reasons, luke at dose paws."

"Snuff, are you sure his name isn't Sir Lancelot?"

"Bear is a hero alright," says Harry, "but do you think he is pretty enough to be Sir Lancelot?"

"I think he's handsome." Bear blushes as Harry expected. "Let me get you another round of beers. It's on the house this time. Then I'll wipe up this mess," as she glances at the floor.

Just then Heinz rushes back into the tavern. "Doc, come quick! That guy has been stabbed."

The tables clear as all the patrons go out to see what happened. Hess is lying on his back in the middle of the street. As Sheriff Mitlstrasser just happens upon the scene, a conspiracy of ravens low on the wind bears witness to the commotion.

"Took a knife high under the ribs; I'm not getting a pulse," says the doctor. He takes a clean handkerchief from his coat pocket; places it over the wound and applies pressure with his hand as he looks into Hess' eyes, whose pupils are dilated. Lifting up the handkerchief, he stares directly into the wound. There is no pulsing of blood.

"Is he gone?" the sheriff asks.

"Afraid so," says de Barton, as if he was just awakened. "Apparently stabbed as soon as he stepped through the door. See the trail of blood. He's all yours now."

"If someone has something to tell me, now is the time," says the sheriff. Someone confirms de Barton's remark, that Hess just left the tavern. Many start to drift away.

Katarina had been reluctant to join those rushing to see Hess, wanting no part of him, but her curiosity gets the best of her and she appears in the doorway. No sooner than she does, Walker Hess attempts to bend forward, blood gurgling from his mouth and belly, and just as quickly he falls back, this time for good. The doctor, the sheriff, and Katarina look at each other in disbelief. *"You haven't seen the last of me wench,"* reverberates in her mind. She has now. No one ever escapes this life without some unfinished business.

CHAPTER 10

THE CONFESSION

May 9, 1556 (Saturday)

It is an overcast morning bestowing a weary pallor on the hamlet and there is little reprieve. Despite the candles, the main interior of St. James' is rather gloomy. The lines to the confessional boxes, one on each side of the church, are quite small and there is only a suggestion of movement. Two veiled women kneel at the altar rail, quiet and remote, apparently saying their penances.

An elderly woman, her hands mottled and skin wizened by the rigors of her abject life, has just knelt in front of a tiered rack of white votive candles set in dull black, metal holders. The clank of her coin falling into the offering box is heard before she reaches for a taper to transfer a flame to an unmolested wick. Their light softens this dark recess of the church and she bows her head in prayer. A certain quietude engulfs her, a peaceful refuge from the sober reality outside its walls.

Harry muses that, if it were not for the women, the Church would be a mere shell of itself. It is the women who rear the children in the faith. It is the women who see to it that the family attends Mass. It is the women who devote their time and energies to raising funds to support the Church. It is the women who volunteer and do the menial jobs.

Harry is kneeling in a pew on the left side, the side where Father

Franz von Clausen is hearing confession. Father Johann Carberry, on the right side, is now gone. Usually, he simply asks the penitent, *"Are you truly sorry for your sins and resolve to sin no more?"* Upon receiving an affirmative answer he will say something like, *"Say the Act of Contrition, three Our Fathers, go in peace."* Stern lectures from him are not the norm.

Harry is beginning to feel apprehensive and is starting to get cold feet. *This borders on sacrilege. But what will the guys think if I chicken out?* A vertical slice of light pierces the back of the church and then a large door is heard to close. Harry twists in his seat to see Snuff standing there watching a teenage boy, the last person in line, go into Father Franz's confessional box. Snuff, his eyes trying to adjust to the darkness, stares at Harry; he moves forward and kneels in the pew directly behind him.

"Yuv bin ear a haf hour. Whut yah waiten fer?"

"I don't want anybody else in line in case von Clausen goes off the deep end."

"Deep end. Whad yah talken bout? All eel do is tell yah sum garbage."

"If you're so sure, you go in."

"Yuh said yud do it. Don't chicken out. I bet ah lot of coin on yuh."

"Somebody say I wouldn't?"

"If yuh must knows, ja."

"Great!" Harry says facetiously as he continues to fret.

"Thah kid's cummin out already. This muz be ah speed record fer Franz. Orr thah kid's a saint. Probably made up sumpin just to have an excuse to receive the sacrament."

"The kid must be a real straight arrow, alright," says Harry."

Snuff tugs at Harry's shirt to get him up and points him towards the confessional; he stays on Harry's heels to make sure he doesn't back out and pushes Harry through the door. Harry falls forward making a terrible racket. The women up front turn towards the commotion with looks of consternation. The old lady decides that it is time to go. Franz slides open the square wooden panel covering the screened window between him and the penitent. Harry is barely perceptible to him in the shadows and Franz is a mere silhouette to Harry.

"Are you all right, my son?"

"Ja Father," says Harry as he fumbles his way to the kneeler but loses his balance again making even more of a racket. Another woman beats it through a side door. Snuff laughs to himself as he waits behind a pillar; someone has to keep Harry honest.

"Have you been drinking?"

"Just a slip, Father, my apologies." Harry manages to get both knees planted.

"You had just a sip?"

"No, a slip. I slipped. No sip."

"My word… proceed."

"Bless me Father for I have sinned," Harry whispers. "It has been six months since my last confession," Harry lies; it is more like sixteen years. "Father, a strange thing has happened to me. I need your guidance, your help."

"Go on!"

"Well Father, I lost my member."

"Lost your member?"

"Ja, Father."

"Your'e talking about your, your…."

"Ja, Father."

"I have read of such things, my son."

"Then perhaps you can help, Father."

"When did this happen, my son?"

"Just the other day, Father."

"Were you involved with a woman at the time?"

"Well Father..." Harry pauses for effect.

"You must tell me everything, if I am to help you."

"Well I didn't want to bring the lady into it."

"The lady may be very much a part of it. Does she know about your loss?"

"Very much so, Father." Harry pauses again.

"Go on my son!"

"Well Father... I am guilty of... of fornication. What I mean is, well, we fornicated."

"Fornication is a grave sin. Do you know her well?"

"Just met her."

"Anything unusual about her?"

"I think she's a nymphomaniac."

"I am not surprised."

"You aren't?"

"My son, all witchcraft comes from carnal lust which in woman is insatiable."

"It is?" says Harry with a trace of hope in his voice.

"I refer you to the Old Testament, Proverbs 30. There are four things that are never satisfied and the fourth thing that the Bible refers to is the mouth of the womb. To satisfy this lust, women will even copulate with devils and make pacts with them."

"I didn't know that the Bible says that about women."

"It is obvious that women are more carnal than men because of their many carnal abominations."

"Carnal abominations?"

"Copulation with devils. Many times have witches been seen upon their backs in the fields, naked to the waist. While the Incubi were only visible to the witches themselves, passersby could tell by the placement of the witches' legs and agitation of their hips that they were engaged in the venereal act. A black vapor could be seen rising from the witch, admittedly on rare occasions, after orgasm had been reached. The vapor was of the stature of a man."

"Whoa! I didn't know this. And you think that I was seduced by a witch, Father?"

"When did you discover that you had lost your member?"

"After she got mad at me."

"Why did she get mad?"

"After we, we...," Harry feigns embarrassment.

"Fornicated?"

"Ja. And, well, I was satisfied but she wasn't."

"Even though you had intercourse with her?"

"Ja but that wasn't enough for her."

"Wasn't enough?"

"Women need more than intercourse to be satisfied."

"They do?"

"She wanted more foreplay. That insatiable thing."

"What sort of foreplay?"

"I don't think I should go into it here."

"She got mad because you didn't give her more foreplay."

"Right."

"Then what happened?"

"I fell asleep."

"That made her mad at you."

"It didn't help."

"I see. Then what happened?"

"When I woke up my member was gone and she was too. I looked under the sheets and the bed, all over, and I couldn't find it."

"My! My! Then what?"

"I went looking for her. When I caught up with her I asked her what she did with it. She laughed. I grabbed her arm and twisted it. She then said that she put it in a feed bucket in the blacksmith's stable."

"And?"

"I forced her to come to the blacksmith's with me; I'm not stupid. I wasn't going to let her out of my sight."

"Wise of you, my son."

"When we got there she said that she put the bucket up in the hayloft. I went up the ladder and found the bucket. There must have been two dozen penises in there."

"Two dozen!"

"At least."

"Did you find yours?"

"I grabbed the biggest one but she said that I couldn't have it because it belonged to a parish priest."

"A parish priest!!! May the saints preserve us. Then what?"

"I got scared and ran away."

"Scared! Why?"

"Because when I looked further into the bucket, the penises had begun squirming about and started eating the oats in the bucket."

"My word."

"Your word! My penis."

"Ja. Ja."

"What am I to do Father?"

Franz remains silent for a few moments. Then, after some deliberation, says "This is a very remarkable story to say the least, comparable to one in Malleus Maleficarum. And you can be sure that I will do all in my power to help you. But before I can make use of the weapons of the Church, so to speak, to combat this evil, so to speak, I must be able to tell my superiors that I have verified your affliction, so to speak. They will want confirmation."

"Verify my affliction? So to speak."

"Ja."

"You mean...."

"Ja."

Harry starts to sweat. "You want me to take down my pants in the confessional?"

"It will be discreet, my son. Just pull your trousers down and I will come around for a quick look."

Harry's mind is racing. *I'll make excuses and just leave.*

"I am stepping out now. Just open the door a bit when you are ready," Franz says as he emerges from the confessional.

I'm trapped, Harry thinks. *Why did I let those guys talk me into this?* Then it comes to him. *The time the guys were skinny dipping in the river last summer. Snuff did it. It just might work.*

"Everyone has gone from the church, my son. It's alright. Are you ready yet?"

"Ja, Father, you may open the door."

"My word, and no testicles." *All those disbelievers in witchcraft should see this,* he thinks. Franz returns to his seat in the confessional and Harry pulls up his pants and buttons them. "My son, sin is the root cause of your affliction. This is the price of your fornication. Through the prayers and sacraments of the Church you had at your disposal the certain means of thwarting the diabolical arts of witches but you strayed."

"I'm a sinner."

"You are here to mend your ways; is that not correct?"

"Ja, Father."

"It will behoove you to seek out the witch who caused this treachery. She is still in the area?

"No, she's long gone."

"Too bad. You might have pleaded with her in soft and gentle words to restore your member; your best hope. Mind you, however, it is forbidden to use witchcraft to cure a bewitchment."

"I don't understand Father."

"I mean that you cannot seek the aid of another witch to work her magic to counteract what has already been done to you."

"Why not Father?"

"Because witches receive their power by entering into pacts with the devil. Consorting with the devil is offensive to God."

"I see Father."

"There was a defect in the formation of the first woman for Eve was formed from a rib of the breast, which is bent. Because of this defect woman is not a perfect person and she is given to deceit."

"Was Adam not a perfect person? His ribs were bent."

"Don't quibble with me. Through their first defect in intelligence and their second defect of inordinate passions, they search for and inflict various retributions by witchcraft."

"Women have enticed me, Father."

"The devil can suspend the local motion of any organ. Since original sin passes from generation to generation through the venereal act, God permits the devil more latitude here than with man's other functions. And, of course, it is easier to bewitch a man in this activity than a woman."

"That's an interesting analysis."

"Are you prepared to make a good confession and sin no more?"

"Ja, Father."

"For your penance you are to say the Our Father one hundred times. In addition, an hour before the first Mass of the day on Sunday two weeks hence, you are to come to the church sanctuary for your exorcism. Now say the Act of Contrition!"

"My exorcism!!!"

CHAPTER II

THE RECTORY

May 9, 1556 (Saturday evening)

Adding Toki Nubutu to St. James' staff had been one of Cardinal Gerhardt's better ideas. Her imperturbable good humor and outrageous wit melt even the most irascible curmudgeon. The high cheekboned, ebony face zippered with two rows of gleaming white teeth stretched in a broad smile demands an answer in kind. Just mention Toki's name and a smile automatically spreads across the listener's face.

Of mixed West African and North African descent, this thirty one year old delight was brought to Innsbruck from Spain by Cardinal Gerhardt. On a papal mission there less than a year ago, he too had been captivated by her provocative, candid eyes and irrepressible smile. She had a way of incorporating herself into your inner circle without being invited. He had offered her round-trip passage to Austria, free room and board, an adequate monthly allowance, and two ounces of gold at the conclusion of her commitment, if she would serve as house manager of the rectory for at least two years. She accepted.

Toki, familiar with some German, is quickly moving towards fluency in her new environment with some inevitable misspeaks. Gerhardt is pleased not only for this refreshing new personality but because he likes having a young damsel around. He fancies the ladies and he enjoys telling Toki risqué jokes, something he could never do with the nuns. While Franz is embarrassed by this, he cuts the cardinal some slack; Gerhardt has a certain je ne sais quoi. As the cardinal leaves for the evening in his more secular clothes and wanting some of his shoes in his closet shined, he tells the sexton to have them polished. This is a long standing request and something Manfred does either in the evening after a final security check of the buildings or in early morning. Little Manfred, as he is referred to, is a church caricature because of his size but he has an over the top personality. Being a dwarf with no formal education doesn't stand in his way of enjoying life; he gives everyone an enthusiastic greeting and makes them laugh with his self-deprecating antics.

Looking back decades, however, to the morning Effie Eberle was murdered, Manfred never saw Willem von Clausen enter the chancery with Effie. Willem had realized at once that Effie was in a very agitated state. What he didn't know was that she was wrestling with a personal problem as well as a nagging dilemma. As to the latter, her father had informed her on his death bed that, when he had returned from Nag Hammadi, Egypt, he had brought with him one of several copies of the Gospel of Thomas that had been found there. He never mentioned this to her before for safety reasons, he said. There is credible evidence, he continued, that Thomas predates the canonical gospels of the New Testament, namely Matthew, Mark, Luke and John. If so, this could possibly alter Church history. Also, he noted, this could very well be why it was ordered destroyed over a thousand years ago and denied canonical standing at the Council of Nicaea of 325. That same council rejected the notion circulating in the Eastern Church that Jesus was not divine. The Gospel of Thomas does nothing to confirm his divinity.

Her father was about to tell her where he had kept it hidden but passed away before he could finish the thought. She searched and searched for days until she stumbled upon it in plain sight, in a crate covered with various hand and garden tools. She liked Cardinal Gerhardt and on impulse blurted out that her father came upon the gospel but regretted her revelation the instant she began uttering it. Her father was warning her of how explosive the codex might be; wasn't he? She had to think this through. *Would the Church destroy the gospel? Should I give it to another biblical scholar? Am I in danger now if I don't give it to the cardinal? Yes, there is someone I can confide in.* She made excuses to the cardinal, saying that she didn't know where her father had it stored but she sensed that he knew she was having second thoughts. There followed a coldness and she sensed a diabolical side of him emerging. One time he squeezed her arm so tight that it was painful and all but insisting that she retrieve it and bring it to him. Just as quickly he softened and asked her to keep looking. Her fondness of the cardinal had been replaced with trepidation.

As to her more personal anguish, she dropped a *'load of bricks"* on Willem the morning that she was killed. Effie had discovered that the von Clausen firm had been skimming Church monies from time to time and she was conflicted about telling Cardinal Gerhardt and hurting her fiancée. She felt it was her duty to do so. She reminded Wilhem of how he had told her that maintaining a large estate was very costly and sometimes became quite a burden meeting the monthly expenses. However, if that was the case, it was certainly no excuse for stealing, especially from the Church. Willem insisted that pilfering Church funds for personal use was a way of life for the Church hierarchy and besides, his firm was only making up for the steeply discounted compensation they had been charging. Effie said that they should have just raised their fees then; he could rationalize all he wanted but to her it was flat out stealing. They argued and

Willem finally stormed out of the room to control his temper, in the process banging his shin on a stool so hard that he gasped.

Limping down a long hallway and into another room, he closed the door and nursed his bruise. His mind raced to figure a way out of this potential catastrophe. He agonized over his stressed relationship with Effie and the potential harm to his family. Glancing out of a window, he noticed snow beginning to fall. With renewed determination he returned to confront Effie once again. Finding her lifeless body on the floor and totally bewildered, he knelt next to her while surveying the violent scene. He was dumbfounded and caressed her cheek. His clothes became stained with her blood and he panicked. *What will the sheriff think? Certainly not the clergy. What if I'm seen leaving the chancery?* He slipped from the chancery into the rectory and past the kitchen without being seen and then into the cathedral, where he exited. He had left his horse sheltered from the cold at the unattended stable. The snow was swirling as he rode a circuitous route home. I say all this based on what Willem had told me long after the fact. But is this an unadulterated story?

At that fateful time Manfred had been charged with attending to the cardinal's shoes. At daybreak he had taken some prayer cards for placement on the table in the vestibule of the cathedral where he discovered that the cathedral doors were unlocked. *Did I forget to lock the doors last night? I locked them. Or was that the night before? Did I do the shoes before or after the security check?* He quickly locked the doors and took a quick look around. Everything was intact, he assured himself. He retreated to the rectory hoping against hope that no one knew of his dereliction of duty; his oversights were legendary and Cardinal Gerhardt threatened to fire him more than once. When the murder was discovered, Manfred knew that he dare not disclose his lapse. And he already locked the door to the chancery by the time he left to get the sheriff. Upon repeated questioning he stood fast. Sheriff Mitlstrasser never discovered this missing piece to the puzzle and had no incriminating evidence. The cardinal subsequently requested permission to go to Effie's home to get a hymn book that he said she had borrowed; this drew no special notice but bore him no fruit.

Now, all these years later, the rumors about the gregarious but spendthrift and philandering cardinal were about to take on a new life. Father Franz, having returned from meditation and prayer for the afflicted, is in the rectory kitchen giving Toki impromptu instruction in the faith. Father Johann is in the adjoining dining room for a post dinner snack.

"Everyone has a guardian angel," says Franz, "per *Psalms 91:11 and 91:12. 'As long as you stay in the state of grace, this heavenly spirit will protect you.'* " He speaks quietly, as though he is still in church but his focus is on polishing an apple.

"From what," asks Toki? Her focus is on slicing a tomato.

"From Satan and his minions. Just last year we had that ferocious storm, too terrible to be anything but a punishment from God. Considering other recent happenings, undoubtedly witchcraft was involved." Johann looks up from eating his strudel but doesn't say anything.

"I thought it was called weather," she makes a small, perplexed gesture with her foot.

"You are not schooled in these things, my child." He begins his assault on the apple. Toki is amused that he refers to her as "*my child*," even though Franz isn't a great deal older than she.

"Have you ever encountered a devil?"

"It is not important that I have or have not encountered a devil," he answers with an edge to his voice. "The Bible speaks of devils and that is sufficient for me and should be for anyone else for that matter."

Just then there is a loud knock at the door and Toki goes to answer it. She returns to tell Johann that there is a man in the vestibule who will only talk to him. Johann takes the last bite of strudel, puts the plate in the sink and proceeds to the vestibule. After some excited chatter, the front door is heard to shut as the two men exit the building.

⌘

The next day the name Cardinal Gerhardt is on every tongue. It seems that he had been seen dining alone at the Boar's Head Inn the prior evening. Here, I am told, is how it unfolded. While having his appetizer, a well-groomed woman, also alone, was being seated at a nearby table. She glanced in his direction, made eye contact, and then returned to her menu. He signaled the Herr Ober, Fritz Freihofer, and requested him to inform the woman as to who he was and invite her to join him; no need for both to dine in solitude. She demurred, saying that she was in mourning and would not make good company. "Nonsense," the cardinal replied. "A glass of wine, a good meal, and a sympathetic conversation is just what you need to comfort you at such a time," Gerhardt, now standing, held a chair for her. Although slight, she was heavy with poise and self-assurance. She nodded acquiescence and Fritz escorted her to the cardinal's table.

"Fritz, I was going to have some soup. I see that cream of tomato is the soup de jour." Turning to his dinner guest, "Perhaps the lovely lady would like the same?"

"That would be nice, danke."

The waiter quickly adds another place setting. The soup, kept hot in a large pot, is ladled into two bowls and brought to the table immediately by Fritz himself. The waiter removes the almost empty basket of bread and replaces it with a full one.

"The soup is delicious. It and your kindness are comforting."

"Ja, cream of tomato is one of my favorites. And the pleasure is all mine."

"My husband recently passed away and this is my first time into town since. Had to deal with some estate business and it took longer than I thought, still not finished. I decided to stay in town overnight. Luckily I packed a few things just in case." Her voice has a soft, timeless quality.

"Well your misfortune is somewhat fortunate for me, if I may put it that way. I was to meet someone for dinner here but there was a message waiting for me expressing regrets. I hate to dine alone and I am enchanted that you consented to join me."

"You are very kind, Karl."

"Karl! Few in these parts know me as Karl, my lady," a quizzical look comes across his face.

"I think I'll order the goulash," she says to the waiter. Turning back to Karl, "Would you like the same?"

"Yes, the same," he nods to the waiter.

"As I recall, it was a favorite of yours some years back." His senses and memory are beginning to race now. *She looks so familiar.* He pauses and stares awkwardly. "Is the Tyrrhenian Sea as beautiful as you expected," she adds?

"Anna? Can it be? But your... pardon, I..."

"My nose, Karl? Sometimes things happen for the best. I had broken it not long after you left but it was my good fortune that the doctor was then able to straighten it for the better."

"Yes, it is my Anna. And your nose was just fine the way it was," taking her hands in his.

"You didn't forget, then?"

"How could I forget; you were so wonderful," he gushes. He pulls the blue handkerchief from his pocket and hands it to her. Tears come to her eyes as she holds it.

"You still have it! I don't believe it."

"I often have it with me. It reminds me of you and the new life I began almost forty years ago. It's a bit worn now but I refuse to part with it."

"I'm so touched... that you still carry it... oh Karl..."

"You are my fondest memory."

Anna looks down to regain her composure, then snaps back. "But I must say, I never pictured you as a cardinal."

"Neither did my family," he laughs. "The pope sent me here on a temporary assignment. I went to your place but you weren't there. The owners didn't even know of you. They had bought the place from someone whom I never heard of. Then Innsbruck grew on me and I talked the pope into letting me stay."

"I believe it did change hands more than once. It wore me down; it just became too much. I didn't have a handsome young man to help me anymore."

"I suspected that you didn't have a brother. Am I right?"

"You figured that out, huh? A girl has to be careful with strangers." They laugh.

"Tell me about yourself, Anna. You say that you lost your husband; I'm so sorry to hear that. Do you have any children?"

"Yes. I mean no. I mean yes, my husband and I were childless. Being with you after all these years has me flustered." The waiter arrives with dinner and then places two glasses on the table. Fritz follows and pours some Bardolino wine.

"Danke, Fritz, so gracious of you."

"My pleasure, Your Eminence. May you and the charming lady enjoy your meal. Dedrick is one of our best; he will take good care of you."

"To our reunion, Anna. It is long overdue." Karl raises his glass in toast.

"Yes, to our reunion," as they clink glasses.

Each silently reminiscing the past, they eat quietly for a bit. Finally, "I've thought of you often, Anna."

"And I of you, Karl." More silence... "I had hoped that you might come back to me. You probably knew that."

"I thought about it. But..."

"But God won out. I had a hard time competing with the frauleins of Innsbruck. How could I compete with God," she smiles. Karl's response is a muted grin. "But Cardinal Gerhardt, there are rumors about your celibacy. Or should I say your lack of celibacy. Word has it that you are a rascal. But a likeable rascal, if that is a saving grace."

"Anna! Anna! People love to gossip, they misinterpret; even a cardinal isn't immune. Is this something you heard recently?"

"I've heard it for, let's say, a very long time." Dedrick interrupts asking if everything is to their satisfaction, allowing him some room to deflect the allegation. He is waved off.

"You were still in this area all along? You knew I was here all this time?"

"I was going to contact you several times. I decided to leave well enough alone. After all, you being a cardinal."

"The Lord forgive me. You were so kind and generous to me. I don't know what to say."

"You don't have to say anything, really. You don't owe me any explanation. Really, Karl, you don't."

"Well, I want to think of you as a friend. And I want you to think of me as a friend, a very dear friend."

"You are my friend, Karl." she laughs. "We better finish the goulash before it gets cold."

"We can't have that, it's almost as good as yours. Let's not waste any."

The minutes pass. Outside of please pass the salt or a comment on the flavoring, they don't say anything. Dedrick comes to clear the dishes. He returns with a pot of tea and the pastry the cardinal likes, also asking if they care for anything else. Karl looks at Anna; she shakes her head.

"No Dedrick, just put it on my bill."

"What are your plans now that your husband has died?"

"Well, people are always asking me to help out here and there; I don't think that will change. I still do some knitting."

"What did your husband do?"

"He was a carpenter, a good man who provided a good home." Tears come to her eyes. "Karl, it's been a long day; I'm going to retire to my room." She grabs her purse and opens it. "Here, let me give you this for my meal, which should cover it."

"Absolutely not! It's about time that I did something for you."

"Well danke. It is wonderful getting together after all these years," a trace of melancholy in her voice.

"I'll walk out with you," putting his tea down.

As they approach the front desk, Anna turns to a porter, "Some packages from The Mill Shop were to be sent over here for me, did you receive anything?"

"Yes, they are right over here. Let me get them." There are several of them and they are bulky. The porter tries to carry them but one or the other keeps falling off. "I'm so sorry, I better get another porter."

Karl picks two off the floor. "No need, I'll go along with you."

The porter leads the way to Anna's room. Karl follows them into the room and puts his packages next to the luggage rack holding the others. He thanks the porter, who then heads to the door.

Karl turns back to say goodbye to Anna. She comes up to him and kisses him on the lips. "For old times' sake." He embraces her and kisses her passionately. She acquiesces. He picks her up and carries her to the bed and starts to unbutton her blouse.

"No Karl. This isn't what I had in mind," she protests almost politely. He turns on his side, flips his shoes off and then his pants.

"It isn't over, it can be just as before."

"Karl, I said no!" now getting agitated.

"Anna, it can be like before," as he reaches under her dress.

"No! Karl. It's not the same now. Stop!" She tries to push him off and wiggle free but is unsuccessful. "Damn you Karl, I said no. Don't! You son of a bitch. Don't!"

The door, still ajar, a married couple walking in the hallway hears Anna's shouts. After pausing to assess the situation briefly, the man cautiously walks into the room and finds Karl, apparently having withdrawn from Anna. He immediately returns to the hallway and tells his wife to alert the manager and get the sheriff. Meanwhile others coming by ask of the commotion. The door is wide open and they see Karl disheveled and tucking in his shirt.

Fritz and Katarina come into the room and see Anna composing herself and tears running down her face. Katarina introduces herself. Fritz takes Karl by the arm, walks him into the hallway and closes the door.

"I witnessed everything," the man says.

"The sheriff has been sent for," Fritz whispers to the cardinal.

"Why it's Cardinal Gerhardt!" someone in the hall cries out.

Back in his office, Fritz has Karl sit down and regain his composure. "It's all a misunderstanding," says Karl. "People misinterpret."

"What I think doesn't matter, Your Eminence. The sheriff, however, has been summoned. Wait here please! I'll be right back." Fritz finds the porter and dispatches him to get Father Carberry. He then puts a pot of hot tea, a cup, a slice of cake and a napkin on a tray and takes it upstairs. Knocking on Anna's door, he announces himself. When Katarina opens it, he hands her the tray.

"Shall I send for a doctor?" Katarina looks to Anna, who shakes her head.

"Tell her I am very sorry. Whatever she wants is hers. And everything is on the house." Fritz then returns to his office but Karl is gone.

Sheriff Mitlstrasser is shown to Fritz's office and within minutes Father Johann arrives. Fritz fills them in on the details. Mitlstrasser sees no pressing need to pursue the cardinal at this hour; he is a prominent figure and easy to find. He does seek out the witnesses and Anna.

Returning from the inn, Johann finds only Manfred about. Inquiring of the cardinal, Manfred gestures that he went to his room for the night. Johann proceeds to the cardinal's room; cracking the door open, he finds the cardinal in bed and to all appearances asleep.

❧

Cardinal Wolfgang Karl Gerhardt gets up especially early. He goes to his study and carefully writes a letter to Pope Paul IV. The pontiff hates the Spaniards and the Habsburgs. Cardinal Gerhardt had participated in his machinations to renew war between them and France. The cardinal has reason to believe that he will receive immediate papal support. A second letter is written to the attention of Rafer Schilling, whom he knows to be back from an excursion through the Vosges Mountains to Lorraine. Toki is dispatched with both to Rafer's chalet. Although she doesn't know it, the pouch she is to give to Rafer for his compensation contains several nuggets of pure gold. It is a tidy sum to insure prompt and exclusive action.

Breakfast is more like brunch on Sundays, with the priests not eating until their respective Masses are over. This particular Sunday, however, they have to prepare it themselves as Toki has not as yet returned. As they are doing so, Johann informs Franz of the preceding night's misadventure and he is dumbfounded.

Cardinal Gerhardt enters the dining area off the kitchen shortly thereafter in a cheerful and almost theatrical manner, as if nothing is amiss. Franz perfunctorily mentions that Toki is absent; his expression is stoic and distant. The cardinal replies that she has gone on an errand. "I see that you have managed without her; may I?" He takes a plate and helps himself.

The two priests choose to remain silent as each eats his meal, waiting for the other to volunteer some information about the preceding night. They avoid each other's eyes and busy themselves getting butter or milk or something else they did or didn't really need. Johann pours everyone a second cup of tea. Finally, Franz breaks the silence.

"Cardinal," this is how the priests usually address Gerhardt, like a military person addressing a superior by his rank, "I am preparing for an exorcism in two weeks hence, since a parishioner has lost his member." Karl and Johann stare at him as if he has two heads. "If you will give me the name of a priest designated to perform such rites, I will proceed to make the arrangements." Johann registers incredulity once again but the cardinal sees his options broaden.

"Are you saying that he is bewitched, Franz?"

"Yes, Cardinal." Franz fills them in with as much detail as he feels that he can without violating the confidentiality of the confessional.

"You know about glamours, gentlemen. This is an illusion created by the devil. This man did not, in fact, lose his member. Of course, this poor, albeit sinful man, perceives the loss as real and has no sense of touch there." says Gerhardt.

"But I did not see it, either." Franz's remark is ignored.

"You all know, of course, last year's storm was certainly the result of witchcraft." Gerhardt looks each priest directly in the eye. Franz nods affirmatively but Johann looks away, which doesn't go unnoticed by the cardinal. "Couple that with the incident a short time ago with the changeling and now this; it leaves no doubt that witches are pervading Innsbruck. Who knows where the treachery will stop. Yes Franz, I'll get you an exorcist as quickly as possible."

The conversation continues in a casual way. Franz glances at Johann on several occasions to see if he is going to broach the subject but Johann pays him no mind. Franz can't stand it any longer. His face takes on a troubled pallor. "Cardinal, a messenger arrived here last evening. Johann was called to the Boar's Head Inn for an emergency. Your name was mentioned."

"My name was mentioned? An emergency?"

"Apparently there was some sort of problem; so I am told."

Gerhardt shrugs. "A problem at the Boar's Head Inn? I dined with an old friend but she departed and I returned to the rectory."

Franz looks at Johann. "Tell the cardinal of your summons there!"

"Perhaps the cardinal will address this in his own time," Johann replies.

"Gentlemen, get to the point please!"

Franz stares at Johann as if he must be daft. *Certainly the story is absurd; the cardinal knows nothing of it,* he thinks. But Franz feels compelled to blurt it out since his colleague refuses to fill the pregnant pause. "It seems that a woman was accosted in her room last night. Witnesses say it was you. It's nonsense, of course."

"Me! Ridiculous!" Gerhardt looks at Franz and then at Johann. His indignation turns to a quizzical smile. "This is some sort of joke. A bad joke, I might add."

"I was stunned when Fritz told me the story," Johann finally replies. "I told myself that this couldn't be happening. Werner had been called, however, and was told the same thing."

"Fritz told you. This is nonsense!"

"A witness claims to have seen you in the act."

"What diabolical nonsense is this? If this is a joke, gentlemen, it has gone too far."

"Nein." Johann shakes his head.

"My word, this is preposterous. Tell me more. Mistaken identity, of course."

CHAPTER 12

THE EXORCISM

May 22, 1556 (Friday)

It is a very cold night for May and it arrives awkwardly, challenged by the wind. Huddled figures drift through the streets like flotsam past an abandoned wharf; the wetness of the driving rain putting a chill in their bones. Lightning strikes give vision to reality and illusion. Father Franz von Clausen, brushing from his face a wayward strand of hair, puts another log in the fireplace and jostles it with a poker; the flames help make him somewhat comfortable. The parlor of the rectory is a drafty place but he is content to read his breviary there by the glow.

Harry Schmidt's exorcism is to take place in two days. Franz remembers being told in the seminary that it is more difficult to cure one who is bewitched than one who is possessed. As much as he is chagrined about Harry, it is nothing compared to the torment generated by those giving witness against Cardinal Gerhardt, who has been confined to the rectory since the incident.

Two trotting horses are heard coming to a halt outside. Franz puts his breviary down and pulls the curtain aside. Raindrops on the dirt streaked window blur his vision. Steam comes from the snorting nostrils of the animals, each straddled by a man in a slick, black cape.

Water rolls off the brims of their tilted hats as they dismount. One helps the other remove his saddle bags and lugs them to the front door. Then comes the knock. As Franz opens the door, he can see one horseman riding into the darkness with the other horse in tow. The interior light shines on the high cheekbones and deep set eyes of a formidable presence.

"My name is Dietrich, Father Hans Dietrich, inquisitor for the Tyrol." Dripping wet, he decides to brush past Franz and leave any further explanations until ensconced inside. Franz had no idea that he was coming and watches as Dietrich puts his bags to the side and removes his hat and outer garment. He stands there until Franz realizes that he is expected to take the clothing, which he does. Dietrich's very bearing commands compliance. His face is weathered and appears fiftyish in age; hair combed front to back. Trim and muscular, a build you would expect more of a soldier of fortune than of a priest. His tall frame moves in long strides to the fireplace to take in its warmth. Without turning his head from the fire, he says, "Please inform Cardinal Gerhardt of my presence. Then, if arrangements can be made for a hot meal, I would be much obliged."

"Certainly," Franz replies as he moves to hang up the dripping garments.

Finally, turning to Franz, "Forgive me, it has been a long and hard trip. What is your name, Father?"

"Franz von Clausen. You taught me theology at the seminary."

"My apologies, Father. There have been so many students; I only seem to remember the querulous. Please take that as a compliment, Franz. May I call you that?" as if there was any real question.

Dietrich sits in the chair that was recently occupied by his new associate and makes himself comfortable. Franz goes to find Toki. "We have a special guest in the parlor, Toki, who may be staying awhile. Please boil some water for tea. If you would be so gracious as to prepare some hot soup and re-heat the tafelspitz from our meal earlier in the evening. And some dessert. Meanwhile, I will find the cardinal and tell him of the unexpected arrival of this priest."

Cardinal Gerhardt responds to the news of Father Dietrich's arrival with some animation. "An inquisitor. What religious order is he?"

"I think Order of Friars Preachers. He taught me at the seminary."

"A Dominican. Inquisitors are either Dominicans or Franciscans."

Dietrich is already at the dining table eating his soup when Gerhardt and Franz walk in. The cardinal comes over to him with a broad grin and an extended hand. "Father Hans Dietrich, I understand." Dietrich rises to accept it and kiss his ring. Gerhardt pours on the charm. "We are absolutely delighted to have you come to our humble and troubled diocese. You have met Toki, of course. I will see that she spoils you as much as she spoils the rest of us," he laughs. "We have a wonderful room for you and you are welcome to stay as long as you wish or feel necessary. Praise the Lord that you have come to us."

"That is most kind of you, Your Eminence."

Inquisitors are often unwelcome and receive cold receptions. Some bishops and cardinals feel that they are an intrusion and usurpers of their power. Still others consider them misguided trouble makers. However, this won't be the case here.

"If anyone is about the Lord's work," Gerhardt says loudly for all to hear, "it is the inquisitors. And I regret to say that this bishopric is the devil's playground and needs your help more than most."

Toki takes Dietrich's empty bowl of soup and substitutes a plate of boiled beef topped with raw horseradish and apples. Gerhardt asks if there is any rostkartoffeln. Before the words are out of his mouth, Toki brings the roasted sliced potatoes and spoons some onto Dietrich's plate.

"Please tell me about it, Your Eminence."

"You wish to enjoy your meal and rest up, I am sure. It can wait until tomorrow." The cardinal doesn't want to give the impression that combating witchcraft requires alacrity for personal reasons.

"But as you said, Your Eminence, I must be about the Lord's work. There is much to do and so little time. Please go on."

As the cardinal and Franz relate the pertinent happenings, Toki pops in and out of the dining area to look after them. Finally she places a tray of knodl, the tiny sweet variety, in the center of the table. "I have a task to tend to but I'll be back shortly gentlemen. Just leave the dishes. Anything else before I go?"

"Toki, you have made my first evening here a wonderful repose after a hard day's journey. I am most grateful. And that tea, exquisite. By your dress, I don't take you for a nun."

"I'm not but I might as well be; I don't get none." Doing an about face she leaves with a smile. Ordinarily, Gerhardt would laugh. Franz blushes. Dietrich goes deadpan. As they finish the knodl and take their final sips of tea there is an awkward silence as they wait for embarrassment to excuse itself.

"Your Eminence, all of a sudden fatigue is catching up to me. Perhaps we can continue tomorrow with a private chat." He brushes his hands together to signal a finality to the evening.

"Certainly. Franz will show you to your room."

*

Word of Father Dietrich's arrival had come to Johann Carberry through me. Early that afternoon Johann had come to stay the night and the next at our chalet. It was just going to be Dad and him for some chess. My arrival that evening was a mutual surprise, even for our itinerant household mouse.

After Dad excused himself and retired for the night, Johann told me of the scandal brewing over the reputed actions of Cardinal Gerhardt; I had left town before the gossip had spread. Johann's curiosity, however, was first aroused when Dad had told him of Toki's previous visit and my mission.

"After all these years, he still recognized me," I tell Johann. "I still sense some animosity. He is as fit as ever. We came upon some bandits. Without hesitation he rode with the abandon of a seasoned cavalryman until we lost them in the blackness of the woods."

"It's a wonder you and your father endure after all these years in that profession. What did you talk about?"

"We hardly spoke the whole journey. When he did, he spoke past me. He has an intangible elusiveness about him. Though he did ask a few questions about Innsbruck."

"What kind of questions?" Johann pours himself some Marillenschnaps and sips slowly.

"What the town is like. Is it prosperous? What the people are like. Are they God fearing? Are they superstitious?"

"Are they superstitious? I can guess his context," half closing his eyes in forewarned anticipation.

"I thought that I would sound him out on that. I asked him what he meant. He said, '*undisciplined religion, religion observed with defective methods in evil circumstances.*' I asked him to be more specific but we were distracted and never returned to the subject."

"And he was cold to you?"

"Well, he wasn't seeking camaraderie with a fellow traveler."

"I remember that he wasn't a Premonstratian or Augustinian. What order?"

"Dominican." It is almost imperceptible but Johann is startled; his eyes linger on me a bit longer than one might expect. Then the word *inquisitor* flashes across my mind as it does his. I should have antici-pated this but inquisitors usually aren't invited by the presiding prelate.

"This is serious, Rafer," Johann tops off his glass once again.

ↄ⊃

Saturday is quite a departure from the day before. A fog now loi-ters in favored low places but reluctantly succumbs to the brighten-ing sun. Warm air replaces cold and the temperature rises quickly to the low-sixties. After breakfast, Cardinal Gerhardt gives Toki the afternoon off and she uses the time to do some personal shopping in town. Father Dietrich and Cardinal Gerhardt have the rectory to themselves and engage in earnest discussions that will bear heavy consequences.

On Sunday, Father Johann is back in the rectory. A black dachs-hund scurries down the hallway and into the kitchen; the smell of ba-con is still in the air. "Well hello, Impy," says Toki. "Father Carberry's home," she yells before he even comes into sight. The dog is a recent acquisition.

"I taught him a new trick, Toki? He will pee on command. Come outside and I'll show you."

"This I have to see," she curls in laughter. "Did you two have a good time at the Schillings'?"

"We sure did. I understand that we have a visitor."

"Yes indeed. And a lot of activity around here this morning." Toki doesn't know how understated her word "*activity*" is. It will be a day to remember.

ↄ⊃

As previously directed, Harry Schmidt arrives in the sacristy of the church prior to the early morning Mass. He doesn't want to go through with the exorcism but he feels it could be dangerous not to. Franz and another priest designated to perform the rite are there to meet him. Snuff has also come along; it had been suggested that Harry bring a close relative or friend to lend his support.

"Father Bernd Desmond will perform the exorcism," Franz tells Harry. "I will say a Mass simultaneously and ask the congregation to pray for your deliverance." Harry registers some concern. "No! No! Your name won't be mentioned." Franz proceeds to a far corner to don his vestments; he motions Snuff to accompany him.

Father Desmond turns to Harry. "My son, are you under any bond of excommunication? And if so, have you failed to obtain absolution from your ecclesiastical judge?"

"Oh no, Father. I have never been excommunicated."

"That is good, my son. I will hear your confession now." Harry says that he feels that he has been exemplary since his last confession so it ends quickly.

"My son, the first thing that you must do is take this lighted candle. Now kneel here on this kneeler." Father Desmond then summons Snuff and whispers some instructions.

Father Desmond dons his stole and retrieves a chalice containing a consecrated host. He peers into the church proper; Father Franz is already on the altar with his acolytes. The Mass has begun. Desmond returns and gives Harry Holy Communion. A methodical and punctilious man, he immediately returns the chalice to its designated place, then back again to Harry and Snuff.

Father Desmond stands in front of the kneeling Harry. Snuff stands to one side, centered and facing an imaginary line between the two; he holds a mortar and pestle containing Holy Water. Taking the pestle and sprinkling Harry, Father Desmond begins:

> "*I exorcize thee, Harry Schmidt, being weak but reborn in Holy Baptism, by the living God, by the true God, by God Who redeemed thee with His Precious Blood, that thou mayest be exorcized, that all the illusions and wickedness of the devil's deceits may depart and flee from thee together with every unclean spirit, adjured by Him Who will come to judge both the quick and the dead, and who will purge the earth with fire, Amen… Let us pray.*"

"*Let us pray,*" Snuff responds.

Father Desmond begins the Litany for the Sick: "*Our help is in the Name of the Lord.*"

Snuff responds, "*Haste thee, O God, to deliver me,*" and thus they continue to the litany's end.

The words of exorcism resume:

> "*O God of mercy and pity, Who according to Thy tender loving kindness chastens those whom Thou dost cherish, and dost gently compel those whom Thou receives to turn their hearts, we invoke Thee, O Lord, that Thou wilt vouchsafe to bestow Thy grace upon Thy servant who suffers from a weakness in the limbs of his body, that whatever is corrupt by earthly frailty, whatever is made violate by the deceit of the devil, may find redemption in the unity of the body of the Church. Have mercy, O Lord, on his groaning, have mercy upon his tears and as he puts his trust only in Thy mercy, receive him in the sacrament of Thy reconciliation, through Jesus Christ*

Our Lord. Amen.

"Therefore, accursed devil, hear thy doom, and give honor to the true and living God, give honor to the Lord Jesus Christ, that thou depart with thy works from this servant whom our Lord Jesus Christ hath redeemed with His Precious Blood."

The faithful attending Father Franz's Mass are especially devout this morning. "Your prayers will be instrumental in relieving this poor soul of his affliction," he had told them at the start. They are at once startled at being in the near presence of one who is bewitched and humbled at being part of the exorcism.

Father Desmond quietly beseeches God for personal strength to deal with this devil before commencing his second exorcism of Harry. Sprinkling Harry with Holy Water, he begins again:

"Let us pray. God, Who dost ever mercifully govern all things that Thou hast made, incline Thy ear to our prayers, and look in mercy upon Thy servant laboring under the sickness of the body; visit him, and grant him Thy salvation and the healing virtue of Thy heavenly grace, through Christ our Lord. Amen

"Therefore, accursed devil, hear thy doom, and give honor to the true and living God, give honor to the Lord Jesus Christ, that thou depart with thy works from this servant whom our Lord Jesus Christ hath redeemed with His Precious Blood."

Desmond takes the lighted candle from Harry and puts it aside. He turns to Snuff and tells him to get the Holy Candle and rope. Harry notices a smirk on Snuff's face.

"My son, the Holy Candle is made to the length of Christ's cross. For the third exorcism, you will be tied naked to it." Harry is flabbergasted. Snuff can hardly contain his joy. "Your clothes will be searched for any superstitious object that may have been placed there by the witch. If found, all will be burned."

Harry feels indignant. He looks at Snuff and then to his own crotch. "*What happens when Desmond finds me intact?*" he mouths as Desmond turns to the side. Snuff now registers some concern.

Harry starts to squirm. "Father, I have sensation there. Your prayers may have been answered. Maybe two exorcisms were enough."

"Praise be to the Lord," says the priest.

Harry pulls down his pants. "Praise be to the Lord," says Snuff.

"Amen," says Desmond seeing that Harry is intact.

"Bless you, Father," says Harry as he quickly pulls up his pants. "I must go now and celebrate my deliverance." Harry falls all over himself trying to get to the back exit. As soon as he and Snuff leave, Father Desmond joins Father Franz on the altar and informs him of what has happened.

The Mass is now over and Franz prepares to exit with the acolytes. Before he does so, he turns and faces the congregation. "Father Desmond has just informed me that your prayers have been answered. The bewitchment has been removed. Praise be to the Lord." There is a rumble of astonishment. Franz proceeds to give them his blessing and the parishioners return to their knees.

The news spreads quickly. And nowhere is it more welcome than in the rectory's dining room. Cardinal Gerhardt and Father Dietrich listen intently to the two priests weave the tale into one narrative.

Toki, overhearing all this, feels compelled to ask. "Does an exorcism ever fail?"

Father Dietrich quotes the text of Malleus Maleficarum. "When a person is not healed, it is due either to want of faith in the bystanders or in those who present the sick man, or to the sins of them who suffer from the bewitchment, or to a neglect of the due and fitting remedies, or to some flaw in the faith of the exorcist, or to the lack of a greater trust in the powers of another exorcist, or to the need of purgation and for the increased merit of the bewitched person."

"Really?" is the only reply she is ready to render.

∛

Cardinal Gerhardt readily sees this as an opportunity not to be missed. He dispatches all the clergy and lay people at his disposal to inform as many townspeople as they can that he will appear at the last morning Mass and make an important announcement, knowing full well that the message will circulate exponentially.

His first public appearance since the scandal, coupled with the dramatic declaration of the successful exorcism, fills the pews and aisles. It is already fifteen minutes after the appointed hour. He will not start until every person that can be admitted is admitted.

The pipe organ sounds a brief introduction and seated parishioners come to their feet. Two acolytes take the lead from the sacristy to the kreuzaltar. Father von Clausen follows immediately, then Father Carberry, Father Dietrich and Cardinal Gerhardt in solemn procession. All bow in unison towards the tabernacle and, with the exception of Cardinal Gerhardt, proceed to sit in the chairs on each side. The cardinal stands with head down in front of the altar for a full minute while he ostensibly prays. Then, with head high and authoritative strides, he moves stoically to the pulpit and ascends the few steps as softly as a whisper in the dark. As heads turn, he competes for attention with a disrespectful dove flying about the ceiling.

His face hardens. He does not speak. With a challenging presence, he slowly looks at those on one side of the pulpit to those on the other. They look at each other in silence and skepticism. Some are singled out in his gaze, seemingly in an eye-to-eye confrontation. He still doesn't speak. He is taking the measure of the congregation and they don't know what to make of it. He touches his right hand to his forehead, then to his chest, and then to each shoulder. Many of the parishioners respond with the sign of the cross themselves.

"Blessed be God," he pauses for effect. "A few weeks ago there was much clamor in the diocese and I was caused great humiliation. Now, the Vicar of Christ on Earth, the Holy Father in Rome, has seen fit to send an inquisitor, Father Hans Dietrich, to Innsbruck." A roar of surprise and apprehension fills the cathedral along with loud murmuring. Gerhardt doesn't interrupt and waits for quiet to be restored. "Father Dietrich has been directed by the Holy Father to carry forward the papal bull of Pope Innocent VIII, Summis Desiderantes Affectibus, written over seventy years ago but just as apt today as then. May God have mercy on us.

"Last fall we were ravaged by an extraordinary storm. Orchards, vineyards and crops were laid waste. Homes ravaged by wind, rain and floods; people left homeless. Walking the streets of Innsbruck, I had wept at my own inadequacy. Father von Clausen. Father von Clausen," he repeats, this time hanging his head in grief, then looking up with a tear in his eye. "If I only had the clarity of your good Father Franz. It is he who warned me of this scourge and through benign neglect, I failed to heed his warnings." Gerhardt is the picture of remorse. "Recently he told us of the changeling." His voice slips momentarily, as if he lost control of it. "And my initial response once again was dithering." Franz listens curiously; he had no idea that he would receive special attention. "And only this morning, Father von Clausen and Father Desmond, through the power of their faith, were the vehicles in curing a fellow parishioner of his bewitchment. I am humbled to be in association with these saintly men.

"Witches, we are plagued and defamed by these wretches because the sin of one redounds upon us all, as though we are of one body. I am to blame for the extent of the infestation for it is said that all bishops and rulers who do not essay their utmost to suppress crimes of this sort, with their authors and patrons, are themselves to be judged as abettors and are to be punished. I hope that you can find it in your hearts to pray for me." The congregation is not sure of what to make of it. "Father Dietrich is here out of Divine Providence; he will address you now."

Father Dietrich puts a friendly hand on Gerhardt's shoulder as they pass each other. Upon ascending the steps of the pulpit he looks to heaven and then back down to the faces in the crowd. "Praise be to God," he growls with his head nodding so as to demand acquiescence. The congregation responds in kind. He makes a slow and deliberate sign of the cross, then....

"There are three kinds of witches:

There are those who injure but cannot cure.

There are those who cure but cannot injure.

And there are those who both injure and cure.

"All witches, regardless of kind, deny the faith. All witches, regardless of kind, copulate with devils. Such abominations are of great offense to God and must be eradicated. Thou shalt not suffer witches to live, so says the Bible. Of those witches who can do harm, there are some capable of working magic and casting spells. They can delude the senses and create illusions." He pauses and looks around the cathedral, from one end to the other. "Do you hear what I say? They can assume shapes and create illusions. I say again. They can assume shapes and create illusions."

Dietrich points to Cardinal Gerhardt. "This holy man, though not entirely free of sin, none of us are, known to you as a pious and honest man, has shamelessly been subjected to slander and ridicule. Singled out so as to besmirch his good name and that of the Church." He looks at the cardinal who in turn bows his head and reverently makes the sign of the cross yet again. "And ye of little faith, the scandal mongers who have been perpetuating lies these past weeks. Quick to judge without consulting the proper authorities." Dietrich snickers in contempt.

"This is not the first time that such a thing has happened. Certainly some of you must be acquainted with the history of St. Silvanus, once the Bishop of Nazareth. He suffered the exact same indignities as Cardinal Gerhardt until the devil confessed his duplicity at the tomb of St. Jerome. History repeats itself." People look at each other. A few heads are bobbing in agreement.

Anna, dressed in muted grey and white, a black net shawl over her head, stands to the side near the back and listens in disbelief. *Certainly Karl knows that I will know of what is being said here.* She has no desire to cause Karl any trouble and told the sheriff as much; she feels that she is partly responsible for what happened. *Am I being called a witch? Karl wouldn't accuse me of that?* Beginning to fear the unknown, she slowly weaves through the crowd towards the door. Some nod in her direction.

Dietrich waits for the murmuring to cease and the people's attention to return to him. "Obviously, you need to know more of witches for your own protection," he says condescendingly. "Witches kill unbaptized children and make unguents from their limbs. They apply it to brooms so that they can ride through the air and attend their sabbats. Satan, in human form, presides over these sabbats. A God fearing man, a trapper, told me this very morning that he found evidence of a satanic ritual in the nearby forest." This stirs the people to the point that they abandon their hushed tones and simply talk openly among themselves.

Father Dietrich continues to reference Malleus Maleficarum. "Simply with a look, the Evil Eye, witches cause death. Cooking their first born sons in ovens enables them to withstand torture in silence;" gasps are heard. "They can lay on their left sides and discern secrets in their dreams. They drive men to extreme hatred or excessive love. They do all these things of their own free will."

Johann shakes his head... *Some people, even intelligent and learned people, can be taught to believe anything,* he muses. *Intelligence is not synonymous with correct conclusions. Intelligence doesn't guarantee good judgement. Intelligence doesn't preclude prejudice. Intelligence doesn't presuppose independent thinking. Intelligence doesn't assure honorable behavior.*

Dietrich reaches below the lectern and then, thrusting some scrolls over his head declares, "This is the general citation of the inquisition. With this document we will begin the restoration of Innsbruck to oneness with God." Turning to the deacons standing nearby, he commands them to take and post the citation to the walls of the church. As they are doing so, he continues...

"Deacons Konrad and Sigmund have cut shavings from the Blessed Candle used in the glorious exorcism of this morning. A few slivers for each household is available to you as you exit the Mass. Cast these shavings within your homes as protection from evil spirits!

"As the pontiff's emissary, I have the privilege yet heavy burden to preserve the people, who are entrusted to our care, in the unity and happiness of the faith. To fulfill that awesome responsibility and to stamp out heresy and the plague of witches, I especially demand the cooperation of all the clergy of Innsbruck and surrounding hamlets.

"*By virtue of my pastoral authority in this region and by virtue of holy obedience and pain of excommunication, I give this treble canonical warning. I command and admonish that within twelve days of this order, the first four days of which shall stand for the first warning, the second for the second, and the third for the third warning, that any person, regardless of his station in life, must reveal to us if he has seen or heard of any person reputed to be a heretic and/or witch.*

"*I command that any person suspected of causing injury to man, beast or the fruits of the earth to the detriment of the State be revealed to us. May the wrath of God fall on any who do not come forth during the stated term. Let him be cut off from the Holy Mother the Church by the sword of excommunication, which sentence we impose from this time forward. We reserve to ourselves the removal of any such sentence with no right of appeal.*"

Dietrich descends from the pulpit and takes up a vessel of holy water. Threading his way down the center aisle, he sprinkles it on the congregation while invoking the Holy Trinity. He then returns to the altar and faces the people. "My dear parishioners, no unclean spirits can abide Holy Water or Blessed Salt. As a further precaution, carry with you at all times a cross bearing the words, Jesus of Nazareth, King of the Jews." He nods to Johann to begin the Mass. The wayward dove settles on the abandoned pulpit, an unconcerned bystander.

CHAPTER 13

THE DIALECTIC

Sunday Afternoon

Cardinal Gerhardt is pleased with how things transpired at the Mass just said. His exoneration by the pope's emissary is as much as he could have hoped for. And the inquisition will now be the focus of everyone's attention. But Gerhardt is not one to leave anything to chance. He becomes anxious and brusque, summoning his subordinates and directing them to stroll about the town and try to get a sense of prevalent reaction to the morning's events. "Report anything and everything to me no matter how detrimental."

Johann and Franz leave the rectory together and make for the long, partially walled road by the river just a block away. It is a beautiful, warm day. Some washed clothing hung out to dry is being taken in. An elderly frau in a long, colorful Bavarian dress is primping the flowers at her stand. Four children tossing a ball nearby spot Johann and rush to him jumping with joy. "Father, Father, show us another one of your magic tricks," yells a girl with a face as young as yesterday. Johann takes a coin from his pocket and places it in the palm of his hand; closes it only to open it with a flourish to an empty hand. The children squeal in delight. Then the coin reappears as he seemingly takes it from the little girl's ear. They all giggle. Johann says that he and Father Franz must be off but he will give the first one with the correct answer to seven plus twelve a piggyback ride as far as the corner shop. A little boy no bigger than Johann's leg comes closest and as he is carried along as the others skip behind.

The effort of the twosome will be understated, simply ascertaining the public reaction to their very presence. The friendliness, or lack thereof, of the people and how people interact with them will be the primary measuring stick. Johann, at least, has no intention of being direct with anyone.

Neither has said a word to each other since they left the rectory. Franz feels that the day has been won but would like confirmation. He isn't going to get it from Johann; he knows him too well for that. Johann, other than his interaction with the children, is not his cheerful, upbeat self and he knows that his colleague senses his discontent.

Johann suspects that Gerhardt has pulled it off and that many of the faithful will accept the word of a papal delegate. It is a simple truth that many are almost childlike in their acceptance of authority figures. Even the learned, with rare exceptions, don't explore the foundations of their religion. Going to church, paying the tithe, and taking the sacraments, purchase their tickets to heaven they prefer to believe.

Outside of some polite nods, people just hurry by. The two priests amble on aimlessly. They come to a more rustic stretch of the Inn River on the northwest edge of town open to rolling hills and overgrown fields with broken fences. A forsaken animal pen stands lonely and untended on the hillside. Johann motions Franz to sit on a weathered bench with him. Across the river rests the lingering shadow of the mountain. Johann leans forward and rests his elbows on his knees. Looking out over the river, he says, "The cardinal is an affable man, Franz, but of dubious character, a life you can't come to terms with. I fear that he puts his own welfare above all else. And that character defect is about to set neighbor against neighbor and leave a trail of torture and death."

Franz is taken aback and somewhat flustered. A reflexive anger consumes him and his demeanor darkens. "What a terrible thing to say," he finally blurts out. "You can't be saying that there are no witches in Innsbruck after all that has happened?" Johann remains silent. "Besides, I don't agree with your insinuations. You are presumptuous and uncharitable to the cardinal. He has a few flaws but he is a good and prayerful man. If you had any doubts, they should have been dispelled by Father Dietrich."

"The cardinal is a hypocrite and not solid on truth, Franz, and I'm afraid your charitable words and expedient thinking aren't going to change that."

"What are you talking about? And what has the cardinal to do with the inquisition? He didn't call for it; his Holiness did;" Franz replies with some sharpness.

Johann sits upright and looks Franz in the eye. "Do you really believe that?"

"I certainly do!"

"Two weeks ago he dispatched Rafer to Rome, who brought Dietrich to Innsbruck. If you doubt it, ask Toki. Rather extraordinary, don't you think?"

Now it is Franz's turn to gaze out over the river, not looking at anything in particular, drowning in his own thoughts. Silence separates them. A hunched figure, he rubs a hand against his cheek, contemplating. An egret labors to emerge from the mud. "Someone accompanied Father Dietrich to the rectory the night of his arrival. It was dark and raining but it could have been Rafer, now that you mention it."

"There was a public uproar and our superior, I use the word lightly, was at the center of it. How better to divert attention?"

"But we do have a serious problem with witches; you are ignoring that," his voice regains its strength.

"Witches?" Johann huffs indignantly.

"You scare me, Johann. Your attitude on these things borders on heresy." Franz has not wanted to accept the fact that his closest friend and a fellow priest considers all witchcraft nonsense. It's as though an ailment unacknowledged is an ailment that doesn't exist. *I have personal experience with witchcraft. What is wrong with Johann? And what of my primary duty to my Church?* "You cause me great anxiety." Johann heeds the implication, a virtuous man choosing between friendship and obligation.

"Franz, I don't have to tell you that witch hunts are based on passages in the Old Testament. They have been energized these past seventy some years by that obscene volume Malleus Maleficarum."

"Remember, two Dominican theologians wrote that book. And appended to it is an official letter of approbation from the theology faculty of the University of Cologne."

"Regardless of any official letter or not, I should point out that those same Dominican theologians asserted that we no longer observe the ceremonies and legal procedures of the Old Testament because such things are to be understood figuratively."

"The truth is made known in the New Testament," replies Franz.

"So we don't take an eye for an eye now; do we? What I am getting at is that priests should not be ecclesiastical enforcers, especially of questionable teachings."

"It's the Church's responsibility to assist the faithful in attaining their eternal reward. This requires discipline and punishment."

"Jesus offered a way of life, a code of conduct, not a new state. The Church has become just that, a governing entity bent on enforcing its own canon law."

"Are you denying our scripture? The establishment of the Church itself?"

"Well, if you want to bring scripture into this discussion. We point to that celebrated passage, that key passage upon which the infallibility of Holy Scripture rests, 2 Timothy 3:16, namely, '*All scripture, inspired of God, is profitable to teach, to reprove, to correct, to instruct in justice.*' But which books, which scrolls, to be more specific, are really Holy Scripture?"

"What do you mean? Really Holy Scripture?"

"Paul, in his second epistle to Timothy, refers to scripture inspired of God but there is no scriptural or other proof specifically certifying as scripture any of the numerous scrolls which are now bound in one volume, the Bible. Paul essentially is saying that these works equip the man of God for God's work."

"Everyone knows that the Bible is inspired."

"Oh! Perhaps you need to limit your statement to the Old Testament, the Hebrew Bible, then. The New Testament wasn't in existence in Paul's time and the idea that it was scripture didn't occur until a century or so later." Franz is taken aback.

Perplexed, Franz just blurts out, "The Jewish and Christian versions of the Old Testament are virtually the same, a few exceptions."

"Well there are a few more exceptions now. The Latin Vulgate, the Catholic version of the Bible, primarily constructed by St. Jerome in the late 4th century A.D., was recently changed by the Council of Trent. Some of the Apocrypha, books written between 200 B.C. and A.D. 100 and of a mysterious nature; hidden from public use; absent from Hebrew canon; have been added to the Latin Vulgate. Jerome opposed their inclusion. Why a change now? Because the Protestants have been castigating the Church for its practice of praying for the dead and for claiming the remission of sins through good works. There had been no basis in scripture for that. So the Church adds new layers of scripture from part of the Apocrypha. So you see where scripture comes from."

"I believe that previous councils affirmed some of the Apocrypha."

"Affirmed some but not added."

"Are you saying that the Council of Trent was speculating?" Franz is somewhat indignant. "Have you forgotten the living, teaching authority of the Church?"

"The Church, *as to* its *living, teaching, authority*, may take it upon itself to declare which books are scripture and which are not but neither the Old nor the New Testaments define themselves nor are there other corroborating documents. And there is no indication that it was really considered important."

"What do you mean, it was not important?" He looks at Johann as though he has lost his senses.

"Just that! Why do we feel it so important today to define that which is scripture if the Old and New Testaments did not define themselves or scripture defined by God Himself? *What I am saying is that faith did not come from scripture; scripture came from faith. People lose sight of that fact.* And a mindset has occurred that if something is in the Bible then it must be so."

"You question the Bible? I can't comprehend this." Johann has come to the realization that believers don't want to hear the facts because they can't change them.

"The men of the Bible had no Bible; I'm speaking of the Old and the New Testaments. They were of whom the Bible was written. They had an oral tradition. In fact, the oral tradition had been given more credence because it was felt that, as Paul later stated, *'the letter killeth, but the spirit giveth life.'* "

"What is your point?"

"The oral tradition was not dogmatic like the Hebrew religion eventually became and our religion is today. It was local, personal and fluid. And that which has since been written has been subject to revision and editing over generations and even centuries."

"What, for example?"

"Most of the Old Testament as we know it today. As to the New Testament, there are scholars who are convinced that Matthew and Luke used the writings of Mark in the preparation of their gospels. Also, it is apparent that they used other common source documents. In other words, the material derived from such sources can hardly be considered the product of inspiration."

"Who said that every word had to be original?"

"Well, are the gospels inspired or simply religious accounts? There is no record that Jesus ever directed or even approved composing a written gospel let alone a New Testament. All evidence, cultural or otherwise, points to the contrary. It is inconsistent that the authors of the New Testament would be *inspired* to document what is known of Jesus."

"But Jesus said: '*Not an iota, not a dot, will pass from the law until all shall be fulfilled.*' "

"But Jesus was speaking of Old Testament law and he denied the literal meaning in favor of a spiritual meaning and fulfillment."

"My Lord! I am very uncomfortable with all this, bewildered actually." Franz stands, his body feeling unnaturally heavy.

"Don't you think it extraordinary how understated 2 Timothy 3:16 is? '*All scripture, inspired of God, is profitable to teach, to reprove…*' that the Bible is to be declared divinely inspired based on this isolated, stand-alone sentence. I would think such a contention would be confirmed repeatedly and emphatically by the biblical writers if it were so important. And then again, assuming that Paul meant inspired of God in the literal sense as opposed to a pious gesture to the Old Testament authors being inclined to set their thoughts and recollections to paper. On what authority is Paul asserting to Timothy that the Old Testament is inspired? We know that Paul never met Jesus."

"He had a vision of Jesus on the road to Damascus, his conversion," Franz replies.

"His conversion! What we know of Paul is entirely from the New Testament itself and from his own letters. In Galatians 1:15-16, Paul says: *'But when it pleased him who separated me from my mother's womb and called me by his grace, to reveal his Son in me that I might preach him among the Gentiles.'* Was that essentially an inward experience? It's plausible from his words, which smack of predestination and a delayed calling since initially he persecuted Christians."

"He speaks of it in The Acts of the Apostles."

"That's something else that is puzzling. The prevailing thought is that Acts was written years after Paul's death, circa 67. The account of Paul's conversion in Chapter 9 of Acts is a third person account by St. Luke the Evangelist. Yet the story of his conversion is repeated in Chapter 22 in the first person as if Paul wrote it. What's going on here? At the very least it demonstrates the difficulty attesting to the accuracy within these texts and it leads to all manners of speculation. Yet over time, the questionability of them fades and people start treating them as a given.

"Also, in Acts 9:7, Paul's companions heard a sound but didn't see anyone. In Acts 22:9, Paul and his companions saw a bright light but his companions did not hear the voice at all. More anomalies."

"Writers don't always get it exactly right."

"Wouldn't you think that an event as significant as this would be gotten right? Why did only Paul hear the voice? If the others did hear it, why was only he able to understand it? His companions would be witnesses to Jesus' address to Paul. Why was only Paul blinded for three days? Why did Jesus come in yet another vision to the disciple

Ananias to have him cure Paul's blindness by laying his hands upon him? It is all so convoluted. It leads one to believe that they are likely misconstrued stories? There is so much that is hard to rectify."

Franz stands there motionless. He doesn't reply.

"Another thing, aren't you inclined to wonder about the credibility of accounts of persons such as Moses and Muhammad, who report interaction with God or with His surrogate, Gabriel, with no substantiation but their own claims?"

"Where is your faith?" Franz demands, his hands reach to heaven only to drop in exasperation.

"Well, it isn't in Church canon."

"I look to our superiors for guidance."

"Our superiors appear very fallible to me. I've been studying the history of the Bible for years now, Franz. Did you know that when the Jews returned from their Babylonian exile in 538 B.C., the Jewish state no longer existed and their religious spirit had almost evaporated; soon after there was a common feeling among the Jews that the succession of prophets had ended?"

"And?"

"The Great Synagogue, a council of 120 fervent Jewish men formed by Ezra, was established to reconstruct the Hebrew religion. To do this they set about collecting those scriptural scrolls that were not destroyed or lost at the time of the exile. This led to what exists today as the Old Testament."

"So you are saying that we do not have Hebrew Scripture in its entirety?"

"I am saying more than that. I am saying that the principle that actuated Ezra in making what would, over time, turn into the first Hebrew canon of the Old Testament, the Law or Pentateuch, its first five books, was a religious and patriotic one. The word canon, of course, actually being a much later Christian term. Ezra, however, certainly didn't consider it canon in the sense that it was inviolable. His treatment of the oldest law books infers that he did not look upon them as inviolable by the very redaction to which he submitted them.

"It is safe to affirm that he added new precepts and practices and even substituted some in place of older ones. Some things he removed as unsuited to the altered circumstances of the people; others he modified. He threw back later enactments into earlier times. Venerable they were, and even sacred, but neither perfect nor complete for all time. In his view, they were not unconditionally authoritative. Nor does the idea of an immediate, divine authority appear to have dominated the mind of Ezra and the Great Synagogue in the selection of books. Like Ezra, these scholars reverenced the productions of the prophets, poets, and historians to whom their countrymen were indebted in the past for religious or political progress but they did not look upon them as the offspring of unerring wisdom. How could they, while witnessing repetitions and contradictions in the books collected."

"You are making the Old Testament into something subjective," replies a riled Franz.

"Of the three divisions of the Old Testament, the Law or Pentateuch was the most venerated of the Jews. The Prophets, or second division, occupied a somewhat lower place but read in the public services as the Law had been before. The c'tubim or Writings, the third division, was not looked upon as equal to the Prophets."

"Some were given greater emphasis than others. I have no problem with that."

"It is generally accepted that these divisions were 'canonized' in the same sequence. The Pentateuch or Torah, if you will, circa 5th century B.C., followed by the Prophets circa 200 B.C., and then the Writings perhaps in the 2nd century B.C. or maybe not until the late

1st century A.D. I am saying that men who belonged to different periods and possessed different degrees of culture worked successively in the formation of what would amount to Jewish canon, which arose out of the circumstances of the times and the subjective ideas of those who made it."

"Why are you telling me all this?"

"The Bible, New and Old Testaments, are man-made and subject to error. They shouldn't be accepted as sacrosanct. Canon should be open to challenge, re-examination and change, especially those elements which advocate capital punishment."

A toxic stillness hangs in the air. Distraught and confused, Franz feels like an itinerant trying to escape the dark; turning, he walks off without saying another word. Johann stares after him unsure of what he has wrought.

CHAPTER 14

THE ECCLESIASTICAL
TRIBUNAL

May 28, 1556 (Thursday)

What is unique about the inquisitorial process is that normally there is no accuser or informer coming forward to initiate legal proceedings. It is founded on rumors and a general report of heresy being practiced in some town or place. The Church, in its zeal to stamp out these perceived threats to the faith, appoints an ecclesiastical judge or deputizes a secular one. The judge must then proceed, not at the instance of any party, but simply by virtue of his office. The local bishop or cardinal usually directs events from behind the scene with the inquisitor there to advise on procedures and technicalities.

But Cardinal Gerhardt wants no loose cannon running his ecclesiastical court so Father Dietrich is given the dual responsibility of inquisitor and judge. As is customary, Father Dietrich is then assigned a notary and two honest persons to assist him in his legal capacity. These persons can be either clergy or laymen but in this case only the notary is to come from the lay ranks. The other two are Fathers Franz von Clausen and Bernd Desmond.

It is Thursday, the fourth day of the first canonical warning, and proceedings commence in the chancery of St. James'. Father Dietrich is about to hear the first witness. As with all legal proceedings, he begins with an acknowledgment to God.

"In the Name of the Lord, our Savior, Jesus Christ. Amen," he says with head bowed. Then, picking up the document on the judge's bench in front of him, he begins to read from it. "In the 1556th year of Our Lord, on the 25th day of the 5th month, to the ears of Father Franz von Clausen, there came a persistent public report and rumor that Wilma Colmarz, of the town of Innsbruck had caused the violent fall storm savoring of witchcraft. This act is counter to the faith and the common good of the state and was set down according to the common report." Dietrich then looks up; turns toward Franz and nods.

Franz motions to Oskar Konig, who comes forward and stands in front of the witness stand. He is the only person present, except for the aforementioned members of the court, for in a charge of this sort the usual method of judicial procedure is abridged. The accused does not get to face the accusers and the accusers are not made known to him or her. The rationale behind the statute is that grave harm can come to them if the witch is aware of their identities.

Konig raises three fingers and depresses two of his right hand in witness of the Holy Trinity. He places his left hand on the four gospels and repeats after Franz. "I swears under oath and to the damnations of me soul and body that I will speaks nothing but the truth."

"Be seated," Franz says and then moves aside.

"Herr Konig," Dietrich begins. "According to your deposition, you do not personally know the accused, Wilma Colmarz. Is that correct?"

"That is correct, Yer Grace. But I seen her a few times."

"I am not an archbishop, Herr Konig. Your Reverence or Father will do. Now, do you know anything of her?"

"Ja, Yer Father. Tis common knowledge she's a witch."

"Just Father will do. Who told you of this?"

"People whispers it when she's about. Nasty, she is."

"What do you know of her habits? For example, does she attend church regularly?"

"I never sees her in church. But I heards that she attends Mass once and takes the Host under her tongue. Not on her tongue minds you. Shortly she spits it out. Can anyone imagines such a thing?" Oskar bows his head and blesses himself with a hand as darkly tanned as his face.

"But you say that you have seen her on occasion. Did you yourself ever notice anything sacrilegious?"

"I certainly dids Yer Grace. Was a Friday. She was eatin slices of beef on Friday. Imagine, eatin meat on Friday gainst the laws of the Church. Two days later I sees her telling people that she's fastin. They could cares less, of course, except everyone knows that you don't fasts on Sunday."

"Would you say that she was deliberately flaunting sacred traditions to mock the Church?"

"I certainly woulds Yer Grace. No doubts about it."

"Not Your Grace. Your Reverence. What of her transvection? Your deposition says that you saw her fly through the air."

"Well, ja. Me brothers n me are shepherds, you see. Well, just befores the big storm last fall; you heards of the big storm, of course?"

"Very much so. That is why we are here."

"Well, there's three of us. Me and me brothers." Oskar looks to Dietrich for acknowledgment.

"Ja. Ja. Go on."

"Well, the three of us was tendin our sheep, as shepherds do. You sees. All was calms and peacefuls like."

"Excuse me, Herr Konig. Let the record show that this was the morning of September 28th of last year, a Saturday. That is correct, is it not Herr Konig?"

"No doubts about it, Reverence. As I lives and breathes, I will never fergets that day. Women flying through the air n all. Then wind, rain n hail."

"You say women, plural?"

"Well, we only sees one. Pardon."

"You must take care to be accurate," Dietrich says sharply.

"Absolutely, Yer..."

"Go on."

"It was like a vision. Me brothers n me were standin together in a valley just outside town here. The sheep were all calm and peaceful, grazin n all. And we looks up nears the crest of the hill, we sees this Colmarz woman flyin through the air in an upright position with her hands extended out. She was bobbins n swayins n shriekins. I was staggered, Yer Grace."

"How far away were you?"

"Maybe a hundred yards. Maybe a bit more. More or less, maybe. Maybe more. Probably."

"Ja. Ja. Then what happened?"

"Well, when she nears the top of the hill, she disappears briefly."

"She just vanished?"

"Well, I won't quite puts it like that, Yer Grace. She floats behind the top of the hill. Next thing we know she's on the very top hunkering down, moving her arms about. And there was like a mist nearby."

"Then what?"

"Well, she wents back behind the hill n within minutes the storm begins to rise. The wind comes up but I had to sees what I could. I mean it was so unusual. So I runs to the top. Me brothers shouts for me to comes back but I had to looks."

"And?"

"I sees a small hole with piss, where she was."

"Urine?"

"I sees piss. I smells piss, Yer Grace. Piss it is."

"You said she was moving her arms about."

"There was a stick there. We all knows that witches stirs piss to cause storms. I'm sure that's what she was doin. And the dark shadow, no doubts the devil. The devil's always nearby."

"My word. Why didn't you come forward then?"

"The devil might do me harm." He looks down as if embarrassed by his fear.

"And your brothers will testify to this?"

"As God is me witness. They saws the same thing."

"Before you leave, tell the notary where they can be reached."

"Ja, Yer Grace."

"Your Reverence. What else can you tell us?"

"Just the storm. I never sees a storm rise so quick. I never sees so bad a storm. I found meself in the middle of a whirlwind. Lucky to escapes with me life, me was. Alls n these parts knows of the storm. Never seens the likes of it. May God have mercy on us all."

"What made you come forward with this information?"

"Pain of ex communication. Warned of witches at Mass. Comes across Father von Clausen walkin down the strasse. He beings a holy man, like yourself, Yer Reverence. I got it now Yer Reverence," he smiles. "Told him what I sees and that someone says her mother was a witch. If anybody knows what to do, it woulds be Father von Clausen."

"Do you hold any rancor for this woman, Wilma Colmarz?"

"I ain't holdin nothin of hers."

"Has she ever done you any wrong? Before or after the storm? Are you resentful of her?"

"Like I says, Yer... I don't even knows her. Wouldn't even calls her n acquaintenance."

"Were you suborned to give information? Did anyone put you up to testify?"

"I was perfectly sober and nobody helds me up to testify."

"Did anyone pay you to come forward with information?"

"Nobody paid me nuttin, Yer Father."

"Anything else?"

"Nein, can't think of nuttin," Oskar says scratching his head.

"You have done your Christian duty, Herr Konig. This court is deeply indebted to you. But I must warn you, and by virtue of your oath, you must keep secret whatever has been said here, by me or what you yourself has said. Speak to no one of this, not even to your brothers; we may approach your brothers separately. Do your brothers know that you came here this day to address this tribunal?"

"Nein, Father von Clausen tolds me to says nothin to nobody. But they laughed at the time."

"Thought it was funny? This isn't to be laughed at."

"Nein, nein, Yer Father. This is not to be laughs at."

"Your... never mind. Go in peace!"

After Oskar Konig leaves, Dietrich takes it upon himself to instruct the other members of the court. "I and all who are associated with me at these proceedings, including those present at sentencing, must keep the names of witnesses secret under pain of excommunication. This is done for the safety of the witnesses. Does anyone have any questions before we bring in the accused?"

"The Blessed Wax?" asks Franz.

"Yes, I have it here." Dietrich passes the priests and notary some wax containing blessed herbs and salt consecrated on Palm Sunday. A cord runs through it so that it can be worn about the neck. He puts one around his own person. Other officers of the court about to enter have done the same. "The wonder of these glorious Church artifacts, the witches themselves have affirmed their protective powers against their machinations."

"I understand that the defendant doesn't have an attorney representing her; isn't this an oversight?" asks Father Desmond.

"Father Desmond, this is the trial of a witch in the cause of the faith," Dietrich replies. "It must be adjudicated in a plain and summary manner without a superfluous number of witnesses and the impertinent contentions of advocates. Only under exceptional circumstances, at the prerogative of the court, is one appointed."

"My apologies, Father."

"Then have the officers bring in the accused!" If one is to associate Dietrich's demeanor with the eight beatitudes, he is not a candidate to inherit the earth.

The officers had been given strict instructions as to how this is to be done. The accused is not to be permitted to look upon the judge or his advisors before they look at her for this will enable her to alter their minds and engender a listless demeanor in them towards her. They would then be predisposed to set her free. So with two burly men on each side of her, being held firmly by straps on her arms, Wilma Colmarz is led into the courtroom backwards.

A craggy and fierce peasant with eyebrows as thick as a forest, a face hauntingly grey with coal black lines reaching out from the corners of each eye, not uncommon gaps in her soiled teeth, she has an athletic bearing nonetheless, especially for a woman in her forties. Tall and angular with bony hands, she seems to look right through you. Her expression declares where you stand in her eyes and most do not fare well, especially the clergy.

Frightened about how she was taken into custody, she clings to the false hope that she has done nothing wrong. What of her two children, their lives have been difficult as it is. Would her absconded husband's parents take them in if it comes to imprisonment or death?

Dietrich motions with his finger for the officers to turn her to face the court. She is turned slowly counter clockwise like a turret traversing its mount and she rakes those in her line of sight with impertinent eyes. Father Desmond unconsciously takes a step backwards in keeping with his reticent nature. Dietrich's chiseled features, set like a clay mask, harden for the expected confrontation. The look which passes between them is mutual hostility. Neither speaks. Franz finally looks to Dietrich to open the proceedings but it is she who assumes the initiative.

"What false acts are to be heaps on me today?"

"Wilma Colmarz, you have been brought here today for a General Examination. Take the witness stand! Father von Clausen, administer the oath!" His tone is cold. There will be no courtesies.

"I takes no oath."

"It will be of no benefit to you if you don't. Sit down!" The officers forcibly sit her down.

"All testimony that you shall give in this court will be considered as testimony under oath and at the peril of your very soul. Lie and you will reap the consequences of the civil authorities and Almighty God," Father von Clausen declares.

Dietrich proceeds. "You live within the limits of Innsbruck, do you not?"

"You already knows that, does you not?" she disdainfully replies. She tugs at a strand of hair.

"From whence did you come to Innsbruck?"

"Pfaffenhofen."

"It says here Constance." Dietrich then looks to Franz inquiringly.

"She was born in Constance."

"Why is I here?"

"The children of witches are themselves offered to Satan. You moved to Pfaffenhofen after the execution of your father for heresy. Did you not?"

She stiffens. *They knows of me parents.* Woken to the full menace of her situation, she suddenly feels old and wasted and a captive of bygone circumstances, her lungs seem to collapse. Perspiration forms on her brow yet the room is cool. Her expectations already contracted, a cry of desperation struggles to be contained. Trembling, she tries to speak coherently through her terror. "You killed me father. You took me father, you did." Her voice quivers from relived fears and tears fall.

"What have you to say of your Mother?"

"You murders her too. You want to kills me now, don't you? Just for be'in born."

"You speak of murder. She murdered a baby in the womb. Your mother laid her hands on a pregnant noblewoman's stomach as others are given to do but as she did so the baby was delivered malformed and dead. The woman's husband was Catholic in name only, I should mention. The loss of his child was a punishment from God."

"Me mother wasn't responsible for that; it just happens."

"Colmarz is not your given name, is it?" You are the daughter of the witch Rebecca Dahlmatz. Are you not?"

"Leaves me alone! Leaves me alone!" Already distrustful of people from the terror of her childhood, a husband that abandoned her and their children, she is now embraced by total desperation.

"We must not leave you alone. We must preserve the faith."

"I ain't done nothin. I ain't done nothin," her voice trails off.

"We have witnesses that say otherwise."

"Youse can't. Youse can't."

"But wese can. Wese can," Dietrich responds derisively. Her eyes drift from person to person looking for someone to understand. "You conspired with the devil, performing supernatural acts."

Wilma closes her eyes and hangs her head. After a pause, "Says who? Says who?"

"You shall not be given the name so that you can do harm. A person of faith. A good person."

"A lying person of faith. Who?" she shouts.

"We are not here to answer your questions. You are here to answer ours. Remove the accused."

Wilma having been taken away, Dietrich turns to the Notary. "When you have completed setting down this whole process in writing, conclude it with a statement that the proceedings were conducted under the purview of Cardinal Wolfgang Gerhardt. Enter today's date, the name of the witness, and sign the document. Court is adjourned until the Particular Examination on Monday, June 1st."

CHAPTER 15

THE INQUIRER

May 28, 1556 (Thursday evening)

Nothing mattered now but our passion. I was driven to take and she was as anxious to submit. Our legs overlapped as she arched her back and my hand moved deliberately to her naked breast. I kissed her neck as I rolled onto my back taking her with me, my hands now clasping her buttocks. I turned her yet again and slide my hand up and along her inner thigh; I lingered as she reached back, grabbed the brass rungs of the bed, and closed her eyes. Finally...

"I'm going to take you now. Is that what you want?"

"Ja, that's what I want."

❦

We lay there side by side. "You have a great suite here. Fritz gave you one of his best."

"Fabulous view, don't you think?"

"That little blue and pink blanket with the gold broken heart, any reason for the broken heart?"

"I'll tell you about it after you tell me more about the broadsheet. What are you calling it, the Inquire?"

"The Inquirer. I've been planning it for a long time, though I didn't have an inquisition in mind."

"You're taking on the Church, Rafer. And in this hostile atmosphere no less."

"Somebody has to do something."

"And you think you can stop it?"

"I can try. Have you heard the name Wilma Colmarz?"

"Nein."

"She appeared before the ecclesiastical tribunal earlier today. She is being held over for a Particular Examination."

"How do you know all this? I thought such things were done in secret."

"I have my sources."

"I want to help."

"You can but indirectly, by diverting attention away from our operation when necessary. I want to limit direct involvement to as few as possible. Abetting heresy is a capital crime."

"Where is the printing press?" She tosses her hair back as if necessary to receive the information.

"It's in the cellar."

"Here? I didn't see any press in the cellar."

"You wouldn't. It's in a concealed room constructed when the inn was first built. A clandestine hideaway, like you find in castles."

"And I'm to divert attention. I'll have to know more than that if people will be coming and going."

"I'll tell you who is involved but that's the extent of it."

"Fritz must be up to his neck in this."

❧

May 29, 1556 (Friday)

The thick, cellar back wall, part of the Boar's Head foundation, is fronted in part with shelving housing all sorts of things. Hidden hinges are installed on an end section serving as a door to the underground room behind it, the now covert news operation. The cellar itself can be entered from the kitchen above or the storm cellar doors in the alley.

Fritz taps a small cask of Riesling, pours a modicum into several glasses sitting on the composition table and hands one to each of us as though part of a solemn ceremony. He then looks to me and I take the cue. I raise my glass and look into the eyes of each in turn to convey the importance of this initiation:

> "We gather here as friends and comrades, dedicating
> ourselves to truth and the common good. Our charter
> is to separate fact from fiction and light the way to a
> more humane tomorrow. By our actions, which we set
> in motion today, may our town in particular become a
> better place, and like a stone thrown into a still pond,
> let them create a ripple of sanity that proceeds from
> Innsbruck and rushes like a wave across Europe."

"Well said," says Harry Schmidt with the straight-faced reverence of a convert.

Katarina kisses me on the cheek. We bring our glasses together in unison and then sip the wine, applauded by distant thunderclaps approaching the valley.

"Basil, your distributorship is our circulation department. That the Boar's Head has been a regular customer is all the better. What of your employees and the inherent risks of exposure?"

"Only Harry, Snuff, Bear and I will be involved with the broadsheets, no one else. Bear will be the only intermediary hauling the broadsheet cases between this cellar and the warehouse; I'll lock them in a closet in my office. The unloading and loading of broadsheets will be done when the other employees are gone. Only Snuff will do the transfers between the warehouse and the three collaborating shop owners. The cases for the broadsheets have diagonal wooden slats nailed to each side to distinguish them from the others. All cases, regardless, will be labeled appropriately."

"Publications will be sporadic so there will not be a pattern," I add. "And let's be clear on this, any operation is to be aborted at any point if anyone suspects a glitch."

"Security is paramount," Basil continues. "As to the cooperating shop owners, each is to disseminate their small bundle of broadsheets after dark while walking home or to the stable and never leaving them in the same places. They have been instructed to carry them in ordinary shopping bags with other goods and only empty them if and when out of the line of sight of windows and others. Our first delivery to them will be this afternoon. Today only, the transfer will be made directly from here in Snuf's wagon."

"By Sunday the clergy will be calling down the wrath of God on us. Fortunately, God will be making up His own mind on that." All laugh. "Everybody but Snuf can be on their way now. Fritz, when I get done printing you can tell me the latest gossip about the Walker Hess murder; I'll look for you upstairs. My memory of him goes back decades, a bizarre incident."

❧

May 30, 1556 (Saturday)

The townspeople come across the broadsheets which had been disseminated helter-skelter. We depend on word-of-mouth for mass circulation. The headlines and script are meant to be provocative and so they are received:

Innsbruck Inquirer

Volume 1   *Saturday, 30 May 1556*

Church Indicts "Witch" – Ignorance Reigns

The Particular Examination of Wilma Colmarz, for allegedly practicing witchcraft, is to begin on Monday and the accused is not permitted a defense attorney. The Inquirer finds this difficult to comprehend from the Church that allegedly sets the standard for righteousness and justice. Frau Colmarz must stand alone against the monolith.

What has she done? This middle aged woman reportedly flies through the air and stirs up tempests, with the help of the devil of course. Never mind that there have been countless renowned Church leaders such as Ulrich Molitar, the fifteenth century Doctor of Roman and Canon Law, that brand transvections as nonsense. According to Molitar, such beliefs got started in the vivid imaginations of disturbed women, the result of self- deception. Still others say that corporeal flights of witches are nothing but illusion and superstition. But Cardinal Gerhardt and his henchman, Father Dietrich, insist on perpetuating this legacy of ignorance and ecclesiastical terror. In light of all that has happened, one questions the cardinal's motives.

It is common knowledge that Cardinal Gerhardt assaulted a woman in her hotel room; the only illusion is his incredulous defense. The best defense is a good offense, right Cardinal. There is always a core of believers who will maintain that the hierarchy can do no wrong. The Inquirer has no doubt that this is our prelate's strategy.

Some other particulars of note are...

And so Volume 1 continued, unrestrained; they can only put us to death once, no reason to hold back. Those parishioners who adhere to the pronouncements of the hierarchy in lockstep fashion are appalled by this broadsheet. Those who question some of the Church's teachings and practices are astonished to see this overt assault. More so, they are curious to see how it will play out.

Father Dietrich is furious. The belligerency of the article is bad enough but what has him absolutely livid is the leaked information. Someone in the courtroom obviously must have violated his vow of secrecy so he orders all parties to his chambers this very day. Each is confronted one on one, even the priests are not spared. What is so perplexing is that all categorically deny divulging any information and all appear to be sincerely chagrined by the episode. Was someone spying on the proceedings? Is one a consummate liar? What he doesn't realize is how one familiar with such proceedings can piece the story together if he is proximate to the comings and goings of the parties involved, if he is privy to unguarded conversations and unattended documents. Dietrich consults with the cardinal.

"Better to deal with the challenge head-on. Blunt the criticism. Take back the initiative," says Gerhardt. "Let's find a suitable attorney for the defense and find one today." Dietrich argues that they are a contentious nuisance but to no avail.

Dolph Zimmerman has just returned from the woods east of town and is pleased to have bagged a buck, leaving it at Heibel's butcher shop to be dressed. Leaning his long bow against the door of his home, he brushes dirt from his britches and shoes. A messenger from Cardinal Gerhardt approaches and informs him that the cardinal would be pleased to see him at once. His sixth sense tells him why; he was told of The Inquirer.

There are a couple of older, more experienced, and better known lawyers in Innsbruck. He has been in Innsbruck a little more than a year now and he has handled a grand total of three cases. Law is an avocation to him; hunting and other pleasurable distractions are his main endeavor. He comes from a more leisured heritage and plans to keep it that way. Both his parents have passed but they have left him in comfortable circumstances. His significant inheritance easily covers his living and office expenses. At twenty five years of age, with no attachments, he is enjoying life to the fullest.

"Counselor," Gerhardt says, "I have heard a great deal about you." Dolph can't imagine what. "A sharp, young attorney with great potential, they say. We have been searching for a person such as yourself to familiarize himself with and handle Church affairs. Possibly you might be interested." Dolph isn't sure that he is. "Do sit down," Gerhardt gestures.

"That is quite an offer, Your Eminence. Who is my patron saint?"

Gerhardt smiles broadly and exudes charm. "Let's just say that you have come to my attention. The Church needs competent people, good Catholics zealous for the faith. I understand that you are such a man." He did register as a parishioner; pays the tithe and occasionally attends church for appearances sake.

"Ja, Your Eminence, righteousness is my very calling. What specifically do you have in mind?"

"You may have heard of Wilma Colmarz?"

"I heard of the broadsheet."

"Ja, an instrument of the devil himself. Well, contrary to what it claims, we have been considering representation for the accused and thought you might do nicely."

"I had the impression that you were offering me a position with the Church administration, Your Eminence."

"Well, first things first. In this instance you will appointed and paid by the Church to represent the witch." Dolph takes note of his choice of words, "*the witch*," a foregone conclusion.

"The inquisition. Of course. Any advocate for the accused would be appointed by the judge."

"We understand that you are not one to quibble, introduce legal quirks or bring counter accusations to stymie the process." The cardinal is saying that, if Dolph is a good boy, he might expect bigger and better things. Gerhardt stares at his hands as if deep in thought, an offer made but subject to withdrawal. There is a pregnant pause.

"Well, I…"

Gerhardt interrupts. "The Church will not be one to quibble either. We will pay the customary fee plus ten percent, plus ten percent more if, shall we say, the case is handled efficiently."

Dolph ponders the offer. A not so subtle incentive to go through the motions. If the cardinal is brazen enough to stack the deck against the accused, I am brazen enough to defend the accused in the real sense of the word. "I will need the names of the witnesses against Frau Colmarz, their depositions, and the opportunity to visit with her."

"Of course. You shall have it by tomorrow. Peace be with you." Dolph is summarily dismissed.

CHAPTER 16

OVERHERD

May 30, 1556 (Saturday Afternoon/Evening)

Father Johann is looking out his bedroom window troubled about what is yet to come. A lonely dark cloud encroaches on a cerulean sky and donates a shower to freshen the air. Mellow green domes mingle with red roofs above the narrow, asymmetrical streets, which seem to compress the buildings into gangly networks of fractured neighborhoods.

The golden gargoyles of the Hofburg Castle, built in the last century, had obediently received the harvest of the clouds only to rudely spit it from their affluent mouths. Streaking sunrays chase after the departing shower and glance off these gilded creatures like burnished spears flung by angry gods. A man in the courtyard below apparently has said something humorous and his companions start to giggle.

Austrians are good and friendly people who embrace their guests. No people are capable of greater elation and, when they play, merrier. He will volunteer his opinion, whether asked for or not. He is thoughtful and considerate and has an unfailing sense of humor. Treat him with respect and it will be reciprocated. If you don't, he will take you to task. She is curious to a fault and has no reservations about being direct. If there is a need for something to be done, however, she will move quickly to fill the gap.

As the sun drops close to the horizon, Johann decides to take advantage of the enticements of the taverns to maintain his avenues of communication; at this stage, Franz is one window he dare not close. His last significant tête-à-tête did not go well so he invites Franz to Mad Herman's Rathskeller for supper. The intimation is to just relax together over a good meal. Franz welcomes the opportunity to abandon the rectory.

Chunks of Vorarlberg cheese, olives and marinated mushrooms are placed on their table hardly before the two come to rest in their booth. A long loaf of bread with a flaky crust comes next leaving a sensuous aroma trailing from the kitchen oven. Johann orders glasses of chilled white wine leaving the selection to the waiter, "as long as it is dry, crisp and not to make one a pauper."

Little is said between the two, some small talk about the weather and food. Franz mentions that the cardinal asked him if the Visintainers left for Salzburg yet but he didn't know. Did Johann? Johann says yes they did, a while ago.

A mutual glance of approval is given when both sink their teeth into the Vorarlberg. Beet soup with a pinch of exotic pepper and an unsweetened knodl on a side plate appear shortly in front of each of the clergymen. This is what makes life worth living each thinks as their palates are being teased. More mushrooms, this time fried, slaw, and sweet & sour red cabbage seasoned with caraway are served in individual bowls. The salted meat dishes start with pork roast followed quickly by veal garnished with a slice of lemon and potatoes with parsley and butter.

The high, wood partition between their booth and the one adjoining at the side offers some privacy. The occupants on the other side have been a bit low keyed and their voices garbled, not enough to disturb their tranquility and hearty appetites. But now, as the priests make their final assault on some apple strudel, a couple of interlopers approach their neighbors and the voices grow raucous and laughter erupts. Clear, coherent sentences are easily distinguishable. Satiated, the two clergymen sip the last of the wine and listen; they can hardly do otherwise. The words belong to Snuff, they ascertain. It was Fritz's suggestion that the boys patronize other places at times to divert a possible connection to the Boar's Head in case any of them came under scrutiny.

"I didn't want Harry tuh get cold feet, yah see. So I pushed him tuh Father Franz's confessional. Father Franz and I goes back a lung way by thuh way. I push Harry in thuh box and it makes a hell of a rackut. Some ol woman lightin candles up front panics and runs for thuh door. Ya shoulda seen it." The laughter from the others encourages Snuff. "Franz, you know him as Father von Clausen, then accuses Harry of be'un drunk. Don't ee Harry?"

Harry takes a seat at the table and course corrects the tale to these reprobate chums. "He thought I might be drunk but he was more discreet than Snuff lets on." Johann, hearing this starts to get up to leave so as to curtail the likely damage but Franz grabs his wrist to settle him back down.

"Then Harry starts off saying it's only been six months since his last Confession. Hell, Columbus was still on his first trip to India since Harry's been to Confession." Harry laughs and makes no attempt to rein in Snuff's hyperbole. "Harry then tells im that ee as sinned; like that's a revelation to anyone." A few more snickers. "Harry then tells im that his member as disappeared. E says that e lost his member an wunts to know if Franz can do sumthin about it." The table goes wild with laughter.

"So then what happened?" someone asks, impatient for more.

"You tell 'em, Harry, it's your story."

"Well... he asks me if there was a woman involved..."

"Harry then says that, not only wuz air a woman involved, ee's bean dating a nymphomaniac an they fornicated. Fornicated! Harry, yah devil." Snuff can't remove himself from the tale to the delight of himself and everyone else.

"Fornicator! Fornicator! Fornicator!" The chant goes up from the rest of them.

"Keep it down," says Harry, getting a bit concerned.

"So yoose think Franz gets all over Harry, right?" Snuff pauses and looks around the table. "Wrong, ee says wimmin just can't get enough."

"He got into all sorts of weird stuff," says Harry, "witches being seen in fields on their backs, naked to the navel, black vapor in the shape of a man."

"But what of your lost member?"

"Oh! This is great," says Snuff. "Franz tells Harry that ee's got to verify that Harry's really lost it. So ee tells Harry to take down his pants and then waits outside the confessional."

"I thought I might have to brush right past him," says Harry.

"Tell em what yuh did, Harry."

"Well, me and some of the boys were at the river last summer, skinny dipping. All of a sudden Snuff comes from behind a tree with a couple of melon halves for boobs and his hogan sequestered. He's walking pigeon toed and knock kneed towards us with his hips swinging side to side. It was a sight to behold. Well, except for the melons and the dramatics, that's what I did."

One of the men stands up and imitates the moves. "Yeah," says Harry.

Another still doesn't get it. "What?" he says throwing his hands up in the air.

Snuff becomes impatient. "Harry grabs his member and family jewels an tucks em behind his legs," slapping the guy on the back of his head to show his exasperation. "Looks just like a, you know."

Franz's face is now beet red from embarrassment. Not only has he been duped but he had compounded the foolishness by staging an exorcism and then proclaiming a cure to the congregation. The incident was another spoke in the wheel for the inquisition underway.

Notwithstanding all the charity his demeanor can muster, Johann realizes that his own presence adds to the mortification. Here he sits, three feet away and eyeball to eyeball, as Franz's gullibility is laid bare. "Let's go Franz," he says in a whisper. "We can discuss how to handle this on the way back to the rectory." He puts some coins on the table to cover the bill. They get up with Johann taking the lead and heading for the stairway up to the street, hoping that his friend is close on his heels. Franz, however, a model of studied self-control, walks around the partition to the table of bounders and addresses Harry directly.

"You will pay dearly for this, sir." He then gives his old friend, Snuff, a withering look for his complicity before storming out and leaving them stunned

❧

May 31, 1556 (Sunday)

Getting out of bed in the half-darkness of the morning, a shutter bangs intermittently from the vicissitudes of the wind; the courtyard is strewn with curled, green leaves. His room is small but nicely furnished except for the cracked ceramic basin which the cardinal promised to have replaced. He woke with the echo of their laughter in his ears. His face expressionless, Franz lights a candle and moves about in its faltering light, the candle a silent observer to a vital man or an unforeseen witness to a vanishing spirit. Looking old and drained, he is a man not loved, a confused and desolate disciple drawn in upon himself. A rigid adherent to canons, affection has vacated his soul. He feels a need to hurry but he does it slowly.

At the conclusion of the day's Masses, Franz requests a meeting in the cardinal's study. Sensing the gravity of the occasion, Cardinal Gerhardt closes and carefully locks the door behind him; he gestures to three chairs facing each other. Taking his seat last, Gerhardt just smiles at Franz and waits for him to speak. Franz, shaken, relates his recent encounter to Cardinal Gerhardt and Father Dietrich. The cardinal, at first, is taken aback but he quickly recovers; he has a discipline of mind tailored for crisis. Calamity diminishes others; he is energized by it, the steady hand on the helm in rough seas. Franz is relieved that the cardinal is not given to anger and deprecation.

They question him thoroughly about the details and then ask if there is anything else that he would like to add. "Only that the record be set straight and that the perpetrator be brought to justice before an ecclesiastical tribunal." They thank him for his forthrightness and say that he should remain readily available the rest of the day. Franz retires to his room and tries to rest; pursued by a nagging loneliness.

Supper passes normally with all the clergy present. Toki out does herself in the culinary arts and as a special surprise produces a magnificent, multi-layered birthday cake. From previous small talk with Father Dietrich she had deduced that today is his birthday and he is especially pleased. Just as delighted is the cardinal. To him, such courtesies are part of ingratiating politics. When the group starts to disburse, and after expressing their thanks to Toki, Gerhardt whispers to Franz that he would like to see him in his study. He hands a cup and saucer to Franz, grabs another and the pot of tea, and departs the dining room with Franz following.

"Have a seat, Franz," the cardinal says pointing to a chair at the end of a low table fronting a couch. After pouring tea for both, he puts the teapot on the table and moves to the window behind his desk. He takes a sip of tea from his cup as he looks out; the sun still reluctant to set. "I made some inquiries this afternoon. It seems that this fellow, Harry Schmidt," he pauses, "is better known as, pardon my French, Horseshit Harry. It's no mystery how he got that name."

"He's a heretical lout by whatever name," replies Franz.

"Maybe. Or maybe just a sacrilegious lout. I know this type. They are more interested in a good time than anything else. Mean no real harm. Of course, they often do cause incidental damage. And this is serious; he must be punished."

"He ridiculed all the Church stands for."

Gerhardt turns to face his subordinate. "*Vengeance is mine, so sayeth the Lord.* But we do have procedures to follow, don't we. For now, he is just suspected of heresy."

"But, but… what are you saying, Your Eminence?"

"A canonical purgation."

"He is more than defamed of heresy." Franz's voice is vehement and confident, for the first time it has a tone of self-assurance.

"Well, maybe more than that. You might even say strongly suspected of heresy. But keep in mind, if he fails the purgation, we turn him over to the civil authorities for the extreme penalty. If he abjures the heresy and later relapses, he is a backslider and meets the same fate."

"He has done enough to convict him of heresy."

"Under ordinary circumstances, you may be right. But at this time and place the negatives outweigh the positives."

"What do you mean?"

Gerhardt walks closer to Franz. "This could taint the whole Inquisition. You know and I know that there are witches about, Horseshit Harry or no Horseshit Harry. This Colmarz woman is a witch. She caused that storm, no doubt about it. But if we come out now and say the Schmidt bewitchment and exorcism were a hoax, well?"

"What if Harry and his chums make it public?"

"They won't. It was a prank. They don't want the heat. They would jeopardize themselves. They would be open to Church sanctions and a backlash from the faithful. Frankly, under the circumstances, I wish that I could ignore the incident."

"What if it does leak out? What if the Inquirer gets hold of it? But more importantly, justice demands punishment."

Gerhardt sits on the couch and places his cup and saucer on the table in front of him. He leans back, crosses his arms, and looks at his subordinate. "Franz, one of the demands of my job is to look after the spiritual welfare of the faithful. And part of that is perception. What is the congregation, the town, going to think if I take to the pulpit and deny the exorcism? Say that we were duped. You and I know that these things can happen but to the simple folk, well, they will see it as a loss of credibility. It will be a drag on the Inquisition. If there ever was a time for expediency, it is now. Expediency is the lubricant between the ideal and reality." He reaches for the teapot and holds it towards Franz, who waves him off. "Of course, we must never refer to this incident again. We can't point to it as an example of witchcraft ever again. Not being true and all."

"This...ah, Harry person and his accomplice... I know the latter very well."

"Let's stick to Harry; he is the main culprit. I propose a secret canonical purgation. A public purgation is not called for since it is not a public matter."

"Not a public matter?"

"Canon law calls for a purgation to be held where?"

"All places where one is known to be defamed."

"Correct. And we are talking about a very tight circle here. Believe me, those close to him will know about the purgation, secret or not."

Things have always been pretty much black and white to Franz. He has a disdain for expediency but he knows that he has no choice in the matter. A secret canonical purgation it will be.

CHAPTER 17

THE TRIAL

June 1, 1556 (Monday)

It is an unusual, colorless and harsh morning sky for June, perhaps an omen of things to come. The exhausted wind swirls in lame gusts on the dim streets trying to rise above the mist and contributing to a remote stillness. As to the Particular Examination, the setting and personnel are the same. Dark circles have formed round Wilma's dark eyes adding to their daunting intensity. She is understandably more anxious than initially. Now it is no longer that prosecution is contemplated; it is real. Flashbacks to her parents' fate cause an involuntary shudder.

"What were you doing the day that vicious storm arose last fall?" Dietrich demands.

"I happened to be riding me mule."

"More like an oven fork, wasn't it?"

"I does no such thing. I'm not a witch," she shouts.

"Why do you lie to this court? We have witnesses."

"They is liars," she screams.

"There is strong evidence against you. Who holds mortal enmity towards you?"

"I don't knows. I don't knows," her voice trails off in despair.

"I have a list of twenty persons. Perhaps some or perhaps none of these persons have given depositions against you. Tell me if you recognize any of the names and, if so, would they spuriously accuse you of the villainy of heresy and witchcraft putting aside all fear of God."

Wilma closes her eyes and resigns herself to the monologue. At the fifteenth name there is a noticeable reaction and her eyes reopen. She lets Dietrich conclude.

"Well?"

"The only name me knows is von Hoffen. They is the ones that accused me mother of killing their baby. So she's the liar?"

"You are quite certain that there is no one else?"

"I is certain of nothin." Hunched, friendless, abandoned by the world, a tear runs down her cheek.

"Katarina von Hoffen, so noted." *This is of no consequence*, thinks Dietrich. *She isn't a party to the proceedings.*

The questioning continues for another hour, asking essentially the same questions but in a different way. Dietrich is mildly disturbed that her answers are consistent. "The defendant may step down. Fathers von Clausen and Desmond please approach the bench." The consultation is brief and Dietrich proceeds.

"We, the judge and assessors, having attended to and considered the details of the process enacted by us against you Wilma Colmarz, of the town of Innsbruck and in the Diocese of Innsbruck, and having diligently examined the whole matter, find that you are equivocal in your admissions. On the whole, your responses are elusive and deceitful."

"Elusive 'n deceitful?" Wilma retorts.

"Wherefore, that the truth may be known from your own mouth and that henceforth you may not offend the ears of your judges, we declare, judge and sentence that on this present day you be readied for rigorous interrogation." Wilma's body tenses at the mention of the term; she knows it well.

"Nein! I does nothin wrong. You can't. You can't."

"Take her away!"

Only now is Dolph Zimmerman summoned to chambers. Upon arrival, Father Dietrich gives him a copy of the Process against Wilma. "Herr Zimmerman, the court will reconvene thirty minutes past one. You may meet with your client at that time and address the court as you see fit." Dietrich gathers the scattered papers on the judge's bench then rises from his chair causing Dolph to look up from perusing the document.

"Another Inquirer appeared this morning. It calls for a public trial of Frau Colmarz." Dietrich walks off without responding.

Wilma is shoved ignominiously into a penal cell. Three burly matrons strip her and search her clothes for any instruments of witchcraft that might be sewn into them; instruments supposedly fabricated from the limbs of unbaptized children for the purpose of sustaining her power of silence under rigorous examination. Rigorous examination is the euphemism for questioning under torture.

Next, and for the same purpose, the hair on every part of her body is shaved and every orifice is checked. As if this isn't enough, three times a morsel of Blessed Wax is placed in a vessel of Holy Water and she is compelled to drink it. One of the matrons invokes the Holy Trinity each time. It is said that this latter method, by the Reverence of God, causes many a witch to break her silence when all else fails. It is odd that people accept this as perfectly normal yet scoff at the tales of West Indian voodoo rituals. One man's sanctity is another man's superstition.

❧

Dolph pours over the Process again and again as he snacks on some cereal, almond milk, and smoked herring hastily retrieved from his cellar. *What is my line of attack? What can I do to divert the tribunal from its foresworn conclusion? What? What time is it? Time to return to court.*

With its embarrassed hinges squealing softly, the door opens into an all-white interior except for the crimson frieze rounding the walls. A spider is waiting patiently at the edge of its web in a neglected corner of the ceiling as an unmindful fly buzzes nearby. Dolph wonders if the fly or Wilma has a better chance surviving this courtroom. The odds favor the fly. The striking appearance of Wilma is even more dramatic now that her head is shaven. The spectacle of her being brought into the courtroom backwards, if not for the serious circumstances, is comical to Dolph.

"Your Reverence," he proclaims, "must the court indulge in such vanity? Doesn't doctrine plainly state that a sorceress loses her power when she is taken into the hands of public justice?" Dolph at once paints himself as an arrogant upstart even though his tone is quite soft. The frosty stares of Fathers von Clausen and Desmond are accompanied by disapproving grunts. Dietrich's demeanor becomes measured and deliberate but he does not scold.

"With regard to the past, Herr Zimmerman. But she may receive fresh powers from the devil at any time. And let me caution you, Herr Zimmerman. Do not disdain such precautions lest you risk eternal damnation. As sayeth the Lord, '*If I had not come and spoken unto you, then you would have no sin, since I have spoken to you, you have no excuse,*' John 15:22. And it is underscored in Acts 17:30-31... '*In the past God overlooked such ignorance, but now he commands all people everywhere to repent.*' " Dietrich speaks patiently, like a forgiving uncle to a recalcitrant nephew.

"Does that apply to Original Sin?"

"This is not a theology class, Herr Zimmermann. Stick to the issues!"

"Didn't John Duns Scotus, the renowned theologian of the 13th and 14th centuries, maintain that witchcraft operates only while there is some physical manifestation of it? He seemed to believe that witches had a fondness for bent needles or similar devices as I recall. Surely Frau Colmarz has been searched for any such artifacts?"

"She has."

"And?"

"Nothing has been found."

"I see. Nothing has been found. She is in the hands of public justice. You wear Blessed Wax about your necks. But she is still brought in backwards. And these precautions are just in case she is a witch?"

"We can't be too careful."

"I see. So she has not been prejudged?"

"Herr Zimmerman. These precautions have been taken because there is sufficient reason to believe that she is a witch. But nein. The purpose of this court is to decide the facts."

"Thank you, Your Reverence. As you know, this is the first opportunity I have had to meet my client." Dolph turns towards her. "My good woman, I am your advocate." He makes a slight bow towards her.

"Couldn't they finds anyone younger?" Wilma says cynically. Dietrich suppresses a smile.

Dolph walks over and sits beside her. "I'll do all that I can for you," he whispers. "My aim is to use the Church's own experts against them. Let's hope that they will succumb to reason." They look into each other's eyes. A tear running down her cheek is the only response she can render.

Dolph picks up his copy of the Process from the table in front of him and turns a few pages. After a quick glance he puts it back down.

"Your Reverence, do I have your permission to reveal the identity of the principal witness in this case to the defendant?"

Dietrich considers the fact that the Wilma Colmarz is in custody. She has been strip searched. She has been shaven. Other precautions have been taken. When the witness' name was read with the others, she stated that she had not recognized it. "This court will be lenient, if not wise; you do."

Their voices are muffled but the words "*I never heard of him*" are clear and distinct for all to hear. Incredulity defines her face and indignation her posture. Dolph presses for more details. Finally, with a nod of undeterred resolve, he rises to his feet.

"Your Reverence, the defendant never heard of this shepherd, Oskar Konig. Not only doesn't she know him, his assertion that she flew through the air is preposterous."

"Herr Zimmerman, we must then accuse Herr Konig of conspiracy because two others witnessed the transvection, also."

"But according to the Process, they never testified, there are no depositions."

"Herr Konig is a man of good reputation and a regular communicant, as are the others. Father von Clausen here has testified to that. Oskar Konig can certainly speak for those others. The evidence is clear, Herr Zimmerman."

"A woman's life is at stake. The court must put forth direct, concrete evidence and not speculation in the pursuit of justice, which I might add, is only as good as its administrators."

"Thank you for your observations, Herr Zimmermann. However, God cloaks the innocent with angelic protection so that they do not come under suspicion even for lesser crimes such as theft. More so He protects the innocent from suspicion of witchcraft."

"That is the Church's position, if one is suspected, she must be guilty. Why bother with trials?"

Dietrich's face reddens. He tilts his head forward and glances down over the bridge of his nose at his papers. Dolph thinks he has him in a philosophical corner and has done major damage to his legal position.

"One suspected of witchcraft," Dietrich mutters without changing his composure, "is guilty of witchcraft but not necessarily of the specific act of which she is accused. And the purpose of the inquisition is to search out all witchcraft practices."

"With all due respect, Your Reverence. Since none of us are divine, we are all capable of error. We may mistakenly suspect someone of witchcraft or theft. And if God permits the innocent to be harmed by witchcraft, certainly he must permit the innocent to be wrongfully accused."

"Your premise is false, Herr Zimmerman. Only the sinful are harmed by witchcraft."

"What of innocent children, below the age of reason? I have heard priests speak of such cases from the pulpit. Children being egregiously harmed."

"Such punishment is for the sins of the parents."

"At the child's expense? Not only do the parents suffer but also the innocent child. Do you really believe this of a just, loving and great God?"

"A direct quote from Exodus, Herr Zimmerman, '*I am a mighty and jealous God, visiting the sins of the fathers unto the third and fourth generation.*' In other words, contracted guilt in children born from their parents' sin and of imitators of their fathers' crimes. And so was the fate of the children of the men of Sodom, who were exterminated for the sins of their fathers."

"A jealous God? You take this literally? It is a contradiction of terms. Who possibly could God, the Creator of the universe, be jealous of?"

"God will not tolerate sin."

"I think of our basic concepts of what is right and wrong. That which is noble and virtuous. I think of how people would react if the courts imprisoned or flogged members of one's family for the crimes of another member. It defies common sense. How can any honest person accept this illogical premise?"

"In the metaphysical scheme of things, it is not so black and white, Herr Zimmerman. If you were a theologian, you would know that the punishment of God is of two kinds, spiritual and temporal. Spiritual punishment is always accompanied by guilt. Not so with temporal punishment. However, temporal punishment is always accompanied by sufficient cause."

"Accompanied by sufficient cause? Would you elaborate, Your Reverence?"

"As Saint Jerome once said, '*whatever we suffer, we deserve for our sins.*'"

"Deserve for our sins is not the same as for the sins of another."

"We all bear the burden of Original Sin," retorts Dietrich. "The crime of a father brands his yet unborn children with shame, and entails upon them a share of his own responsibility."

"We all suffer temporal punishment on account of the Original Sin of Adam?"

"Exactly."

"But certain persons, such as innocent children, are singled out because of the sins of their parents? Just for temporal punishment, of course?"

"This is long established Church doctrine. If you were learned in theology you would be familiar with the works of prominent thirteenth century Church leaders. William of Auvergne, for example, once the Bishop of Paris and author of *De Universo,* which greatly influenced the development of theological studies in Paris, insisted that demons, with divine permission, killed children to punish their parents. Then there is Caesarius of Heisterbach, author of *Dialogus Miraculorum* in 1225, he speaks of devils taking the form of women and killing children with mere looks. Stephen of Bourbon, an inquisitor, said the same. You best stick to the law Herr Zimmerman and leave theology to the theologians. You are out of your element."

"Theologians are fallible and quite possibly operating under false premises. In that same century the Mongol hordes were sweeping over much of Asia and Europe slaughtering thousands of men, women and children as they went. Butchering everybody and anybody. I say again, everybody and anybody. Annihilating whole towns for the sake of power and territory. This was said to be God's will because of the sins of the people. In other words, fiendish atrocities on a continental scale committed to right other supposed wrongs. Temporal punishment? Where is the sense of proportion here? How does this square with '*thou shalt not kill?*' We are awash in contradictions. How long must others continue to suffer because of such distorted thought? Nein! A woman's life is at stake here. She is not being tried on proven facts but on questionable biblical doctrine and inexplicable teaching. Also, I do not subscribe to the contention that the ecclesiastical judicial system, comprised of men and not the divine, is unerring when it comes to witchcraft or anything else. That innocent people have never been wrongfully suspected of crimes flies in the face of reality."

"May I remind you, Herr Zimmerman, you are in an ecclesiastical courtroom. This is not a course in biblical criticism and you are egregiously in error. "

"This case should hinge on nothing more than proven facts."

"Common justice requires that a witch not be condemned to death unless she is convicted of her own confession."

"Of her own confession. I have not heard the defendant confess."

"The defendant will be exposed to rigorous examination. This is a very compelling method of getting at the truth for the mind doesn't have the facility to consistently lie under such circumstances. Her crimes will likely be revealed to us."

"Her crimes! God only permits the guilty to come under suspicion! The defendant is not prejudged? Why do I have the feeling that something is amiss here, Your Reverence?"

"Because you are contentious and wish to distort God's plan. Do you have anything else to offer, Herr Zimmerman?"

"I may be contentious but you, sir, are captive to specious teachings no matter how illogical."

"And your insolence knows no bounds, sir. I have a mind to remove you from this case," his voice vibrating with throttled anger. Rules of procedure allow for this; Dietrich may continue the case without a defense advocate. He has been very tolerant for an inquisitor. But there is the cardinal's mandate to project an image of objectivity.

"You may or may not be aware, Your Reverence, that Dr. Ulrich Molitar, the well-known Church canonist, published in 1488 a memorandum on witchcraft at the instance of the then Archduke of the Tyrol, Sigismund. Molitar maintained that no credence be given to statements made under torture. Anyone, which means even you Father Dietrich, through pain and fear might confess things that he has never done just to escape the immediate pain. Yet despite the statements of Molitar and others, torture is being used to this day."

"What others?" asks Dietrich.

"Johann Weyer, a prominent physician connected to the court of Julich-Cleves. He says the same. He denounces prisoners being dragged from their dungeons time and again to undergo torture until they confess. He says anyone would readily trade such bitter treatment for death. In his experience prisoners admit to anything suggested to them just to escape the torment."

"Well let me tell you and Weyer what the policy of the Church is on this for that is all that matters."

"All that matters?"

"This is what we are dealing with," snaps Dietrich.

"One.   Witches can be lawfully tortured by the inquisition because the crime of witchcraft is so difficult to prove. Witches act in secret.

"Two.   If there is evidence, direct or indirect, or if there are credible witnesses, and I quote Malleus Maleficarum directly here, *'she is to be exposed to questions and torture to extort a confession of her crimes.'*

"Three.   Likewise, statements of the witch on the rack or other such devices are conclusive evidence of her guilt when supported by confession of guilt afterwards.

"Four.   Some witches are endowed with the power of silence and can resist divulging any truth even under torture. This, also, must be and can be determined and thwarted."

"And not open for discussion, I take it."

"Guards, remove the defendant for questioning!" Dietrich stands, hastily retrieves his papers, and briskly exits the courtroom with Desmond and von Clausen in tow.

છ

Dolph owns a corner building at the fringe of the business district and it serves as both his office and home. The front door on Seidel Strasse is the main entrance to the office but the door on Basen Strasse, a little used side street, is employed as the residential entrance. The dining area and kitchen are in the back part of the first floor with the latter overlooking an alley. The wooden interior stairs leading to the rest of the living quarters on the two floors above creak as you go but it is a suitable sanctuary for a solitary man. He has a penchant for unglazed vases with freshly cut flowers and the walls are hung with eclectic oil paintings, some by his own hand.

He doesn't go directly home but rather wanders aimlessly feeling impotent and frustrated. The street drops abruptly then flattens out and there are echoes of carts rolling over cobblestones. A passerby pays him no mind. Reason has gotten him nowhere but he is reluctant to abandon it. He must shame them into an acquittal.

As he comes upon the Boar's Head Inn he decides to have a brew. A few businessmen sit together, a pitcher and half-filled glasses of beer resting on their corner table. Katarina, helping-out yet again, shows Dolph to a table less proximate to them.

"I've had a tough day in court, fraulein. A tall, cold brew might ease the pain," he says gesturing with his hands. His disheveled hair and distracted look underscore his claim.

"A lawyer?" Dolph nods. "Not the witch trial, I hope? You look a little young to be thrown to the wolves."

"Well, I've been thrown to the wolves nonetheless."

"Well isn't that something! Anything to eat with it?"

"Nein, not much of an appetite." His eyes follow her fluid hips as she disappears from view.

Katarina races to Fritz's office and tells him of their special patron. "Oh! How interesting," he says as he leaps from his chair. "Rafer is in the cellar. Tell him to get up here; I think he should meet him. I'll grab the beer." Katarina is amused at how quickly and deftly the rotund man maneuvers.

"Guten Tag, mein Herr," says Fritz, setting a beer in front of Dolph. Katarina is putting together a small tray of smoked herring, pickles and bread, compliments of the house."

"Very hospitable of you, sir, but there is no need."

"Well, we are here to nourish our guests and brighten their spirits."

"Herr Ober, he's the lawyer in the witch trial," says Katarina as she approaches with the brettljause.

"Well, isn't that special," Fritz replies as the street door opens and I walk in. "Rafer! Come over here! Meet the advocate in the witch trial! Katarina, get Herr Schilling a beer." I stride to the table. Dolph stands to acknowledge me, an oft lost courtesy, and invites me to have a seat. "You fellows get acquainted! Unfortunately, I have inventory to check and much as I hate it, I mustn't put it off any longer. Katarina will be here to look after you. Gentleman."

"Herr Ober," we both respond.

"Rafer Schilling! The famous mountain guide?"

"I'm a mountain guide. But you confuse me with my famous father."

"Both of you are held in high regard."

"Danke schoen. Nice of you to say so. And you have been appointed by the Church to defend the witch. You must be honored; you're such a young man."

"Everyone keeps telling me that."

"Some are quietly skeptical of its reality, witchcraft, that is."

"Even some clergy have denied it," adds Dolph.

"I've heard the same."

"Well, it's my job to present every legitimate argument I can to defend this woman. To be candid, I don't feel adequately prepared. I wish I knew more about doctrinal criticism as it pertains to witchcraft."

"I happen to know somebody well versed in doctrinal matters. Might be able to arrange a meeting if you want. But I question the value. To my knowledge the Church has solidified its position on this issue."

"Is it St. Jude? The patron saint of lost causes."

"Where can you be reached?"

"My office is on the southeast corner of Seidel and Basen. But tell him to use the entrance on Basen."

"Basen Strasse, you got it. Tell me a little about yourself. How long have you been in Innsbruck?"

ço

Wilma stands with her arms overhead and each wrist bound by a thong. She is now in the hands of her jailers, Helmut and Heinz Keiple, round faced identical twins harboring deep set eyes and hairless scalps. The singular distinguishing feature is Helmut's limp right leg, which he drags along. When Dietrich first arrives at the dungeon with his retinue, he orders the two to bathe immediately. Their body odors could be part of the torture for the accused but he wasn't about to endure it.

Washed and back in the dungeon in the bowels of the chancery, the dolts, not encumbered by the thought process, are instructed by Dietrich. "When I indicate that you should apply some engine of torture, you will proceed at once but not joyfully. Feign, if you must, that you are vexed by your duty." He turns to Fathers von Clausen and Desmond, then to the notary. "Torture is one of the best tools at our disposal yet it is not a panacea. It works most of the time. Other times the results are questionable, not precise. Some of these Godless creatures are so weak of spirit, at the least application, admit to anything. Some have the power of silence or are so recalcitrant that no matter what is done to them, nothing will be forthcoming."

"Then how can we be sure?" asks Desmond with idealistic discomfort.

"We will know," replies Dietrich. "Also, if she confesses under torture, we will question her again, removed from the chamber. We will demand that she repeat her confession when not under pressure."

Desmond looks quizzically to Franz, bewildered by the last remark. Franz doesn't acknowledge him. "This power of silence, Father. Would you elaborate?"

"Through a pact with the devil, she will be so insensible to pain that one could pull her arms from their sockets and she would not reveal the truth. This is all explained in Malleus Maleficarum. Of course, God could send a good angel compelling the devil to withhold this help."

"This is very perplexing," says Desmond.

"There is no real consistency here. Some do not have this capacity; the devil not rendering any assistance to the tortured witch. The devil sometimes tests them to see if they denied the faith in word only. The devil can only conjecture the sincerity of the witch; he cannot know her innermost thoughts."

"It is all so uncertain," says Desmond, a moral but dependent man.

It is but a few yards to the torture chamber; the twins lead the way. The clergymen enter quietly, piously, after all, they are about the Lord's work. Helmut and Heinz are now on each side of the cylinder ratcheting Wilma so that her heels leave the floor. Her eyes close but she says nothing as the thongs bite into her wrists. Dietrich looks at his notes and asks, "Why do you deny your transvection when the shepherd Konig and others saw it?"

Wilma keeps her eyes closed and doesn't respond. The question is repeated. Again no reply. Helmut picks up a cane and looks to

Dietrich. The nod is quickly followed by the thuds of three hard strokes across her back. Wilma gasps with each strike and writhes as her feet lose contact with the floor. Her eyes close and head falls forward gulping for air. Desmond winces, failing to hide his uneasiness with the whole affair. Oskar Konig's deposition is then read by Dietrich in its entirety. This gives Wilma time to collect herself and contemplate the consequences of not cooperating with him.

"You won't stop til I admits to yours lies. Let's be done with it. What does you wants me to say?" This is not acceptable to Dietrich but he is willing to play this out slowly. He leaves with his entourage telling the twins to leave her hanging there for an hour to embrace the fear of God.

❦

June 2, 1556 (Tuesday)

"Inquisition's Secret Trial A Sham" is my headline. The text hammers again that the whole business is a farce predicated on superstitious gossip and used to divert attention from Cardinal Gerhardt's assault. That secrecy is maintained to hide the flawed character of the trial from the public. I want to keep the Cardinal on the defensive and put the power of public opinion in play. But Dietrich is reluctant to take the bait.

"We, not The Inquirer, must be in control here. The Church cannot allow itself to be dictated to by this subversive paper."

"Only if it were so easy, my dear Hans," replies Gerhardt, "even the Church, as holy as it is, must be responsive to public perceptions. Perception is reality. Let us be quick to make concessions to demonstrate openness and throw their assertions back in their faces. More importantly, we have eyewitness testimony that she is a witch. A public conviction will give us unquestioned credibility and discredit that shit bucket at the same time."

"And what of these continued accusations against you?"

The devil is my cover story; he reminds himself. "That has already been addressed. Let them wail away. Was that a knock? Is someone there?"

"It is I, Johann."

"Come in Johann!"

"The bulletins are ready for distribution, Your Eminence," handing a finished copy to the cardinal. Although he had composed it, Gerhardt wants to be sure that there are no errors.

"Good, get this around town as quickly as possible! As quickly as possible. Two can play this game. The people must know that I have nothing to hide."

"I'll personally see to it."

"And see that, that attorney fellow, Zimmerman, knows about the postponement immediately, will you?" *How convenient for us,* thinks Johann.

"Certainly. Father Dietrich, anything special on your agenda today?"

"The tribunal keeps me busy every day."

"I understand. Gentlemen, let me carry this forward for you. Good day."

"Likeable fellow, isn't he?" says Dietrich upon Johann's departure.

"Very popular. Everybody likes Johann. And he likes his meals and schnapps as you can see by the size of his girth. Wish he had less food and more fire in his belly. I must rely on Father von Clausen for drive and action."

"And Father Desmond?"

"More the methodical type. Conscientious. An inward fellow. A bit naive. But a good man." *Always try to say something positive.*

"This attorney, Zimmerman. To say the least, he's very problematic. Ordinarily, I wouldn't tolerate his contentiousness."

"I apologize for that. My mistake. Should have stuck with a known quantity. Sorely misjudged that one."

"I'll handle him. It might be for the best. If he puts up a good fight, it will make our victory even more credible. Truth is on our side."

"That's the way to talk, Hans. Turn a negative into a positive. The archdiocese will be stronger than ever by the time you get through."

It is hardly past eight in the morning and so much has already happened, Johann muses as he knocks on the Basen Strasse door. A stray dog emerges from the alley and gives him a cursory once over. Johann reciprocates but the dog loses interest and meanders away. The sky is still stale and heavy refusing to yield its light. The Inquirer had been laid at the rectory door most likely before dawn, possibly by a parishioner, and Toki dutifully alerted the cardinal. He had to give Gerhardt credit; he had made up his mind to go public and had the Church press operating within the hour.

"Herr Zimmerman?" Johann asks as the door opens.

"Ja."

"I'm Father Johann Carberry. Rafer Schilling sent me. So did the cardinal."

"Come in! Come in Father!" Dolph says not sure what to make of his guest.

"Herr Zimmerman, there's been a postponement."

"The trial?"

"Ja."

"The Inquirer possibly?"

"Ja. It stirred things up over there. Taking counter action."

"Come sit at the kitchen table here."

"I brought some tea leaves for you. Hope you have a strainer?"

"Well, how extraordinary. I am much pleased. I happen to have some water boiling. And ja, I do. And I have Zwetschkenknodel."

"Wunderbar. But I prefer schnaps to tea, myself, if you don't think me impertinent?"

"Schnaps it is."

Johann, also, had some trepidation about their meeting but so far he likes what he sees, what he feels. "I understand that you need some counseling on Church doctrine. We can begin this morning, if you like."

"The delay is until?"

"Thursday. And the court will be open to the public."

"Fantastisch!" Dolph brings a bottle of plum schnaps and a glass to the table. He then goes to pour a cup of tea for himself before returning. Johann, seated, hands him Gerhardt's bulletin. Dolph takes the chair opposite and reads it through while Johann delights in his libation.

"Wunderbar!" they both say in unison but for different reasons.

∽

June 4, 1556 (Thursday)

This time Wilma does not enter directly into the courtroom from the side entrance. A partition has been erected channeling her toward the rear of the room so that she has to turn one hundred eighty degrees to face the bench. Dietrich and his advisers, alerted as to her entrance, stare at the end of the partition when she is brought around it, thus eliminating the need to bring her in backwards.

"I see that some renovations have taken place, Your Reverence," Dolph says as Wilma is being seated.

"I must tell you Herr Zimmerman," ignoring his remark, "my assessors and I concur as to the need for still further rigorous examination of the defendant. However, you may present any additional information that you may have pertinent to the defense of your client."

"Thank you, Your Reverence."

"This trial is now open to the full scrutiny of the people of Innsbruck, with seating on a 1st come basis. Cardinal Gerhardt has insisted upon it despite my protestations that it is not necessary. If you can't trust the Church, who can you trust?"

"Indeed, Your Reverence."

"Nonetheless, I feel that a public trial will be instructive and will put the fear of God into the servants of the devil. Proceed, Herr Zimmerman."

Dolph turns towards Wilma, who listens without hope. He gives her a reassuring smile and begins his peripatetic journey to enlighten the court. He will refer frequently to a long checklist he put together from his own instruction on canon law and intense tutoring by Johann. Fortunately, he has always been a quick study.

"Tertullian, the Carthaginian priest and theologian, born a little over century and a half after the birth of Jesus, in his *De praescriptione haereticorum,* indicates in Chapter 17 that scripture was being contested when he wrote his tome and that there were diverse interpretations; in Chapter 34 he states this was so even at the time of the apostles. As the title suggests, he sought to prove that much was heretical. Here is a man living at the time that the concept of a Catholic Church was just being realized. The time that the New Testament was just beginning to be viewed as being on a par with the Old Testament; just beginning to be referred to as scripture itself, the time of Theophilus of Antioch, about 180 A.D." All the priests look at Dolph with stupefaction. He is lecturing them on scripture. But no one interrupts. "So there was controversy in Tertullian's time, so it is today. Tertullian, however, later came to write virulently against the Church and developed his own doctrine of the Holy Trinity and, contrary to his previous inclinations in Chapter 22, repudiates that the keys were left by Christ through Peter to His Church; he came to say that they were just personal to Peter, interpretations from the man who had previously railed against other interpreters of scripture. Do you see where I am going with this?"

"That is the reason for canon, Herr Zimmerman?"

"Exactly, the books were not recognized as scripture until the Church defined them as such. And what became scripture? It was anything that spoke favorably of Jesus. I am saying, Your Reverence, that the production of the New Testament was preceded by a long period of tradition and tradition is a human affair. Written, and the more fluid oral sources, were edited into the books as we now know them by numerous anonymous persons. This being the case, it is impossible to attribute divine inspiration to the written texts in their final form. Therefore, one cannot say that inspiration is personal to a select few, such as Matthew, Mark, Luke and John, who then gave the scriptures to the community."

"So you are telling us that the Bible is not inspired. Incredible!"

"The time alluded to as the time of biblical revelation was long past when the New Testament came into being generations later. As to the Old Testament, almost all of it, centuries after the central events."

"I see where this is going; ignore the command *'Thou shalt not suffer witches to live.'* "

"I am saying that we cannot speak with certainty as to what is sacred text and what is not. If the noted theologian and saint, Thomas Aquinas, his renowned teacher, Albertus Magnus, as well as Peter Lombard, Alexander of Hales and Bonaventure can be mistaken about sacred text, anyone can."

"Oh! And how were they mistaken?"

"Thomas, as did his contemporaries, considered the *Corpus Areopageticum* of near apostolic antiquity, believing that it was written by Dionysius the Areopagite, when we now know that these books were more likely written at the earliest in the late fifth century, in other words, centuries after the passing of Dionysius. Impetus had been given to their supposed authenticity by the 649 Lateran Council, which erroneously affirmed Dionysius as the author. Thomas, through ignorance, cited him over 1700 times. He gave great weight to *De divinis nominibus* in particular. Thus, theological commentaries of Thomas, hinging on these documents, were based on a false premise."

"We are aware of Pseudo-Dionysius," says Dietrich.

"Church councils make mistakes. Theologians make mistakes. All are subject to error. This trial is open to error. I ask the court to proceed with an open mind and disregard prejudgment."

Dietrich is surprisingly unemotional. "So you say, Herr Zimmerman. The fact is, however, that the Church herself has never been proven to be in error on matters of faith or morals."

"The Church promulgates the teachings of theologians such as Thomas Aquinas. Aquinas was a Doctor of Theology; the substance of theologians is faith and morals. In the case of Pseudo-Dionysius, Aquinas relied on a false premise as did the Lateran Council. Both were mistaken."

"What makes you such an expert in these matters? What are your credentials? Why should we look to you to tell us what we should believe and what we shouldn't?"

"My degree is in law, not theology, as you well know. But you are also aware that in the pursuit of my degree, canon law was a significant part of the curriculum."

"A few theology courses qualify you, do they?"

"One need not have a particular degree to know the facts. Let us look at the notion of canon itself. When used in the sense of a *list*, it is a Christian term that did not find favor until the fourth century A.D. The men of the New Testament had no interest in canon. Yet today there is great focus on this thing called canon."

"Canon should be discarded then?"

"I am saying that canon is derivative of what we call scripture but too much emphasis is being given to it. If it were so important, Jesus' posture towards the Old Testament would have been exegetical."

"And it was not?"

"Nein! Jesus spoke in parables. He related to contemporary life. He did not explain scripture but he did allude to Hebrew Scripture to reinforce his points."

"You make light of the Old Testament?"

"The pattern is similar. The Jewish state had a significant oral tradition, especially prior to the Babylonian exile. The death of the nation was accompanied by the near death of the theocratic spirit. Subsequently, the Jewish religion became the domain of the scholars, a thing of understanding, the subject of learned treatment; its essence was reduced to dogmas or precepts. Thus the spiritual component was diminished in favor of a more academic one."

"But the Written Law of Moses pre-dated the Babylonian exile by many centuries!" says Dietrich.

"Absolutely, Your Reverence. And it can be reasonably assumed that some of that law likely existed before Moses. But the Written Law, the Pentateuch, the Torah, if you will, was not central to Israel's constitution as it later became. Until the end of the Babylonian exile, there was no canonization process. There was no process of choosing or selecting among competing scrolls."

"So?"

"There was a dual source of authority in rabbinic Judaism. There was the Written Law, the first five books of the Hebrew Bible, namely, Genesis, Exodus, Leviticus, Numbers and Deuteronomy, which we are told was given to Moses on Mount Sinai. There was also the Oral Law passed down through many generations. But as to the Old Testament as a whole, there had been no hard fast, invariable delineation of what was to be included or excluded. Not until Ezra, Nehemiah and the Great Synagogue anyway. Not until well after the Babylonian exile ended in 538 B.C."

"So scripture is not unconditionally authoritative you say. And the prophets, how do you characterize their utterances?" Dietrich wants to see how far afield Dolph goes.

"Personal. Sometimes set down and sometimes not, often transitory. Sometimes accurate and sometimes not."

"And the Talmud? Mishnah?"

"They underscore my point. They, also, represent a break from oral to literal. They are the written manifestations of the oral tradition of the Jews."

"Anything else?" Dietrich sneers.

"The Talmud is the written foundation for all codes of rabbinical law and it is derived from rabbinical discussions dealing with the law, customs, biblical understanding, and culture. The Mishnah, circa 200 A.D., is the first written compilation of the Oral Law and is a component of the Talmud. The Gemara, circa 500 A.D., the other component, is the rabbinical discussion of the Mishnah. The Talmud is considered just as authoritative as the Law given to Moses."

"So canon is overstated; we shouldn't take it too seriously," Dietrich says pursing his lips, then shaking his head in disbelief.

"I'm dealing with facts here, not conjecture. For the sake of justice, they can't be ignored. Historical facts, Your Reverence, and not speculation. The Bible is a revered tome and I mean no disrespect. My point is, however, that we can't rely on the authenticity of so called inspired canon in light of its true development and especially since this was never the focus of those of the Old or New Testaments. Jesus rejected the literal meaning of the law and instead proclaimed a spiritual meaning. So yes, we shouldn't literally trust in that Old Testament command, '*Thou shalt not suffer witches to live.*' "

"And according to you the Church should ignore acts of witchcraft."

"I am saying that the Church, and more specifically this court, should leave scripture out of these particular proceedings and just deal with material facts."

"I must say that I am shocked by what I have heard here today. It is only for the sake of candor and openness, however, that I have indulged you. If only all of this were as simple as you make it out to be, it is not."

"I appreciate that there is much to consider, Your Reverence."

"As Tertullian indicated, the early Christian movement was degenerating into separate factions. I think of the muddled views ascribed to Papias, Bishop of Hierapolis, by Eusebius, which of themselves point to the need to codify the oral tradition because of pervasive divergences. And, also, dubious written epistles and gospels were prevalent. The Christian community had to sort things out based on available near apostolic references. Lists of writings believed to be of an orthodox nature became New Testament canon. And you think that is extraordinary, Herr Zimmerman? "

"The key words here are '*believed to be of an orthodox nature.*' According to Tertullian, what was labeled canon still had many challengers; it didn't have universal acceptance yet over time that fact has been lost. Church canon and doctrine, then and now, are therefore not irrefutable."

"But Herr Zimmerman, you are completely overlooking the living, teaching authority of the Church," Dietrich says derisively.

"The Roman Catholic Church settles canonicity by the traditions of the Church but tradition is a human affair and it is fluid. The New Testament is largely a product of tradition and tradition is subject to variation over time. Canon ignores this fact and has assumed a synthetic position. And the Church's dogmatizing of scripture and doctrine over the centuries continues today with the rulings of the Council of Trent, which began ten years ago and will likely reconvene again I am told."

"I'll tell you about sacred tradition, Herr Zimmerman," Dietrich barks, "it is Christ's active beneficence to the Apostles faithfully passed from generation to generation. It is the customary means that the faith is communicated as guided by the Holy Spirit."

"Your thesis supports my contention that canon is unnecessary."

"Tradition and scripture confirm each other. The Council of Trent, Disciples of Christ coming together as one, praying over the evolution of Christian thought, gives us the Bible in its final and correct form. He, who does not accept it, whole and entire, is anathema. The Lord Jesus Christ corroborated the authority of the Old Testament. I refer to John 10:35, where it is said that *'scripture cannot be broken.'* "

"Ja I remember. And in that same chapter of John, Jesus said *'I and my Father are one.'* The Jews accused him of blasphemy for claiming to be the Son of God. He said that *'the Father is in me, and I in Him.'* But some say that Jesus was saying that we are all of God and that he was not claiming to be the Messiah. Some say that Jesus was a prophet."

Dietrich pages through Malleus Maleficarum and then uses his quill to stroll line by line with his words in tow... "*The Jews sin more greatly than the Pagans; for they received the prophecy of the Christian faith in the Old Law, which they corrupt through badly interpreting it, which is not the case with the Pagans.*"

"But the Jews set down the Old Testament in the first place! Who better to interpret it?" replies Dolph.

"I say again. The Jews broke their covenant with God." Dietrich presses his main point. "Malleus quotes Saint Thomas Aquinas in the Second of the Second, Question 10, '*...the deeds of the unfaithful, which are of themselves good, such as fasting, almsgiving, and deeds of that sort, are no merit to them because of their infidelity, which is a most grievous sin...not every deed of theirs is a mortal sin but only those which proceed from their very infidelity, or are related to it... For example, a Saracen fasts to observe the law of Muhammad as to fasting, and the Jew observes his feast days; but in such things he is guilty of mortal sin.*' "

"By acting for the glory of God, they sin?" Dolph asks rhetorically. "Jesus left no written texts and none of the original gospels survive. Some biblical scholars maintain that well-meaning but not authoritative additions were made to the gospels by Church leaders. This must be taken into consideration in this trial."

"Let me enlighten you, Herr Zimmerman. Divine revelation is of two parts; Sacred Scripture is one and the other is contained in the depository of the Church, in other words, the unwritten word of God. I refer to St. Paul's second letter to the Thessalonians, specifically 2 Thessalonians 2. 14, a significant statement... '*Wherefore, brethren, stand fast, and hold traditions which you have learned whether by word or by our Epistle.*' Thus, infused with the Holy Spirit, the Church is the sole interpreter of divine revelation in its dual form, Herr Zimmerman," regurgitating the Church's position and ignoring Dolph's contentions.

"So this '*significant statement*' that you refer to is taken from a letter written by Paul. Jesus didn't say it; Paul said it in a letter that he wrote. A letter. If the Church was to be given such awesome authority and responsibility, wouldn't it be reasonable to assume that it would have been proclaimed by none other than Jesus in very clear and emphatic terms as opposed to being buried in one of Paul's letters? Even so, it is not a very definitive statement. Once again, this becomes a colossal stretch for the Church to assume such authority."

"Herr Zimmerman, I am at my limit as to your insolence," his manner sharp and abrupt.

"Your Reverence, it is an attorney's duty to be insolent; it is how we emphasize our points. You certainly are aware of courtroom dialectics." Dolph is now resigned to the fact that he will not open a closed mind; someone so invested in his beliefs that he will even dismiss facts. If he can just plant some seeds of doubt in the public mind. "You quote Thomas Aquinas. Yet Thomas had been excommunicated from the Church. What say you of this?"

"What say you?" Dietrich is exasperated but works to conceal it.

"According to Stephen Tempier, the Bishop of Paris, Thomas, who had been dead for three years, and others, had made erroneous theological statements so the bishop excommunicated them in March, 1277. The next month, Pope John XXI wrote Bishop Tempier condoning his action and condemning those philosophers and theologians who '*presume to dogmatize errors contrary to the purity of the true and catholic faith.*' Talk about credentials; Thomas Aquinas was a Dominican doctor of the Church. Talk about error of interpretation; either the great theologian was wrong or Bishop Tempier and Pope John were wrong. This isn't some slap on the wrist here, we're talking excommunication."

"Well..."

"The point is that theologians, bishops and even popes make mistakes on matters of faith and morals. They misinterpret, so how can we go about putting people to death when we are not absolutely certain of the correctness of our actions?" Dietrich is clearly uncomfortable and seems at a loss for words. "In 1278, the year following the excommunication of Thomas, the general chapter of Dominicans met in Milan and sent Raymond Mevouillon and John Vigoroux to England with full powers as visitators of the chapter to investigate whoever *in scandalum ordinis 'showed disrespect for the writings of the venerable father Friar Thomas d'Aquino.'* These men were empowered to reprimand, remove from office and/or ban from the province those guilty of such transgressions. This is your own order refuting the Bishop of Paris and the Pope."

"There were some differences among some individuals," Dietrich retorts.

"These are more than differences among some individuals, Your Reverence. The Dominican Order endorsed Thomas; the Franciscan Order did not. William de la Mare, who held the Franciscan chair of theology at the University of Paris, compiled a *correctory* of Thomas taking issue with his positions that were opposed to Franciscan teachings and untrue. This *Correctorium* was officially adopted by the general chapter of Franciscans held at Strasbourg in May, 1282." Dietrich seems preoccupied. "That's the bad news. The good news is that no one died over their differences."

"Those differences were resolved, Herr Zimmerman."

"Resolved or simply reversed by those in power and friendly to Thomas? In 1323, Pope John XXII issued the papal bull *Redemptionem misit* proclaiming Thomas a saint of the Holy Roman Church and one who was exemplary in holiness and doctrine. In 1325, Etienne Bourret, Bishop of Paris, lifted the excommunication of Thomas and the condemnation of those propositions that touched on the doctrine of Thomas."

"Herr Zimmerman. It is common for the Church Doctors to have differing opinions, some even contradictory, as to scriptural matters. However, until the Church makes a decision on two diametrically opposed opinions, each may be held by their proponents."

"A decision wasn't made here? Wasn't made here? For almost fifty years some of his teachings were labeled heretical. If he had not already been dead, he would have been burned at the stake if the Franciscans and Pope John XXI held sway."

"You don't have the necessary training in these matters, Herr Zimmerman." Dietrich rocks back and forth in his chair and stares at the ceiling as if what he is hearing is inconsequential.

"Just decades ago Pope Adrian VI wrote in one of his papers that a pope may err personally or even in a pronouncement on matters of faith."

"None of these popes proclaimed that he was making an infallible statement from the chair of St. Peter. He does not speak ex cathedra, infallibly, unless he specifically states he is doing so."

"No pope, as yet, has ever spoken ex cathedra, according to the Church, although there have been a few alleged occasions. Yet decisions are being made by the hierarchy, on matters of faith and morals, as to what is heretical and what is not. People are being tortured and put to death because of those decisions. Infallible or not, who will take responsibility for these irreversible actions?"

Dietrich shifts nervously in his chair. "Individuals have erred on occasion, Herr Zimmerman, and must take responsibility for their own actions. The Church has not."

"Inquisitions have been going on for centuries, Your Reverence." Dolph turns away and begins to walk about. "Individual responsibility? Individual responsibility? Individuals are citing and enforcing canon law. Church law!"

"Don't quibble with me!" Dietrich shouts. "I already told you of the living, teaching authority of the Church." His face is taut and menacing. For just an instant, one instant, he seems to lose his composure.

"Councils make declarations. Popes issue papal bulls. Bishops issue diocesan letters. These are viewed by the laity as teachings on faith and morals. The faithful are expected, commanded, to conform." Dietrich seems to be searching his mind for a pretext to shut Dolph down but Dolph is relentless. "Who is the living, teaching authority of the Church? The Pope speaking ex cathedra? The councils of cardinals? The individual bishops themselves? Who?"

Dietrich's red face portends fury but he manages to control his hostility. His eyes close as he says, "Herr Zimmerman, you are a devious and reprehensible advocate. But I will answer your question for the benefit of those in this courtroom. Infallibility was promised by Christ to His Church and it is the pope who expresses that infallible authority. Definitive teaching is final and unalterable so you can say it is infallible. Infallibility is concerned with the explanation and protection of truths already revealed. Doctrines which are not revealed truths per se but are nonetheless so closely connected with revealed truths are infallible because to deny one would deny the other. As to other doctrine, unless declared ex cathedra, it is not infallible. Do you follow me so far, Herr Zimmerman?"

"Are you admitting that all doctrine is not infallible?"

"The Church cannot err in its teaching of revealed truth only because it is aided by the Holy Spirit. I, also, have done my research." Paging through his notes, "I cite biblical passages quoting Christ addressing the Apostles at the Last Supper which infer the promise of infallibility... John 14: 16, 17, '*I will ask the Father, and he shall give you another Paraclete, that he may abide within you forever. The spirit of truth... he shall abide with you, and shall be in you.'* And John 14: 26, *'But the Paraclete, the Holy Ghost, whom the Father will send in my name, he will teach you all things, and bring all things to your mind, whatsoever I shall have said to you.'* The Holy Spirit, the Third Person of the Blessed Trinity, guarantees that the Apostles and their successors will properly define Christ's teaching. The pope teaching ex cathedra and an ecumenical council subject to the approbation of the pope as its head are distinct organs of infallibility."

"How do the faithful know which teachings meet the revealed truth criteria?"

"If there is a need to so define a teaching, it will be done."

"So the faithful do not have to adhere to all faith and moral teachings of our popes and bishops? Just those designated infallible."

"To the contrary, those who don't observe Church doctrine, fallible or infallible, and its disciplinary laws are subject to eternal damnation, such is the Church's doctrinal authority. For example, even if that eccentric Copernicus is correct with his heliocentric theory, while an ecclesiastical authority which condemned him for that position was wrong, he must faithfully fulfill the external conditions demanded of him by that authority. This is so because of the Church's underlying authority to possibly convert a proposition to infallible teaching. It would be acceptable for him, however, to withhold his internal acquiescence to the ecclesiastical position if he had considerable evidence for his position."

"So if one is excommunicated by the Church, as in the case of St. Thomas Aquinas, for example, it implies that he is likely headed for eternal damnation?" replies Dolph.

"Your contentious arguments about these positions of the Church have nothing to do with this woman's diabolical acts of witchcraft.

Henceforth, your remarks will be so confined or you will be discharged; do you understand me? The court is adjourned until Monday. The guards will prepare the defendant for further questioning."

"So you are saying that, '*Thou shalt not suffer witches to live,*' is revealed truth? It is infallible revealed doctrine?"

"I am."

CHAPTER 18

THE CANONICAL
PURGATION

Late in the afternoon Harry received a letter saying that the Church considered him Strongly Suspected of Heresy. He took it to the warehouse, only Snuff and Basil were there. Since they got him into this trouble, they should get him out of it; Harry told them. Here's how it went…

"By the wording, it's a secret purgation," says Basil. "And anyone present will be sworn to secrecy. That's significant. I doubt they want people finding out it wasn't a real exorcism. We'll have to wait and see if Snuff gets a letter."

"We're talkin bout a canical purge here, not a trial for witches," says Snuff.

"No torture!" adds Basil.

"But I'll be a marked man the rest of my life."

"Ain't sponsors anvolved in these things," asks Snuff, "those to stan up for im?"

"Ja, it says ten of his own station," Basil replies. "For example, Harry is secular, so they must be secular. And the sponsors must be practicing Catholics of good reputation and have known Harry for a considerable time with little interruption."

"Rafer n his father ill stan for you, an the rust of us," says Snuff.

"I don't think the Schillings should be associated with this. The Inquirer… it's too risky."

"Thur's a lot of blokes we knows. They will have tah stretch the truth a bit. Anybody ave a problem with at? Spread a few groschen around." They all look at each other and shrug.

"The purgation is for the day after tomorrow! A real rush job. The good news is that they don't want the names of the sponsors beforehand. No background checks," adds Basil.

❧

June 5, 1556 (Friday)

Harry and his sponsors stand before Cardinal Gerhardt in a side chapel. Father Dietrich stands discretely behind the cardinal. Father von Clausen is appalled at some of the ragtag characters representing Harry and unchallenged by Gerhardt. The cardinal simply has them sign or mark preprinted forms stating that they are practicing Catholics and well acquainted with Harry. Bear, Fritz and a waiter from the Boar's Head are the only church goers known to them. Katarina and Basil, at least, are more than presentable. The rest look like beggars polished up for the occasion. *If they only knew*, thinks Harry.

Franz acts as Notary and reads Harry's crime. Then, looking directly at Harry, says "Behold! According to that which has been read, you are Strongly Suspected of Heresy by us; wherefore it behooves you to purge yourself and abjure the aforesaid heresy." The Book of Gospels is placed before him upon which he places his left hand. He takes in his right hand the abjuration and proceeds to read it:

> "I, Harry Schmidt, of the Town of Innsbruck and in
> the Diocese of Innsbruck, standing my trial in per-

son in presence of you reverend Lord the Cardinal of Innsbruck and the Judge of the territory subject to the rule of Emperor Charles V, upon the four Holy Gospels set before me and touched by my hand, I swear that I believe in my heart and profess with my lips that Holy Catholic and Apostolic Faith which the Holy Roman Church teaches, professes, preaches, and holds. Also, I swear that I believe in my heart and profess with my lips that God permits witchcraft to affect the generative powers more than any other human function because of the shamefulness of the act. And so it is that we inherit the original sin of our first parents by means of that act.

"I swear that I believe that not only will simple heretics and those schismatic be tortured in fire everlasting, but that those above all will be so punished who are infected with the heresy of witches, who deny before the devil that faith which they received in Holy Baptism at the font, and practice demoniac lewdness for the fulfillment of their evil desires, inflicting all sorts of injuries upon men and animals and the fruits of the earth. And consequently I abjure, renounce, and revoke that heresy, or rather infidelity, which falsely and mendaciously maintains that there are no witches in the world, and that no one ought to believe that those injuries can be caused with the help of devils; for such infidelity is, as I now recognize, expressly contrary to the decision of Our Holy Mother the Church and of all the Catholic Doctors, as also against the Imperial laws which have decreed that witches are to be burned.

"Also, I swear that I have never persistently believed in the aforesaid heresy, neither do I believe nor adhere to it at the present, nor have I taught it, nor intend to teach it, nor shall teach it. Also I swear and promise that I will never do or cause to be done the denial of witches or witchcraft and the illusions of the devil of which you hold me strongly suspected as a heretic. And hereafter, which God forbid, I should do any of the aforesaid, I am ready to undergo the punishment provided by law for backsliders; and I am ready to submit myself to any penance which you decide to impose upon me for those deeds and words of mine for which you hold me strongly suspected of the said heresy. And I swear and promise that I will perform it to the best of my strength, and will omit no part of it, so God and this Holy Gospel help me."

Franz tells Harry to step to the side and the sponsors to form a straight line. He then walks to the first in line and stands before him. Cardinal Gerhardt breaks the silence. "Each sponsor in turn will place his hand on the Book of Gospels and shall utter these words, '*I swear upon this Holy Gospel of God that I believe Harry Schmidt to have sworn the truth.*' "

Franz moves from sponsor to sponsor with the book and occasionally has to prompt someone as to the proper phraseology. Dietrich is impassive but Franz can't resist an occasional shaking of his head in disgust. Franz then announces that the abjuration is complete and the sentence will now be pronounced by His Eminence

Cardinal Wolfgang Gerhardt. A somber hush pervades the chamber. Harry stiffens, not sure what to expect.

"We, Wolfgang Gerhardt, Cardinal of Innsbruck, and Father Hans Dietrich, Inquisitor of the sin of heresy in the domains subject to the rule of Emperor Charles V, and especially deputed by the Holy Apostolic See, are of the mind that you, Harry Schmidt, of the Town of Innsbruck and of the Diocese of Innsbruck, has denied the existence of witches and all their powers. But that you may be more careful in the future and not become more prone to the like practices; and that your crime not remain unpunished; and that you may be an example to other sinners; we having consulted with many eminent and learned lawyers and Masters or Doctors of the faculty of Theology; and having before our eyes only God and the truth of the Catholic and Apostolic Faith; and sitting in tribunal as Judges; we condemn, or rather impose penance in the following manner upon you, Harry Schmidt. Namely, that you shall never hereafter presume to do, say, or teach such things. And let there be set down those things of which you have abjured.

"But that you may be an example to others, that your sins may not remain unpunished, that you may become more careful in the future, we your Judges and Cardinal, on behalf of the faith, sitting in tribunal as Judges judging, order that you put on the grey-blue garment as appropriate to such crimes. Also, we sentence and condemn you to 14 days imprisonment plus 4 for public mockery, there to be punished with the bread of affliction and the water of distress; reserving to ourselves the right to mitigate, aggravate, change, or remit wholly or in part the said sentence if, when, and as often as it shall seem good to us to do so. This sentence, given the 5th day of June in the Year of Our Lord, 1556."

Father Dietrich quietly beckons two guards. After a few brief words they take hold of Harry's arms and proceed to lead him to the dungeon. The sponsors are dismissed.

❧

The Angelus rings from St. James' tower announcing the approaching nightfall. A handclap of rain says hello and just as quickly goodbye. An unescorted river mist sneaks from the banks of the Inn into the street below the tavern. I am upset when Fritz tells me what had happened. Since Harry had insisted upon leaving me and my father out of the loop, all felt that they had to respect his wishes. At least things went relatively well.

If Fritz shocked me, I shocked him. "You're not going to believe this, Fritz, but I have it on good authority, Johann, that our cardinal has engaged himself in yet another liaison."

"Really! A new love?"

"Love appears to be the right word. I'm told that he was quite smitten. Happened on a visit to Rome a year or so ago. Thought he would never see her again. Apparently a few days ago he ensconced her at the Visintainer chalet; you know, on the periphery of Zirl. At least this is what Johann surmised.

"Last I heard the Visintainers went to Salzburg and wouldn't be back for months."

"They did. So the cardinal leaves the rectory the other day saying he is meeting an old acquaintance in Zirl but doesn't say when he would be back, which is unusual. Also, he had made recent inquiries about the Visintainer place for some unknown reason. Johann and I are old friends of the family and were asked to check on the place from time to time. Johann decided to kill two birds with one stone, satisfying his curiosity being one of them."

"Voila, he finds the cardinal and his paramour at the chalet."

"Ja, but they didn't see him."

"How did he know about their encounter in Rome?"

"Some unusually frank comments Gerhardt made after that trip. He had mentioned this raven haired beauty that was the temptation of all temptations, his very words. It seems that his attendants had become rude to her attendants as they were all going about their duties and this woman chastised them in no uncertain terms. She was so spirited and beautiful, he said, he was taken by her on the spot. They were staying in adjoining residences and exchanged pleasantries from time to time. At the end of his stay he gave her a large emerald brooch as an apology. She was enthralled to say the least so he invited her to visit Innsbruck as his guest. Apparently circumstances were not right for that at the time."

"And now she is at the Visintainer chalet and wearing the brooch," Fritz proffers.

"But apparently the honeymoon didn't last long. Johann was looking through the window. It seems they just finished eating and were chatting. The cardinal abruptly gets up shouting and paces about. At one point he tears the brooch off her bodice and puts it in his pocket. Then she hands him a letter. Johann felt one or the other might burst out the door at any moment so he left."

"I wasn't aware the cardinal even knew the Visintainers."

"Gerhardt visited their chalet with Johann on a couple of occasions; Herr Visintainer is a generous benefactor of the Church. He hides a backup key to the place outside and both know of it. "

"And this is going on under the nose of the inquisitor," says Fritz in amazement.

"Hold on! Johann's walking in."

"The cardinal has been taken extremely ill," Fritz and I stare at him in surprise.

CHAPTER 19

THE TRIAL RESUMES

June 8, 1556 (Monday)

"*Wizards thou shalt not suffer to live*," Dolph Zimmerman proclaims to the bench. He then turns and faces the courtroom spectators. "That is what the Old Testament tells us; Exodus 22:18. I have been directed by the Court not to further address such things as the inspirational or non-inspirational nature of this or other biblical statements. So, I will not." Dietrich raises an eyebrow at the remark. Dolph continues.

"Peter Lombard was a twelfth century scholastic theologian, Bishop of Paris, and author of the *Four Books of Sentences*, which became the standard textbook of theology at medieval universities. The renowned thirteenth century Dominican theologian, Thomas Aquinas, in his *Commentary on the Sentences of Peter Lombard*, refutes those who say that witchcraft exists only in the imaginations of men. He refutes those who say that there are natural causes for the things attributed to witches, causes which we just do not understand. Thomas says that such thinking is contrary to the teachings of the Church." Dolph looks at Dietrich. "The living, teaching authority of the Church, I presume?" Dietrich nods approvingly. "Thomas says that demons have power over the minds and bodies of us all, when God so permits. In his *Summa Theologica*, he states that witches are the beneficiaries of this power via implicit or explicit pacts with the demons. Also, when a soul is ardently moved to wickedness, as happens with little old women, the countenance becomes venomous and hurtful to children." Dolph looks to Dietrich again, leaving the impression that he now seeks his endorsement.

"Historically speaking," Dietrich feels compelled to add, "It is impossible to deny the existence and power of evil spirits and still follow the teachings of the Church."

"Yet Albertus Magnus, the Dominican philosopher and teacher of Thomas, known as Dr. Universalis because of his wide-ranging knowledge of science and philosophy, said and I quote… '*the prudent scholastic inclines generally to the opinion that magic frequently rests upon deception, that the people are lead entirely by their imperfect mental culture into the association of magic deeds with later occurrences.*' "

"Albertus did not deny the existence of witchcraft," says Dietrich.

"He wouldn't contradict Church policy as prudent clergy are wont to do," responds Dolph, "but he also cautioned against rash conclusions. What is real and what is deception? Wilma Colmarz is accused of causing the great storm some months ago. Did she really or have people just drawn false conclusions? She is accused of flying through the air, transvection. Albertus did not believe in the reality of witch rides. Did she really fly through the air? These are the issues that must be resolved."

"Let's stick to the issues then, Herr Zimmerman."

"Well, Your Reverence, *Questio lamiarum*, written in 1505 by the Franciscan Samuel de Cassinis of Milan, asserts that the devil lacks the power to carry people from place to place. Samuel argues that to perform such an act would require a miracle, that God alone works miracles, that if the devil could so transport persons to sabbats, it could be done only by the permission of God, Who in such a case would appear to favor sin since sabbats are sinful. Here we have an ecclesiastical writer in this century saying that transvection does not exist. Yet this court is accusing Wilma Colmarz of just that. I ask that this charge be stricken from these proceedings," says Dolph.

"The weight of evidence is against this writer. Arnaldus Albertini, inquisitor in Valencia and Sicily, later Bishop of Patti, set down about fifteen years ago a conclusive rebuttal to this argument. Arnaldus insisted that transvection cannot be denied because Christ himself was carried by the devil to the pinnacle of the temple." He leans forward with the delicious smile of one who just declared checkmate, "What say you to that, Herr Zimmerman?" But Dolph anticipated the response.

"Not so conclusive, Your Reverence. You speak of the temptation of Jesus as found in the gospels. It is remarkable to me that in Mark's gospel, Mark just refers to the devil tempting Jesus while He is in the wilderness; no transvection is mentioned. Matthew and Luke go into much more detail and speak of His transvection but there is diversity in their accounts. It is odd that there is no mention of this temptation in the gospel of John. There were all sorts of stories circulating in those days and it seems that anything favorable to Jesus became canon regardless of merit. One must not turn a blind eye to this."

"It matters not that all reports are complete. And it is not contradictory to say that these things occur by illusion and imagination, yet in addition occur in reality. Even the youngest among us, who have reached the age of reason and have taken instruction in the true faith, know that certain angels fell from grace. These bad angels, devils, still retain all their powers according to God's will."

"Is illusion true injury?"

"Even fantasy cannot be achieved without the assistance of the devil. And pacts between witches and devils are not made in dreams or through self-deception. And their purpose, after all, is the doing of supernatural evil."

"About thirty years ago, Paulus de Grillandus Castilioneus, Italian auditor of the criminal cases in the diocese of Arezzo, made an interesting discovery. He found that the Doctors of Laws, for the most part, maintain that witches are not carried bodily by the devil; they say that these women are deluded by the devil. On the other hand, the theologians say that they are carried through the air. Both are talking about the witches in our time. This is a significant discrepancy of fact. How can the Church today rightly prosecute it?"

"So you are saying that we can't be sure about these things and that the charges against your client should be dismissed. Is that right?"

"I am and also science; some argue that there are natural causes for disasters and sickness. If they are correct, what excuse will the Church give for this terrible legacy of torture and death? What then of the living, teaching authority of the Church?"

"Science can't contradict the faith. The successors to the Apostles are without doubt guided by the Holy Spirit."

"So the Church keeps telling us. The followers of Aristotle, the Peripatetics, even denied the existence of devils."

"Many learned men are deceived; would that there learning be good. Bartholomew de Spina, the renowned theologian and the Provincial of the Dominican Order in the Holy Land, who died only a decade ago, addressed this issue as well as anyone. He said, and I quote, '*In regard to witchcraft, its possibility or its actuality, whether it is to be regarded as heresy or not, theology alone can decide what is to be taught and what course of action is to be followed in dealing with witches.*' That says it all, Herr Zimmerman. Proceed with the facts of this case only; do you hear me?"

"Yes, many learned men are deceived," Dolph answers sarcastically. Could the Court enlighten us as to the nature of storms so we can put the alleged actions of Wilma Colmarz into perspective?"

"I will be glad to, Herr Zimmerman." He pauses to gather his thoughts... "St. Thomas Aquinas made some pertinent remarks about this in his commentary on Job. As Thomas says, winds and rain and other similar disturbances of the air can be caused by the mere movement of vapors released from the earth or the water. Yet in the matter of local motion, corporeal nature must obey spiritual nature, therefore the natural power of devils can cause these and similar disturbances."

"When and where do devils actually figure into the equation?"

"That is an interesting question. You mentioned Peter Lombard. His Four Books of Sentences have been referenced not only by Aquinas but also Bonaventure, Albertus Magnus, John Duns Scotus and others of note. According to the Doctors, in Peter Lombard's Second Book of Sentences, Distinction 6, '*bad angels or devils, as ministers of punishment to the wicked and trial to the good, their place is in the clouds of the air. If they dwelt here with us on the earth itself, they would plague us too much so God does not permit it.*'"

"So according to the Doctors of the Church, if we could transport ourselves into the clouds we would encounter devils. Thank God for sunny days. But what of their actions, Your Reverence?"

"Devils operate on the active and passive elements in the air and around the fiery sphere so as to bring down fire and lightning from heaven. And this isn't supposition on my part; so say the Doctors. All of what I say is expressed in *Malleus Maleficarum*."

"Fire and lightning come from heaven. So say the Doctors; so it must be so," Dolph says acerbically.

"The Dominican theologian John Nider, in his *Formicarius*, documented that a certain man who was taken into custody told the judge that it was easy for his kind to cause hailstorms and tempests. But they could not do all the harm they wished, however, because of the guardianship of good angels."

"What of the procedure to do harm?"

"This man would go into the fields and through incantations implore the chief of the devils to send one of his servants to do the harm that they sought. When this call was answered, he would proceed to a crossroads and sacrifice a black cock and throw it into the air for the devil to receive. The devil would then stir the air and bring about storms with thunder, lightning and hail."

"Well then, if I understand correctly, the storm that struck Innsbruck could have been caused simply by the vapors which rise from the earth and water or by the action of witches. If caused by witches, then Innsbruck was not under the protection of good angels."

"That is a fair assessment. But we know that a witch was involved because of the witnesses to the circumstances and the severity of the storm. This was a punishment from God."

"I see, natural forces only generate mild storms," Dolph stares at the ceiling in disbelief. He then turns to his client and nods to her. She nods back indicating her readiness. "Your Reverence, I call the defendant, Frau Wilma Colmarz, to testify." Dolph goes to her and accompanies her to a chair near the bench. Father von Clausen reads her the oath. She nods.

"Frau Colmarz, please state your personal status," says Dolph.

"I is a mother and the sole supporter of me two children. Me daughter is seven, me son six. I have a small place, a few livestock, which provides. I make me own clothes for me and me children."

"Frau Colmarz, testimony has been given that on the morning of September 28th of last year you flew through the air in a supernatural way to the full view of a shepherd just outside of town. Did you really do this?"

"Completely nein. He must of been tanked-up."

"Were you at this place, this hill, on the morning of September 28th?"

"Me was."

"And what were you doing?"

"Ri din me mule, ri din the ways I always does."

"If he saw you, wouldn't he see your mule?"

"Me mule is bigger than me, aint he?" making a wry face.

"Did anyone else see you?"

"Not as I knows. Out fer a brief stint, ats all."

"So why do you think the shepherd says otherwise?"

"He's a liar, nots me. Or else he bears mertal emity to me."

Dietrich interrupts. "It is too late to claim mortal enmity. You have already testified that you did not know your accuser prior to this trial."

Dolph looks at her but she gives no response. He has been reluctant to dwell on the transvection without being able to counter it but feels that he has little to lose. He has to try, at least, to shift the onus to Konig; put his testimony in doubt. "So it comes down to your word against a shepherd."

"Shepherds," admonishes Dietrich.

"We have had only one witness to testify here. The rest is hearsay."

"The Court will subpoena the other witnesses, if necessary, Herr Zimmerman," says Dietrich.

"Thank you, Your Reverence, that won't be necessary." *I'll find them on my own,* he thinks to himself. *I don't need them to testify if they are going to support their brother.* And Dolph had found no one else to come forward and testify as to Wilma's character. Wilma is someone who doesn't need anyone else and people resent her for it.

Wilma is excused from the stand and Dolph asks that she be replaced by Oskar Konig. Dietrich orders that the defendant be returned to her cell prior to Konig entering the courtroom. Wilma's haggard gaze lingers on Dolph as she is led away, her one vestige of hope.

Konig then goes on about the transvection, the stirred urine and other claims. Dolph hammers him about the distance he was from Wilma on the hill and as to how he could be sure that it was her. He is unshakable. Even Dolph has little doubt that Konig really believes what he saw. Finally, Dietrich adjourns the court. Wilma is to be *"examined"* this very afternoon; Dolph wonders if she can withstand another round of torture. The court will reconvene upon further notice, absent a confession of guilt.

☙

The shadows are disturbed and don't go unnoticed by Wilma. Just the sight of the prison guards causes her to tremble now. Heinz opens the door to her cell letting Helmut hobble into the darkness and squat next to her on the straw mat, his drooping ears and bent leg are too ostensible to be overlooked. His clothes are plain, colorless, stained and proclaim a penurious and unkempt life straining for any benefit that might be stolen. His manner is that of one with an abandoned conscience who likes to linger in forbidden places.

"Frau Wilma," Helmut speaks slowly with a slow smile, "tis time for your examination."

"Nein! Nein! I don't does these things."

"Heinz 'n me wouldn't knows. Buts it ours jobs." Helmut stands, his powerful and scarred arms hang like mooring ropes. "Come!"

Resuming their duties in the examination room, they stretch her to the verge of her arm sockets being torn free. She gasps for air only to expel it in sharp and piercing screams. Father Desmond, a shy, courteous man of conscience now damaged, turns aside and vomits.

"Ease off," says Dietrich.

Her bloodshot eyes are half shut and her body throbbing. Franz is pale and expressionless. Johann's words begin to haunt him and he begins to question himself, his Church. He hates people to dislike him. He knows that he is not loved, his feelings always withheld, a person of detachment. *Is mine a life without success?* Not as bright as he would like, he is accepted for his industry, a practical but not an endearing trait. He looks at Dietrich like a child to his father, searching for answers. A shiver runs up his spine; *will I ever know real truth?*

All remain still for two, three minutes, watching the heavy breathing from the sweat drenched and shivering form. Then they hear something, ever so softly, a murmur. Dietrich places his ear near her mouth. He stands upright and motions Franz to come near. "I'm a witch. I'm a witch," and then loses consciousness.

Wilma is given a sponge bath and her bruised and discolored body is dressed in clean, white, worsted cloth by the matrons. Her guards put a cot with a soft mattress in her cell and place her on it, covered by a coarse wool blanket; in short order a doctor arrives to tend to her. She moans and whimpers in agony perspiring profusely while snatching fleeting moments of sleep through the night.

ℝ

Four Days Later (Friday)

Late in the morning Wilma regains a semblance of consciousness and a matron spoon feeds her some warm chicken broth before she lays back once more. Later in the afternoon the inquisitor is alerted that she is awake and his retinue proceeds to her side. Helmut Keiple closes the cell door behind them but stands ready to do their bidding.

"When was it that you abjured the Faith?" Dietrich asks her softly. Wilma just stares at him. "When did you make your pack with the devil? Was it twenty years ago? Eighteen? When?"

"Eighteen," she replies. Franz takes notes. Desmond bears witness.

"At the instance of the devil you performed sacrilegious acts. You spit out the Host of the Lord. Did you not?"

"Ja."

"You ate meat on Fridays."

"Ja."

"You fasted on Sundays for the sole purpose of showing contempt for Church practices."

"Ja."

"You caused your neighbor's cows to go dry."

"Ja."

Dietrich's glance to his colleagues conveys *I told you so*. "And what of the cat, the familiar?"

"Cat... von Hoffen"s cat." Her voice trails off as she grimaces with pain. If she can cast aspersions on that family, she will.

"Katarina von Hoffen? The one who holds mortal enmity towards you?"

"Ja."

"And you flew through the air." Wilma closes her eyes. "And you flew through the air." No response. "Matron, give her some water!" Dietrich anxiously awaits as the matron tends to her, fearing that she will be unable to continue. "You flew through the air. You urinated, which combined with the vapors of the earth and other agents to bring on the storm."

"Ja."

"So you confirm the testimony of Oskar Konig,"

"Ja." Wilma lay there exhausted and burning with pain, unable to move her arms.

"Who were your associates in this?"

"That von Hoffen woman."

"One thing more. For all of those eighteen years, you performed coitus with an incubus devil did you not?"

"Ja." Wilma falls unconscious. They retreat to the cell door and Helmut pushes it open with misplaced ceremony.

"Arrange to have this von Hoffen woman taken into custody. There are issues here and mortal enmity or not, I want her examined," Dietrich tells Franz. "But I want her someplace else. I want to eliminate any chance of them communicating with each other. Any suggestions?"

"My family's castle is close to here. It has a dungeon," replies Franz.

"Let's use it."

☙

June 13, 1556 (Saturday)

Toki has a lot of mouths to feed all at once this morning; usually breakfast is a more staggered affair. Dr. de Barton had stayed the night tending to the cardinal, who is only a bit improved. Two traveling Franciscans had appeared at the door yesterday requesting lodging and were accommodated. Fathers Carberry, Dietrich, von Clausen and Desmond also descend upon the dining area about the same time. Toki introduces the visiting friars to everyone and salutations are exchanged. Each receives a cup of hot tea as soon as he is seated.

"My, what is this?' the more extroverted Franciscan asks.

"Tea, from the Orient," replies Johann. "An exotic beverage we have been privileged to obtain. The cardinal indulges us."

"My word, I've never had anything like it… quite exceptional. Praise be the Lord."

"Tell us doctor. Have you been able to nail down a diagnosis for the cardinal yet?" asks Johann.

"Yes, I've been anxious to tell you about that. It is my considered opinion that he has been besieged by the devil again or poisoned."

"Spoiled food?" Johann follows up, immediately discarding the first assertion.

"Not from my kitchen," says Toki frowning at de Barton. "I didn't serve the cardinal anything that I didn't serve the rest of you or myself for that matter. No one else has gotten sick."

"It is a very disturbing situation," says de Barton.

"It must be witchcraft," Franz blurts out, at the same time becoming embarrassed for thinking that the cardinal could be incapacitated by such.

"Doctor, what makes you think it may be poison?" Johann asks.

"He has experienced a fire in his mouth and throat. Takes cold drafts of water to assuage it but to no avail. He had severe abdominal pains and becomes confused. There appear to be streaks across his fingernails; much like an arsenic case I had some years back in which the perpetrator administered it sporadically in miniscule doses. Some such compounds are colorless and tasteless; he'd never detect anything unusual when ingested."

"We are on our way to Bolzano, Italy," says the talkative Franciscan. "The pope is visiting there. We will seek his intercessory prayer for the cardinal."

"That's kind of you, Father," Dietrich replies. "Franz, do you have anything to report on that von Hoffen woman?" Johann flinches at the mention of Katarina's name.

"I gave her name to the secular authorities yesterday afternoon. We might know something by today or tomorrow," his voice a motionless monotone.

"Is her first name Katarina? Does she work at the Boar's Head Inn?" Doctor de Baron asks.

"Ja, it is; she does," Franz replies.

"Why is she being sought?"

"She may be an accomplice of Frau Colmarz," answers Franz. Johann's eyes widen but he is not about to play a hand.

"It doesn't surprise me," replies de Barton. "There were some peculiar circumstances surrounding the death of Walker Hess. The two argued immediately before he was murdered."

"Maybe I should move on this right away. I'll get some deputies and seek her out myself." Franz responds as Toki puts serving dishes of food on the table.

"Well certainly wait until after breakfast," says Dietrich. "Another half hour won't make any difference." Toki pours him and the others more tea before leaving with a tray for Cardinal Gerhardt.

Impy comes into the kitchen, puts his two front legs up on Johann and starts to whimper. "Some of these men might not get their fill, Impy. And with age-diminished eyesight they might have trouble telling a dachshund from a sausage. I better get you out of here." They all laugh. Johann raises an acknowledging hand to the Franciscans as he and his dog leave. The two make directly for the Boar's Head to warn her.

As they finish breakfast, Dietrich tells de Barton that he would like to accompany him part way on his walk back to his office. The doctor calls up to Toki that he will return before noon. The others disburse at the same time.

Toki returns to the kitchen and is just finishing the dishes when she hears a knock at the rear kitchen door. An elderly, nicely dressed woman presents herself. "Good morning, my dear, my name is Gretchen, I heard that the cardinal has taken ill; I have some experience in the medical arts and would like to help."

"Who are you?"

"One who could very well relieve the cardinal's suffering."

"The cardinal already has a doctor."

"Doctors have their place but also have their prejudices. I often succeed where doctors fail."

"Does the cardinal know you?" A shout is heard from upstairs; it's the cardinal calling for her.

"I'm sorry, the cardinal is very sick and he is not seeing anyone. Thank you for your concern."

"Tell the cardinal that I am a friend of his recent acquaintance and she feels that I can be of help. I will wait outside here."

"No, come inside and wait here."

Clearly in great discomfort, the cardinal is writhing in his bed. "I need something more to drink, Toki," he struggles to talk. "The thirst."

On the night table is a wet cloth in a bowl so she wipes his forehead with it. "Yes, I'll get you something right away. But you have a visitor."

"No visitors!"

"It's an elderly woman. Says she is a friend of a recent woman acquaintance of yours. Pretty confident that she can cure you."

"What acquaintance?"

"She didn't elaborate. She is waiting in the kitchen now."

Things are starting to add up to Gerhardt. "Alright. Something to drink. Bring her."

"I brought some carrot juice, just for the cardinal mind you. Carrot juice with a medicinal tonic," says the woman.

"You read minds, this will do nicely," says Toki, pouring some in a glass. "He will see you now."

The woman is lively for her age and quickly mounts the stairs. Gerhardt is on his side and remains so as she takes a chair beside his bed. She watches as Toki gets him propped up a bit and he sips the carrot juice.

"I'm told you can help me," he wheezes.

"I come from Zirl." This confirms what Gerhardt suspected. "It's apparent that your illness has been caused by a spell of witchcraft."

"Witchcraft, you say." Gerhardt knows immediately that his former "*love*" is still pursuing her extortion plot. She had seen him leaving the scene of the murder of a high government official's daughter, who had been introduced to him during that visit to Rome. She didn't think anything of it at the time but as circumstances were made public, namely that the victim was raped, and now another assault on a woman; she became suspicious. Looking further into his background, she discovered that a woman was mysteriously killed in his chancery decades earlier. Connecting the dots as to the possibility, it was worth a try. When she accused him of the Rome murder, along with other fabricated "*facts*", he became shaken and then menacing. At that juncture, she showed him a letter. "What can you do to cure me?"

"You must make amends and a public appeal to the evil spirits requesting that the witch who brought this on you be countered so that your illness will be transferred to her. In so doing, of course, it will be a mortal blow to her. Of course, any reasonable compensation for my services will be appreciated," giving him a knowing glance.

Gerhardt tries to sort things out in his muddled mind. *The wine we had. She poisoned my drink knowing all along that I would resist her demands. Money is what she wants and she is turning the screws but this public appeal is just adding insult to injury.*

"I am too ill to think," he rolls on his side. "Tell Toki where you can be reached. We'll be in touch."

Toki leads her down the stairs. "Witchcraft is a terrible thing. I do wish the cardinal well," the woman says. "I'll stay in touch with you." Toki walks her to the door then returns to the cardinal's room.

"Get me pen and paper, Toki," he cries out in pain. "You said the two Franciscans are to meet with the pope in Bolzano?" *I can at least mitigate this secondary compromise;* he feebly contemplates.

"Ja."

"Bolzano isn't that far."

"They came on horseback."

"Tell them that I have a letter for the Holy Father and they should leave for Bolzano right away." He groans again. "I will give them some coin to ease their journey. And more for a messenger to make a speedy return. Providing I live that long."

ℝ

Dolph Zimmerman has spent the morning seeking out Oskar Konig's two brothers but to no avail. To his chagrin, they had gone to visit friends somewhere in the Wattal Valley near Stennech. They are not expected to return until Sunday afternoon or evening. Dolph leaves a message that it is urgent that they contact him immediately upon returning.

Johann is having little success finding Katarina. He finds Fritz and alerts him as to Wilma's confession and her implication of Katarina. Fritz tells him that she went out earlier and didn't plan to be back for another couple of hours. He thinks that she might be with me at my place so Johann heads out my way.

As circumstances would have it, Franz and a couple of deputies turn onto Herzog Friedrich Strasse at the same time as Katarina, only from different directions. Katarina is walking alone.

"Father von Clausen! Katarina von Hoffen, I was at the canonical purgation the other day you may recall. We actually met many years ago."

"Ja. You are now employed at the Boar's Head Inn?"

"Why, Ja."

"I must ask you to come with us."

☙

At Zirl, Gerhardt"s former heartthrob is pacing the floor anxiously when her accomplice walks in. "How did it go?"

"Said he'll get back to me. The felon drank another taint of arsenic, so far so good."

CHAPTER 20

THE AUTO-DA-FE
(The Act of Faith)

June 18, 1556 (Thursday)

A wooden platform has been constructed which extends out from the top step of St. James. Along the front of the platform, parsimonious steps traverse to the courtyard itself, which is surrounded by the buildings and opens only to the west side. A podium is on the platform's forward edge, dwarfed by the imposing cathedral doors to the rear. High backed chairs upholstered in red velvet are on each side of it and slightly behind, grand chairs proclaiming the status of the personages who are about to occupy them. To the right and left of them are smaller, unadorned chairs for those of lesser status. The air is warmer, the damp has vanished, and a lenient wind teases the river surface into the syncopated movements of a lonely composition. There is an unexplained aroma of juniper berries.

Sheriff Mitlstrasser's men are positioned all about the courtyard and into the adjoining square; placed there well before the crowd had started to gather. He knew that there would be a huge turnout, after all, the auto-da-fe had been announced at every Mass throughout the diocese with customary indulgences promised to those faithful in attendance.

Dolph had desperately tried to see Father Dietrich yesterday afternoon but was repeatedly told that the inquisitor was not available. Today, in the sixth rank from the foot of the steps, he waits beside the three Konig brothers for the spectacle to begin. I was no more fortunate in my attempts to reach Katarina. Dietrich had given strict orders that there will be no visitation rights. I demanded to see the cardinal but was told that he was so distressed that he would see no one. Johann confirmed this and vowed to keep me informed as best he could about Katarina and Harry.

Now the area resembles a holiday fair. People are sprawled on the ground as jugglers and acrobats move among them. Clowns made up as witches with exaggerated make-up and body parts move about eliciting belly laughs. Vendors of food and drink quintuple a normal days' business. Children wrestle and chase after each other watched by some barn swallows perched on a roof ridge.

Little Manfred, with a habit of looking around as if he suspects he is being followed, pushes the center doors of St. James open and then retreats to its safety. Father Desmond, a man not born to authority, emerges first and sprinkles holy water into the crowd. An acolyte carrying a crucifix on a six foot pole is next to emerge followed immediately by the unusually tidy Helmut and Heinz with Wilma literally in tow. A roar goes up from the crowd. Each twin is holding an end of the rope that had been wrapped and knotted about her chest and arms, her hands bound in front of her. With head bowed she takes one painful step after another as she is put on display a prudent distance from the front of the apron and a chant of "witch, witch, witch," goes up. Even a barking dog appears to admonish her. The bailiff of the secular court and three of his attendants climb the steps at the right and form a semi-circle a few paces behind her, followed by the notary.

Father Desmond now sprinkles holy water on the condemned and her cortege. He then moves to his left and sprinkles the other dignitaries as they proceed in file to their appointed places. Father von Clausen stands in front of the chair on the far left. Schultheiss Hoeteling, the town supervisor, stands before the large velvet covered chair next to Franz. Father Dietrich, the last in the procession, stands before the remaining upholstered chair with Father Desmond assigned to the more humble seat next to him. Parents gather in their children and admonish them to be quiet and the barn swallows take their leave. The entertainers and vendors cease their activities and stand or sit among the others as space permits. Dietrich motions to his associates to sit then moves to the podium. He waits for the crowd noise to subside.

"Our good cardinal, His Eminence Wolfgang Gerhardt, is gravely ill." A murmur rumbles across the plaza. "Cardinal Gerhardt told me to personally convey to you that he is here in spirit." He pauses for effect. "However, once again, because he is such a champion of the Lord, he has been made a target of evil doers." More rumblings from the crowd. "A witch has been avowed as responsible for his infirmity. We find this to be incredible but, the fact is, a cure was being withheld until the Colmarz witch was persuaded to intercede. This she has done, may God rest her soul. The cardinal is being closely monitored now by his physician." Dietrich raises his hands and beseechingly says, "May the Lord be with Cardinal Gerhardt. Let us pray." Dietrich leads the crowd in the Lord's Prayer before resuming.

"We are in the presence of a confessed witch but do not fear, we are protected by the cross of Christ and the holy water of the Church." Another pause. "Let this confession of Wilma Colmarz, heard in her own words by the three priests on this very dais serve to discredit all those who deny the existence of transvections or who say that transvections only exist as mere phantasms. Let her confession of being the instrument of..."

"Nein!" a voice calls from the crowd. "Nein! Nein! Nein!" People look about for the source. "There was no transvection," Dolph shouts as he stands to challenge the inquisitor. Those on the dais shift in their seats as Dietrich stares in disbelief into the eyes of his courtroom adversary. "Herr Konig here recants his testimony. The accused was riding her mule, standing on her mule. His view was largely obstructed by the contour of the hill itself."

"Silence! You make a mockery of all that is holy, sir." Dietrich roars. "This man, for those of you who do not know, defended the witch at her trial, in the process heaping one heresy upon another." He turns again to address Dolph. "The trial is over and the accused has confessed under duress and then absent duress. The trial is over, do you understand? No more chicanery."

"I understand injustice when I see it," Dolph blares.

"Seize that defender of heresy!" Dietrich shouts back, his finger thrust at him like a dagger. Any tolerance of Dolph has long since dissipated. "You will rot in hell before you will ever again slander the Holy Church. Schultheiss, please have your deputies seize him!"

"Don't listen to me!" Dolph exhorts. "Hear the brothers of the witness." It is now Dolph's turn to point. "They have seen her do this before."

The deputies are already upon Dolph and someone who attended the trial shouts, "He dared to deny the truth of the Holy Bible; he's a heretic. Arrest him!" The bloodthirsty element roars in support, not wishing to be denied the spectacle of a witch being dragged about and vilified. The Schultheiss waves his arm to have Dolph taken away. Dietrich nods in approval as the deputies move with dispatch. His gaze shifts to the Konig brothers, who become gripped with fear. I can see

Oskar's right hand shake uncontrollably. They need no further prompting and cautiously scamper to the perimeter and vacate the area.

The tragedy of it all is that Oskar's brothers didn't know until yesterday that he was the linchpin to her trial. It was all a joke to them, Oskar thinking that Wilma flew through the air. She would stand on the back of her mule with hands outstretched as it walked along the dirt path running behind the hill and near its crest. For thirty yards or so all you could see was Wilma from the chest up before she disappeared altogether. Oskar's preconceived notions completed the picture.

Dietrich holds his arms up to the crowd and motions with his hands to those who had stood for a better view to retake their seats. Hoeteling retakes his. Wilma, still in great pain, lowers her head again as another wisp of hope fades into the vortex that has engulfed her.

Dietrich looks at Wilma. "An equestrian acrobat?" he waves his hand in dismissal. Many in the crowd roar with laughter. "Lawyers! Lawyers are artists of deception and contentiousness. Lawyers don't belong in an ecclesiastical courtroom and they will no longer be allowed in mine, except to be prosecuted."

"Lock him up!" someone yells. The mob element, its baseness aroused, repeats the admonition. "Lock him up! Lock him up! Lock him up!"

Seizing the moment, Dietrich calls the notary to the podium. "My good people, the notary will now read the sentence." Dietrich takes his seat.

"We, Wolfgang Gerhardt, by the mercy of God, Cardinal of Innsbruck, and Judge Hans Dietrich, in the territories of Holy Roman Emperor, seeing that we are legitimately informed that you, Wilma Colmarz, of the town of Innsbruck and in the diocese of Innsbruck, have been

*before us accused of the heresy of witchcraft, of which you
were lawfully convicted by your own confession and by
witnesses, we therefore proceed as we are bidden by the
canonical institutions.*

*"And since we wished to conclude this case without any
doubt, we convened in solemn council learned men of the
theological faculty and men skilled in the canon and the
civil law. We now judge that you are a heretical witch
according to the canonical institutions. We, the said cardinal and judges, sitting in tribunal as judges judging,
having before us the Holy Gospels that our judgment may
proceed as from the countenance of God and our eyes see
with equity, and having before our eyes only God and the
irrefragable truth of the Holy Faith and the extirpation
of the plague of heresy; against you, Wilma Colmarz, we
cast you forth from this our ecclesiastical court and leave
you to be delivered to the secular arm."*

Dietrich, Von Clausen and Desmond rise in unison, turn to the center isle and proceed in file back into the cathedral. Only after Manfred
closes the door behind them does the Schultheiss rise. Gripping both
sides of the podium, he tells the fanatical element what it wants to
hear. "Death to heretics!" They respond in kind.

"The crimes of witches are not purely ecclesiastical," Hoeteling
explains, "they are also secular because of the temporal injuries which
they commit. In my dual capacity as a provincial judge, it falls upon
me to carry out the special laws of the state for only the state has
the authority to exercise capital punishment. I will do my duty."
Hoeteling could have added that the inquisitor had also deputed his

duties to him so that he had the authority of the pope as well as that of the emperor. And Herman Hoeteling would take the method of inflicting the death penalty from the sentence of penance given to the accused. All this is set out in the canons on the abolition of heresy.

"I hereby sentence you, Wilma Colmarz, to be taken at two hours before noon on the morrow, June 19th, in the year of our Lord, 1556, to be burned until you are dead. May God rest your soul." Helmut and Heinz hand her to the secular officials and she is taken away to random cheers.

҂Ѻ

The auto-da-fe is hardly over when Gerhardt asks Toki to bring that woman to him as soon as she reappears. She arrives on cue with more carrot juice.

"Come in Gretchen," says Toki.

"Danke schon, I pray His Eminence is feeling better." She puts the juice on the counter.

"He a bit improved but certainly not better. I'll take you to him."

"Ja, indeed."

"Toki," the cardinal says, "give her that purse and then excuse us, please," his hand flails in the direction of the nightstand. Toki reaches for it then hands it to Gretchen before returning to the kitchen. "That is the brooch and also, well you can see, a substantial financial draft;" he rolls his head on the pillow. She looks in the purse then puts it in her bag. "The call for the assistance of a witch has been publicly stated." He gasps. "Now... if I am not cured, I will arrange for my henchman to hound you and your employer until you are no more." Gerhardt is desperate to rid himself of the pain. Only he and his inner circle know that he has received written dispensation from the pope allowing him to use a spell of witchcraft to counter a spell of witchcraft. *It's nice to have powerful friends in high places*, he thinks to himself. "Now, what can you tell me?"

"You will receive a notification shortly, assuming this is acceptable. One other thing, if we are pursued, letters will be released to certain adversarial parties. You were shown a copy at the Visintainer place."

"Get out of here! Get out! His voice trails off as his energy abandons him.

Gretchen re-enters the kitchen, "I'll be going now."

Toki turns from the pantry and says, "Have a good day!" to the closing door. *Now where did the carrot juice get to?*

The cardinal will receive a letter three days later advising him to drink lots of water, eat egg whites and avail himself of laxatives. Just as Dr. de Barton prescribed.

❧

The inquisition gains momentum following Wilma's execution with more arrests as the days pass. True to his word, Dietrich allows no advocates in his courtroom rendering the accused completely defenseless, as if it mattered. Helmut and Heinz trade secret court details to prisoners and their relatives for bribes and favors. Such details, when revealed to the accused, can make them unwittingly more vulnerable because they are not expected to know them unless they are guilty. But I get ahead of myself.

The peculiar circumstances surrounding the murder of Walker Hess had become the central point of Katarina's General Examination. First there was her threat to kill Hess. Then there was that cook at the Boar's Head Inn who saw her stab the molten image. And then there was the testimony of Doctor de Barton.

"Tell us Doctor," Dietrich had asked him, "why do you say that the arrival of the accused at the scene of the murder caused you alarm?"

"Well, Your Reverence, a wound is influenced by the mind of the murderer. An inescapable atmosphere of the murderer's hatred and violence permeates the wound so that, when the murderer draws near, the blood wells up and gushes from the corpse. This is a well-established medical fact set down by the Dominican friar Vincent de Beauvais in his *Speculum Naturale* three centuries ago."

"I know of this medical phenomenon, Doctor. Some say it originated as a curse upon Cain, the first murderer. The gushing forth is the voice of the blood crying from the earth against the murderer who is present."

"I had just finished examining the victim, Mr. Hess, and determined that he was dead. That is when the von Hoffen woman ventured on the murder scene. I noticed her and then, when I looked back at the victim, there was a new pool of blood."

"I see," replied Dietrich.

℘

June 20, 1556 (Saturday afternoon)

Frau Keller hadn't stayed on the premises for many years but she did continue to render services for the von Clausens. She is in the atrium when Franz arrives with Fathers Dietrich and Desmond.

"Franz, my darling. Give me a big hug and a kiss!" A broad smile spreads across his face as he complies.

"This is my second mother," he warmly announces to his associates. "In truth, I saw more of her than my real mother, who was preoccupied helping my father manage the estate."

"Managing an estate is a demanding job. Your mother needed all the help she could get. I was delighted to help and I am blessed. Give me another hug!" Franz gladly obliges.

"This wonderful woman spoiled me rotten. You should taste her pastry. If I had stayed here instead of going into the seminary, I would weigh three hundred pounds."

"Well, if I knew you were coming, I would have put the kitchen to better use. But you should be ashamed of yourself, not coming home more often. I'm here more than you are. This is not going to be just a hello and goodbye is it?"

"Well, to be frank, we are here on Church business."

"Church business?"

"It has to do with the inquisition. Some of the accused are being housed in our dungeon."

"I know. I know. Oh Franz, these things are so upsetting to me."

"It troubles us, my good woman," says Dietrich, "but it is our duty."

She gives him a stern look. "Well, be off then. Franz, give me another hug!"

☙

"Experience has shown us that the more they are conjured, the less they are able to weep. They will take on a tearful mien, even smear spittle upon their cheeks to give the appearance of crying, but they do not genuinely weep." Dietrich explains the tear test to Bernd and Franz as the latter leads the way to the dungeon.

"Why is this so," asks Father Desmond.

"Tears are a gift from God to the penitent."

"Saint Bernard spoke of this," adds Franz. "He said that the tears of the humble can penetrate to heaven; they can conquer the unconquerable. So by their very nature they are displeasing to the devil and the devil does all in his power to prevent witches from realizing penitence."

"Witches never weep?" asks Desmond.

"They do weep false tears," replies Dietrich.

"False tears?"

"When the judge absents himself from her presence and when she is removed from torture, they have been known to weep," answers Dietrich never bothering to turn his head or avert his hollow eyes, his hands clasped behind his back in a tutorial affectation. A confused and bewildered Father Desmond follows them down the soiled, stone staircase into the dingy, friendless gloom, questioning his own motives.

A guard leaps from his chair as they approach and brief words are exchanged. Lifting a torch from its sconce, he leads them the few steps to Katarina's cell. The neglected lock of the black iron door screeches as the key turns and Katarina stiffens at the sound. The incongruity of it all nags Father Desmond but his thoughts are preempted as Dietrich walks slowly to Katarina and stands before her for an unspoken moment; puzzled, she stares back. She has a sensuality which transcends even these circumstances. And then, "Prepare yourself for examination under duress and confession of your sins."

"I have done nothing! What is wrong with you people?" She is pale and forlorn but nonetheless steadfast.

"Torture will elicit the truth," Dietrich replies in a cold monotone. Katarina gasps.

"Father Franz, don't you recall our teenage years? Remember us being together on the day that Albert Freihofer was killed. You know that I'm not a witch." Dizziness now embraces her as the gravity of her predicament is solidified; her mind is grasping at old memories as she tries to find a path out of this nightmare. Ushered into the world with broken beginnings, even a father is absent from her recollections. She looks at Franz but no one is there, his eyes, his self, are not to be found.

Dietrich dramatically places his left hand on her head.

> *"I conjure you by the bitter tears shed on the cross by our Savior the Lord Jesus Christ for the salvation of the world, and by the burning tears poured in the evening hour over His wounds by the most glorious Virgin Mary, His Mother, and by all the tears which have been shed here in this world by the Saints and the Elect of God, from whose eyes He has now wiped away all tears, but if you be guilty that you shall by no means do so. In the name of the Father, and of the Son, and of the Holy Ghost, Amen."*

Another incongruity, thinks Desmond. *A judge is not to touch a witch, especially with his bare hands; Dietrich violates his own admonition.*

Katarina is all the more bewildered. An awkward, ponderous minute passes before Dietrich simply utters, "So you see." He turns abruptly and leads the others from the cell. She listens despondently to the dull echo of their footsteps as they ascend from the desolate chamber. Being alone and unable to reach out is its own adversity.

Dietrich continues, "I want to try a new tactic with this one. As much as possible, I want her cell to be appointed well and with a comfortable bed. She is to be treated with courtesy and kindness and be given good and satisfying meals. Give her anything that she asks for as long as it has been thoroughly scrutinized and can do no harm. Now, who might we send to her to gain her confidence? An honest person who is zealous for the faith."

"She probably won't trust a clergyman," says Desmond; he is met with admonishing frowns.

"I am told that Father Johann is well liked by the entire congregation; he is our man," says Dietrich. "I want you, Franz, to make the cell arrangements but get word through the jailer to the von Hoffen woman that it is Father Johann that is interceding for her."

ɞ

June 22, 1556 (Monday)

Over the weekend the cardinal had received the nefarious verification that he had been given proper treatment all along and the pain was subsiding. By Sunday evening the discomfort was negligible. As time progresses into the wee hours of Monday, he feels relief. *Apparently it's behind me*, he declares to himself and falls soundly asleep.

Quickly dressing at dawn, he proceeds to the kitchen and prepares a light and hurried breakfast. From there he goes directly to the stable and saddles his horse. *It is the usual greed of women,* he thinks to himself. *I'm and old fool. To think she cared for me. She will be long gone but I must tidy up.* He urges his horse on to Zirl.

Gerhardt ties his horse to the hitching post; he can see that the place is showing signs of neglect. The wind picks up prompting the brush to tremble. The garden patch is overgrown. Steps leading to the cellar are covered with clumped, damp leaves. He checks the stable and it is empty except for a scurrying squirrel that is oblivious to his presence.

He enters the chalet with some trepidation, the creaking door announcing his arrival. He looks about. Sheets that had covered some of the furniture are still in a pile in a corner; he replaces them. A small fashionable suitcase in a bedroom contains women's clothes. Are they her's?

Fatigue from his recent ordeal returns. He makes himself comfortable in a striped, upholstered chair that resides near the fireplace. The setting makes him contemplative and, content in his weariness, he realizes that he is not one given to solitude. *Solitude depresses me. When I close my bedroom door the loneliness is suffocating. Is it any wonder that I pursue these liaisons? Johann drowns it with drink. Franz would be content with masturbation. Desmond is probably still a virgin from that.* He listens for the slightest sound without any reason to do so. *Blackmail may flame up again. What are my options?* He dozes off. Meanwhile, the same morning…

"Father Johann," says Katarina, "I've been wanting to talk to you for so long." Her eyes begin to tear. "I understand that you are responsible for these comforts."

"Actually Father von Clausen did it as an accommodation to me, he knows we are friends. Here, Rafer said you would like this keepsake; also, he says he will do all he can for you." Katarina takes her baby blanket. "If only I was more resourceful." Puzzled, Katarina stares into his eyes. It is almost as if she has to console him. *Has he been drinking again?* He looks down. "I did not think it wise to visit you. I felt that I could be of little help to you and, frankly, I believed that I could do you some harm."

"How could you harm me?"

"There's been speculation as to how Dolph was so conversant in biblical criticism during Frau Colmarz's trial. Father Franz has all but accused me of coaching him. Which, as you know, I did. Some of the arguments that I gave Dolph, well, I argued with Franz on other occasions. I thought it possible that my own commitment to the Church was being debated."

"Why do you feel it's alright to come to me now?"

"Katarina, I am not here on my own initiative. I have been sent by the Inquisitor." Katarina recoils.

"Perhaps I bring some good news; I'm not sure myself. Father Dietrich says that he will be merciful even though he feels certain of your guilt. He cites not only your implication by Frau Colmarz in raising the storm but, more importantly, the peculiar death of Walker Hess."

"I didn't even know Frau Colmarz. I don't understand why she ever implicated me."

"She claimed that you had mortal enmity towards her. That, at least, gives a semblance of prejudice on her part against you."

"But why? I never met her."

"From what I am told, her maiden name was Dahlmatz. She is the daughter of Rebecca Dahlmatz. Well..."

"Oh my God!"

"You know the connection then."

"Of course. Her mother was accused of causing an abortion to Baroness von Hoffen. Rebecca Dahlmatz was burned as a witch many years ago, about the time I was born."

"Then you're the daughter of a nobleman no less?"

"I'm not really a von Hoffen. It's a long story. But she must have thought so. The Baron, as I later came to hear, argued with his wife to let things be; he didn't believe in witchcraft. But the baroness and her friends were convinced that Rebecca Dahlmatz caused the abortion by laying her hands on her womb. The town worked itself into a frenzy and the incident became a sensation. You must have heard of it."

"Growing up. It only came to mind recently."

"That is why she named me."

"I can argue the point for you but I'm afraid that isn't your biggest problem. The focus on you has more to do with the killing of Walker Hess."

"I know; they say that I killed him. It's crazy. Someone stuck a knife in him. I was in the tavern at the time. There are witnesses."

"They never found a knife. And one of the cooks testified... but you know all that. They're ignorant fools, Katarina, but their perception is the reality. You must now think in practical terms. You must think of your own welfare. You are in the gravest danger."

"What do you propose?"

"It is not what I propose; it is what the Inquisitor proposes. These accommodations," Johann says as he glances about the cell, "are permitted as a token of his mercy. Now comes the hard part. If you confess to witchcraft now, he promises that he will not condemn you to death but you may never be released from prison."

"Oh my God! And if I don't?"

Johann looks down at the floor. He then raises his head and says with closed eyes, "You will be tortured and burned at the stake."

"But I'm innocent! How can they do this?"

"So was Frau Colmarz. Katarina, Dolph used all my arguments and his own in court and it meant nothing. Good arguments. Sound arguments. I can't get you out of this, no one can. I'm despondent." There is a prolonged silence and she starts to shake.

"Tell them that I confess." Tears start down her cheeks.

CHAPTER 21

THE DISCOURSE

June 22, 1556 (Monday Afternoon)

"Don't tell me you started jause without me," the cardinal says with panache as he strides at a spirited pace into the rectory dining room. "Cold smoked trout, sliced wheat bread, cheeses, cakes, uhmm, looks delicious." His brethren get up from the table in unison and fuss over him. Toki had been left a note that morning and instructed to say that he is feeling better but not to be disturbed.

"I'm amazed," says Father Desmond, "we were set to give you the last rites."

"And I have been prepared to receive them. Thank you Bernd."

"This is remarkable, Your Eminence," says Father Dietrich.

"So good to have you back in good health," says Father Franz, next in the procession to pay homage.

"Gentlemen," Toki announces, "I have taken the liberty to open this beautifully painted jug of sekt. I will pour when you are seated."

The cardinal takes his usual position at the head of the table. The conversation is jovial and Gerhardt welcomes the camaraderie. It is good to be back he tells them. He is sure that Dr. de Barton will give him a clean bill of health. Each has his fill then sits back to sip another glass of sekt. The cardinal then asks to be brought up to-date on the inquisition. After a summary, Dietrich mentions that Father Johann was to talk with the von Hoffen woman today. "I was hoping that he would have reported back to me by now. Has anyone seen him?"

"Speak of the devil," says the cardinal with a snicker as Johann comes into the room carefully putting one foot before the other. They all laugh. "Johann, so good to see you."

"My! My! Your Eminence, you look terrific," his voice is slurred and edgy. "Is this a miraculous recovery or what? The Lord is with you."

"He is. He is. Grab that chair down there. Toki, put some of those goodies in front of Father Johann." He then leans over and whispers, "No one appreciates a well laid table more than our Johann."

Toki puts a large plate in front of him with a sampling of everything. She tops off everyone's glass before putting the near empty jug back on the table. Johann gulps his down. "I have an errand I must run," Toki says. "Just leave the dishes!" She knows full well that Father Franz will at least put them in the sink to soak. He hates untidiness. "Does everyone have all they need before I go?"

"They do. They do, Toki. You get on your way now; we'll be just fine," says the cardinal.

"Auf Wiedersehen to all of you. Cardinal, make sure you take a nap, you hear?"

"I hear. I hear."

"Auf Wiedersehen, Toki," the others respond.

"Thank God for Toki," says Johann almost despondently as he takes great care to empty the remaining sekt into his glass without spilling it but his unsteady hands fail him.

"Amen," the others respond.

Johann has almost finished his plate before Dietrich brings the conversation back to more serious matters; his calculating mind is restless for the news. "Johann, how did it go with that von Hoffen woman?" Sitting at the other end of the table opposite the cardinal, Johann puts his fork down and stares into his plate as if he had been stunned, his elbows firmly at his sides. His face and hands grow pale as he grapples with sequestered conflicts, a man hopelessly adrift with no island in sight.

"Johann?" the cardinal finally says, puzzled.

Sullen and dissipated, he gazes at each face for one last assessment of their characters and convictions, for anything not yet discovered. He wants to say that Katarina is innocent and argue against the notion of witchcraft in a final effort but he knows that it would be futile. He starts to say the words that he dreads but they won't come out. He tries again to no avail.

"Johann?"

"She confesses," he blurts out like a man who just coughed up a piece of meat.

Dietrich is visibly pleased. Gerhardt, still holding his glass of sekt between his long, lean fingers, is surprised and puzzled. *Confesses?* He listens with veiled trepidation to Dietrich's self-complimentary remarks. He has known Katarina only briefly and likes her, such a pretty girl with a slender back and flowing hair, her dusky eyes. *A witch?*

"Excuse me!" says Johann, getting up from the table and knocking over the empty jug. He steadies himself by grasping the edges of the table; his shoulders are hunched and his head is listing to starboard. "Suddenly I feel a little woozy." The others gesture to help. "Nein, I'm alright. I just need to step out for a breath of fresh air. Didn't sleep well the last couple of nights." He has no intention of rejoining them. For a moment they stare after him and share an uncomfortable glance. Franz, alone, has an inkling of his friend's less obvious quandary.

While stabbing a sliver of cheese with a toothpick, Dietrich breaks the momentary silence. "Women are so credulous; so easily seduced by the devil. He promises witches money but they invariably end up with dung or broken pottery and they are never satisfied with their marriages."

"It seems to me women don't know what they want," says Desmond. "Or else they want it all not realizing that to have one thing usually means giving something else up. There is always a tradeoff."

"I once considered marriage," says Franz, "but to some extent the scriptures scared me off. Matthew XIX does not instill confidence to marry. Then I read Saint John Chrysostom's comments. You may recall that he was the Archbishop of Constantinople in the late 4th century. He says that woman is a foe to friendship, an inescapable punishment, a necessary evil, a natural temptation, a desirable calamity, a domestic danger, a delectable detriment, an evil of nature painted with fair colors." Franz stops to ponder. "Oh, one other thing. If it be a sin to divorce her," he says, "then enduring the daily strife becomes a necessary torture."

"And what of Seneca, in his Tragedies," says Gerhardt, "he observed that a woman either loves or hates; there is no third grade. And the tears of a woman are a deception; they may well from true grief or they may be a snare."

"Woe to the lover who abandons her," adds Franz. "She will seethe with hate and say vile things about him."

Desmond pushes his plate forward and rests his elbows on the table. "But marriage is a sacrament. Are you saying that women are a punishment from God?" He is hopelessly dependent on others.

The cardinal gives a sober laugh. "Bernd, I bet they will be saying the same things about women hundreds of years from now. There is an *innate tension* between men and women. I'm speaking of personal relationships, not social relationships. Men and women *think* differently. They *handle* things differently. And they have *different priorities*. The problem is, each expects the other to think and act the way they do and it will never happen. They either go with the flow, that's the way he is, that's the way she is, and focus on the positives or they will keep knocking heads." He decides to change the subject. "Witches! I long for the day when they are gone from Innsbruck." He stands to leave; he has a way of shutting down conversations.

"This will never happen," replies Dietrich to the amazement of all.

"Never happen?" The cardinal raises an eyebrow.

"Not as long as any exist on the face of the earth. Not without the final solution."

"The final solution?"

"There is no remedy for their practices, unless witches be entirely eradicated by the judges, or at least punished as an example to all who may wish to imitate them. Put terror in the hearts of those who contemplate becoming witches."

"Gentlemen, I don't want to overdo it on my first day back in good health. Good day."

☙

A chill visits Innsbruck this night causing Johann's bloodshot eyes to tear but a more affable moon glistens on the fields lighting the way between unmoved clouds. Dad had retired early when Johann, visibly shaken, arrives at our chalet. His eyes are dark with dread and I've never seen him so vulnerable. He is upset with himself and disturbed at having to break the latest news about Katarina. His only consolation, he tells me, is that she is not going to be tortured or die. After putting his horse in the barn and getting settled, I put out some meat pies and wine; I initially brought out fruit juice but he wouldn't have it. He uses his bread to collect the last of the gravy. Our long conversation helps settle him down but my mind is racing.

"Although slim," he says, "at some distant time, if Katarina is repentant, the Church might relent and set her free." My look of incredulity shames him and I am embarrassed for that.

The candles burn lower. My thoughts inexplicitly turn to our youth, a place we can both understand. I ponder how necessity made him more self-reliant with the early death of his father. How I enjoyed his eccentric sense of humor. But reminiscing is a short lived luxury. For hours we discuss every aspect of Katarina's plight. I throw another log on the fire; he sits next to it across from me, filling the whole chair. The wine lets us momentarily distance ourselves from reality. Finally I give voice to what I have believed in my heart from the time that Katarina was first taken.

"Do you believe that there is such a thing as justified killing?"

"Of course, why do you ask?"

"Such as?"

"Self-defense. Defense of others in imminent harm. Repelling an invader." Johann's eyes widen. "What are you getting at?"

"What of a pre-emptive strike?"

"What?"

"I hope to put together a clandestine band of, shall we say, irregulars."

"Irregulars?"

"Force, Johann, you can't move the intractable without force. We must take things into our own hands."

"Such as?"

"Free Katarina and Dolph. Maybe even the others if we ever get public support. I don't want to be too explicit. I want you to have deniability."

"I see where you are going as to Katarina and Dolph. As to anything more, I don't sense any groundswell against the inquisition… but so much is out of kilter. It's madness."

"What do you think needs to be done?"

"Well, the Inquirer is a good start… we must educate people as to what Jesus really intended. He never appointed a pope despite all that *'upon this rock I will build my church business.'* I want to explain scripture to the faithful as it really is. Christianity is a positive way of life, not an institution to be dominated by ecclesiastical princes and a so called infallible head of state. And then there are other myths to be dealt with."

"Such as?"

"I think of the Aquinas paradox. We are told that Thomas experienced a visitation from the Blessed Virgin to assure him that his life and works were acceptable to God. A supernatural event just to say one man's life and works were acceptable. Acceptable? Then we are told, that as he struggled with an inscrutable passage in Isaias, Saints Peter and Paul then appeared to assist him with its interpretation. It is all so fanciful in the grand scheme of things.

"In Naples in 1273, months before his death, we are told that three of his brethren witnessed him being lifted in ecstasy as a voice was heard above the altar saying, *'Thou hast written well of me, Thomas; what reward wilt thou have.'* Again, this is quite incredible that God would manifest Himself to someone that just wrote well of him. And offer a reward no less. We are told that Thomas replied, *'None other than Thyself, Lord.'* Yet on December 6, 1273, he decided to give up his writing. His faithful friend and secretary, Father Reginald of Piperno, questioned him on this. Thomas replied, *'I can do no more. Such secrets have been revealed to me that all I have written now appears to be like straw.'* Secrets no less! Why secrets? Regardless, despite these alleged supernatural assurances of his great contributions to theology, Thomas himself refers to his work as of little value. More likely Thomas had an intellectual epiphany changing his metaphysical perspective. No matter how you interpret his assessment, however, it didn't interfere with his faith, which he gave testimony to on his death bed a few months later, March 7, 1274."

Johann is having a crisis of faith. I fear for his well-being. "Johann, let's get some rest. We're tired; it's not the right time for possible life changing decisions."

"And let this wine go to waste?"

"Just our glasses, the jug is empty."

∽

June 23, 1556 (Tuesday)

Both of us slept later than usual but Dad has breakfast ready for us anyway. He is going fishing and wants us to join him but I tell him that I have some business in town and will accompany Johann back to St. James'. We trot off right after we finish eating. I want to prepare another Inquirer and, if I see him, welcome Harry back now that his sentence is up. Johann tells me that Franz wanted to keep Harry incarcerated indefinitely on the pretext he was connected to Katarina; he still seethes over the confessional incident.

"Any chance Harry will be picked-up again?"

"The cardinal couldn't care less about Harry. Another thing, if you didn't already hear. Remember as kids we came across what looked like a sabbat. Well, that sort of thing is apparently still going on."

"I heard. But I'm more interested in your remark last night about Jesus not establishing St. Peter as the head of the Church. Care to elaborate on that?"

"I was reading manuscripts belonging to Dr. Gunther Eberle; does the name ring a bell?"

"Ja, his daughter Effie was murdered in the chancery… decades ago."

"When I was transferred to Innsbruck early last year, I was initially put up at the Wilten Abbey. My belongings had been sent ahead and stored in the basement. The janitor takes me to them and they are sitting next to a large crate marked '*Dr. Gunther Eberle, care of Effie Eberle*.' According to the janitor, it was discovered at the storage depot long after she was killed. Since Dr. Eberle was known to be a biblical scholar, it was given to Wilten Abbey; put in the basement and soon forgotten. Obviously no one knew their specifics. I do now. Quite revelatory."

"It touches on that quote?" I ask. "To say that Jesus did not establish Peter as the preeminent leader of the new Church strikes at the assumption of future popes inheriting such leadership."

"Ja," Johann replies but seems reluctant to elaborate. We must have ridden a furlong without another word being spoken. He is way out on an ecclesiastical limb and I don't want to be the one that shakes the tree. The inquisition and his studies are disrupting his place in the world. Does he follow Martin Luther's path? It is one thing to think opposition, another to do it.

"It is a matter of truth; isn't it?" he finally says. I sense that it is not a question directed at me. " '*And I say to thee, that thou art Peter; and upon this rock I will build my church, and the gates of hell shall not prevail against it.*' That's a direct quote from the Gospel of Matthew, 16:18. The New Testament was originally transcribed in Greek. Greek was the universal trade language of the Roman Empire. Did you know that?"

"I'm aware of that."

"But did you know that the Greek term for rock used in this text is in the feminine singular form although according to the Catholic Church it's supposed to refer to Peter, which of course would be masculine singular. We have a major grammatical discrepancy here; do we not? Just how important is this discrepancy one might ask?" Johann looks at me more to see my reaction than anything else. He continues. "Our theologians answer that Jesus would have been speaking Aramaic, not Greek; Aramaic doesn't distinguish between genders. Well, maybe he was. Then maybe he was speaking Hebrew or then again maybe Greek all along. Nobody really knows? But even if Matthew was translated from another language into Greek, the translator felt it proper to use the feminine form of rock rather than the masculine."

"Do you know of an Aramaic or Hebrew version of Matthew?" I ask, knowing full well what the response must be.

"If there was, it no longer exists."

"So you infer that the Church reads more into Jesus' words than are there?"

"I'm in good company. St. Augustine, who lived a lot closer to biblical times than we do..." he pauses. "Third, no fourth century?"

"He was born in 354 as I recall, in present day Algeria."

"You should be teaching me."

"You just raised the right question."

"Well, Augustine also understood Jesus' words much differently. Jesus had just asked his disciples, '*Whom do men say that the Son of man is?*' Some said he was John the Baptist. Others were saying that he was Elias. Still others Jeremias or one of the prophets. Then Jesus asked, '*But whom do you say that I am?*' It is here that Peter replied, '*Thou art Christ, the Son of the living God.*' And Jesus answered, '*Blessed art thou, Simon Bar-jona, because flesh and blood hath not revealed it to thee, but my Father who is in heaven.*' Jesus is saying to Peter that he was inspired to call Jesus the Son of the living God."

"Peter is making a confession of faith."

"Exactly, and according to Augustine, it is on this very confession of faith by Peter, that Christ is the Son of the living God, that Jesus is building his church. He is not building the church on Peter himself."

"Jesus was responding to Peter in kind? Peter said, '*Thou art the Christ*' and Jesus replied '*thou art Peter.*' "

"This is also the interpretation of St. John Crysostom, Augustine's contemporary.

"So much is a matter of interpretation, isn't it?" I reply.

"Of even greater significance, if you contend that Jesus was making Peter the head of his church, why isn't there more evidence of this in the New Testament? Why isn't Peter singled out as *the* leader upon the death of Jesus? Why wasn't he treated as such by the others? Why didn't the early Christian writers indicate this?"

"All evidence suggests the opposite; you are saying."

"The very next verse, Matthew 16:19, states, '*And I will give to thee the keys of the kingdom of heaven. And whatsoever thou shalt bind upon earth, it shall be bound also in heaven; and whatsoever thou shalt loose on earth, it shall be loosed also in heaven.*' This appears to give Peter the power to remit sins and is a plausible argument in favor of the special position of Peter. But in John 20:23, this power appears to be given to all the disciples, not just Peter."

"So where does that lead you?" I ask.

"It leads me back to the lack of universal recognition of Peter as preeminent leader in the Christian community... of which there were different branches. This fact seems to overshadow everything. For one thing, in the synoptic gospels, Jesus rarely referred to himself in the first person as he is doing in these two verses of Matthew. For another, it appears that Matthew is voicing his view as to the place that Peter should hold. I say this because, on such a profound issue, it is astounding that the words of Matthew 16:18 are not confirmed by the other gospels; these words that he attributes to Jesus appear to be a well-meaning construction of Matthew."

"Questionable things have a way of evolving into accepted truths. In time, these so called truths become dogma. In time, the truth of the matter is lost."

"There is no supporting evidence to conclude that he did bestow primacy on Peter."

"Did Peter choose a successor?"

"There is no evidence of it," Johann replies. "Evidence does point to him being in Rome when he was martyred."

"Ja, the years 64 or 67 are given as the most likely dates."

"That's another thing. Peter did not found the Holy See of Rome; it was already established before he arrived. Peter was an apostle and shouldn't be confused with the later church office of bishop. The authority of the Apostles of the New Testament was not defined by locality. The power of bishops, on the other hand, is confined to their place, a jurisdictional office."

"In the early centuries the word pope simply meant father," I add. "It wasn't unique to the bishop of Rome. Of course now, whoever is named bishop of Rome automatically becomes the pope as the successor to the apostle, Peter."

"From what I read about the Council of Nicea in 325 A.D.," says Johann, "the bishop of Rome, who was not personally present, was considered of no greater or no lesser status than the eastern bishops. And St. Jerome, a contemporary of Augustine and Chrysostom, all born shortly before or after 350 A.D., wrote that all bishops, wherever they may be, are of the same worth. Now some say that Jerome meant that bishops have the same worth in ordination; jurisdiction is another matter altogether. You can see how afar interpretation can go. Gregory

I, however, a bishop of Rome himself, a couple of centuries after Nicea wrote that, '*whosoever calls himself Universal Priest is in his elation the precursor of Antichrist since he proudly puts himself above all others.*' "

"Certain metropolitan sees, and consequently their bishops, gained greater influence in the universal Church. Rome came into special favor because it was the imperial city," I interject.

"Application of the New Testament texts pertinent to the authority of Peter were used to support Rome's claim to be the universal arbiter of the Church. Also, that is where he last preached and was martyred. In the first century and much of the second century, however, there is no evidence of the presence of an individual bishop in a clear leadership role. There was no bishop of Rome in the customary sense of today. The norm was a collective leadership, even in Rome. If there is an exception, it would be James' leadership of the Jewish Christian community of Jerusalem."

"James was in control in Jerusalem. Not Peter."

"And you know who succeeded him there."

"The blood relatives of Jesus," I reply. "And eventually, Gentiles took over the leadership roles. The papacy is an administrative position, an elective office. No special theological abilities are intrinsic to it."

"Over time, once again, scripture was scoured by the theologians to justify Rome's preeminence. Ensuing power enhanced its stature with the passage of time," Johann adds. "Jesus didn't explicitly establish a deacon/presbyter/bishop leadership structure. Yet the Church continues to cite the list of Irenaenas of Lyons, which is a construction of the 180's mind you, professing to a continuous succession of bishops in Rome starting with the little known Linus following the death of St. Peter. They may have been religious leaders but not what we might refer to as monarchical bishops succeeding one another. Yet some theologians, who acknowledge that the evidence demonstrates a collective leadership, say this isn't a problem because those men would be dominant persons who exercised de facto leadership even though not monarchical bishops per se. To say the least, it is quite a stretch to recognize them as the direct successors of Peter. And the rise of Roman prestige through the centuries did not mean automatic acquiescence of non-Romans to directives from Rome. That and other differences, such as the Roman Church maintaining that the Holy Spirit proceeds from the Father and Son rather than the Father alone, eventually led to the great Greek Orthodox schism."

"And there isn't the remotest chance that they will ever be unified again," I reply.

"Not unless the bishop of Rome renounces his primacy over all other bishops. This concept is so entrenched, however, it won't happen."

"Speaking of the hierarchy," I say, "I meant to tell you. I went to the Visintainer place and it's vacant again."

"Nothing is forever. I take it then that the key is still in place? The rack of antlers over the front door."

"Ya, I went in." We stop in front of the cathedral.

"Would you be so kind as to take my horse to the stable?" he asks. "I have some praying to do."

"Of course." He dismounts and we look at each other realizing the ordeals ahead. He turns and proceeds up the steps.

Succession or no succession of Peter, I had withheld a conclusion that has been with me for a long time. If the resurrection of Jesus is cited as proof of his divinity, why is the verification limited to a few of his associates whom we are told he appeared to? Why didn't Jesus subsequently walk the streets of Jerusalem? That would have gotten everyone's attention. How is it possible, if divine, that he left such an uncertain and ambiguous legacy? Judaism, Islam, Buddhism and Hinduism, to cite other major religions, don't recognize his divinity.

Then there is the virgin birth story, the creator of the universe being born of a woman no less. And a woman who later had other children. Viewed objectively, separating oneself from one's indoctrination since birth, it is overwhelmingly irrational.

CHAPTER 22

THE APOSTATE

Still Tuesday Morning (June 23, 1556)

Having just left Johann, I arrive well before the noon meal so the dining room of the Boar's Head is devoid of customers as is the tavern. No one is in the kitchen so I proceed to the cellar printing room to begin composing a future edition. I am not there long when Basil and Snuff show up via the alley entrance shaking with troubling news.

"Ulrich von Clausen, Franz's father, is on to us," blurts out Snuff.

"What?"

"Snuff labeled the most recent broadsheet cases, the ones with diagonal slats, '*Swiss Pears.*' All the other cases are labeled correctly. When Snuff makes a stop, he doesn't leave the broadsheets in the stockroom with the other delivered goods, he puts that case in the proprietor's office. Ulrich was in the wrong place at the wrong time and noticed what was going on; apparently he got suspicious. For another thing, it's too early in the season for pears," Basil adds.

"Pears keeps well wen stored n the cold. Plenty of cold n the Swiss Alps. Can keeps them all winter and spring," Snuff defends himself.

"If so, von Clausen doesn't know it. Anyway, he follows Snuff on horseback and while Snuff goes in the alley entrance to Stauffer's Bakery to announce his arrival, Ulrich starts snooping around the

wagon. He finds another '*Swiss Pear*' box, pries open the lid, and…"
Basil throws up his hands. "Son of a bitch."

"I comes out to get the deliverables," says Snuff, "and von Clausen
is grinnin ear to ear. He says something likes, we meets again Snuff,
thought I'd buy some of them pears yer selling but apparently they've
undergone a transformation. He holds up a copy. I, of course, acts
bewildered and says I didn't knows they was n there, one of our clients. He says yeah, despites yer special handlin. Then he says, come to
me castle after supper. We needs tuh talk. Don't be late. He folds the
broadsheet, mounts is horse and trots off, he does, not nother word."

Basil insists that we must shut down the operation now and dis-
mantle everything. Snuff fears for his life and wants to leave the area
immediately.

"Nothing will happen before tomorrow," I insist. "We have a
little time to think this through. We may have some leverage." They
look at me in disbelief. I remember my father telling me years ago
that Effie Eberle had once confided in him. She intimated that any
funds channeled through the von Clausen firm were subject to a re-
definition of the laws of property. She started to say something else
but they were interrupted and the conversation never resumed. Effie
was killed shortly thereafter. What I know of Ulrich von Clausen
gives me no reason to believe that what she said was without merit or
that anything has changed.

I ask Basil to post Bear near the castle as quickly as possible to
forewarn of any nefarious activity. Even though Snuff fears being ar-
rested on the spot, he eventually agrees to follow through on von
Clausen's demand.

❧

It's a mild evening as a cloud speeds past the quarter moon but a chill clings to Snuff like the dank air of an overlooked cellar. He dismounts and approaches the last few yards to the castle entrance on foot. His eyes are wide to examine every beckoning shadow; his ears alert to any misplaced sound. A watchman anticipates his arrival and escorts him through the gates only to hand him off to a servant carrying a lantern. The room he is brought to is dim, most of the light coming from a well stoked fire. When the door closes behind him, a figure rises from a high-backed corner chair placed squarely on an Oriental rug. Ulrich von Clausen, his face creased and pallid, sips from his glass of Barolo wine with a confident formality; his shifty eyes are bright with pleasure. Snuff looks at him sharply.

"It is a frightful business, wouldn't you say Snuff? The inquisition I mean." His smile is as cold as a Norwegian fiord. Snuff listens with his eyes. Ulrich shrugs his bent shoulders, waits, and pensively adds, "You can spend a lifetime making something of yourself yet it can be destroyed with one misstep. Wouldn't you agree Snuff?"

There is no closing the gap from centuries of mistrust, the class divide is too great. Still opting not to reply, Snuff steps forward and hands him an envelope; I didn't send him unarmed.

"What is this?" Ulrich holds it to the light, turning it over several times before removing the letter and moving closer to the fire to read that a yet to be named person is aware that church funds have been skimmed by his firm. Also, there are certain parties willing to testify to the inquisitor that Baron Ulrich von Clausen has participated prominently in sabbats, even with an acolyte, the recently murdered Walker Hess. Ulrich turns his head just enough to expose a malicious stare and flushed cheeks. "The line between comedy and tragedy is very thin, Snuff."

"I em willin to cross it," Snuff finally retorts as he holds a charred, wooden chalice in the air. Ulrich falls silent, herding his recollections. Finally...

"There can be no friendship without discretion, can there Snuff? My servant will see you out." Ulrich waves Snuff off with the audacity of not troubling himself to lie. As for Snuff's state of mind as he exits the castle walls, *I've lived an entire bleed'in lifetime tween midday and midnight.*

The lingering question remaining, what is the staying power of our truce? Changes must be made and deliveries would no longer be made from Basil's facility.

❧

June 24, 1556 (Wednesday)

Snuff and I join Fritz at a tavern table and I quietly touch on my intentions to help Katarina and Dolph escape but I don't elaborate. Instead I focus on the logistics of printing future editions of the Inquirer. It is late in the morning and as we are hashing this out there comes a loud commotion at the door.

"Holy horseshit," Snuff says, "it's Horseshit Harry." In he comes, leading the lot of them, heralded as if he has risen from the dead. Triumphant! Fritz and I stand to greet him and he struts over and bear hugs each one of us in turn.

"Free beer for everyone," Fritz calls out." He then disappears into the kitchen only to reappear with a cook and a barmaid, each holding an oversized brettljause. A cheer goes up. I long lost any ability to be shocked by Snuff. He proposes an outlandish toast as much to himself as to Harry.

"Always be'in intact meself, and be'in a boudoir atha'lete xtra ordinaire, with wimmen furever grateful for me services, I wish Harry similar success as he fursakes pris'un leef. Tuh Harry, may he ave his pick of all duh peckers in duh nests of Innsbruck an thot he put it tuh good use."

"Horseshit! Horseshit! Horseshit Harry!" goes the chorus in gleeful retort.

C/3

Not far away Johann is as enraged as we are exuberant. He is a wild man moving swiftly and bursting upon the von Clausen castle unannounced. A familiar face, household staff make way with courteous acceptance as he descends to its bowels. He stomps into Katarina's empty cell then a rumble of profanity proceeds him to Dolph's cell with its dark, dismal corners and the broken, hanging web of an absent spider. "Open this door!" Johann demands as he points to the lock.

"Father, what's going on?" the diminutive jailer asks apprehensively, as he trails behind having put aside a plate of food.

"Just do it!" is the only explanation he will receive; the jailer reluctant to challenge his authority.

Dolph looks into Johnan's eyes searching for a clue as to what is happening. The unspoken response is clear; *do as I say; any explanation will have to wait.*

Servants murmur to themselves as the two make their hurried exit. Riding double, the path rutted and trampled falls away sharply as they move with purpose toward town pursued by an imagined apparition; startled animals mark their progress through the untended woods.

Dropping Dolph at his home, Johann's rage undiminished, he proceeds to the chancery and dismounts, his large riding boots crushing anything underfoot. He goes from room to room and then crosses to the rectory. The door to the cardinal's private study is ajar and he spots the inquisitor there annotating some documents. He shoves the door so hard that it slaps against the interior wall causing Dietrich to bolt upright. "Word has it that Fraulein von Hoffen is on her way to the Diocese of Constance. Why? As if I don't already know," his voice laden with innuendo.

Astonished, Dietrich returns his pen to the ink holder and tries to remain nonplused. "What don't you understand?"

"You promised her mercy. Constance is known for its severity, not mercy. It's run by idiots."

"My dear Johann, I said I would be merciful; I did not say to whom." He reaches for his pen once again implying his retort settled the issue.

"We were speaking of Fraulein von Hoffen, not of '*to whom.*' "

"You understood me to say that I would be merciful to a witch when the Bible calls for their extermination?" The pen is shoved back into the holder. "Why the Church is bound by divine command-ment to their eradication. Merciful to a witch! Never! Merciful to the people, to the state, ja." He stands in defiance with a face of unre-strained contempt.

"You lying fraud," Johann shouts as he throws her baby blanket in Dietrich's face.

"Mind your actions, Father!" casting it aside, both voices now much louder and oblivious to the approaching footsteps.

"You led me to believe that you would spare her life. Don't deny it!"

"But it is no longer in my hands; is it? Her sentence shall be passed by another judge in Constance."

Johann leans forward and grasps Dietrich by his cassock. There is a terrible clatter as he pulls him across the desk and onto the floor.

"You scum," Johann shouts as he smashes his fist into Dietrich's face. Dietrich, strong and fit himself, pulls Johann to him. They roll back and forth knocking into chairs and tables causing candlesticks and crystal to fall on top of them. Both manage to get to their feet wrestling with each other to gain the upper hand, the stems of crystal glasses snapping under them.

The commotion can now be heard all over the rectory. The cardinal and Franz hastily enter upon the scene to witness Johann driving the inquisitor into the bookcase like a bull elephant pinning an encroacher against a tree; volumes tumble from the shelves adding to the chaos. Johann's fury still rages as Dietrich tries to push him away but to no avail. Dietrich trips trying to avoid his blows so Johann kicks him, at the same time profaning his character and integrity. Gerhardt grabs Johann's shoulder only to be rewarded by Johann whirling around and smashing his fist into the cardinal's jaw, knocking him halfway across the room. Franz stares in disbelief. "You fake," Johann shouts at the cardinal after realizing who he hit. "You womanizing fake, if anyone should burn in hell it's you."

Dietrich, blood trickling from his nose and mouth, face discolored, picks-up a walking stick and smashes it into the back of Johann's neck. Toki arrives to see him stumble forward into a small table, spin as if attempting a pirouette, and stare with vacant eyes before he falls gracelessly on top of it with a thud and slides to the floor. As the cardinal struggles to his feet, Toki's hands move to either side of her face and her eyes wide in disbelief. *This happens in taverns,* she thinks, *not in rectories.*

ℭ

The cell is the one that Wilma had occupied. Helmut and Heinz Keiple take a perverse delight in having a priest as their ward. They treat him deferentially, however, unsure yet of his long term status. Late in the afternoon his first visitor arrives; it is Franz. He brings a couple of wooden chairs into the cell. Johann ignores him at first, sitting on the floor mat and staring at a wall. Franz stands behind one of the chairs, his hands resting on the back of it. "Johann, take the chair... we need to talk."

Johann cups his face in his hands. "My expectations were so different when I entered the seminary. What kind of a world is this? Heartbreak has replaced my hopes." Franz walks behind him, reaches down and tugs him to his feet. His hand guides him to a chair like a caring physician tending to an elderly, failing patient. He takes the other chair and waits for Johann to continue. "I'm not sure I want to remain a part of the Catholic Church, Franz," he says painfully. "Not after witnessing what it does to people. Not after associating with the people who run it." Franz doesn't respond. "You just don't understand where I'm coming from; do you?" Franz leans forward in his chair and places his elbows on his knees. He clasps his hands together and rests his forehead on them. It is his turn to stare at the floor, unwilling to condemn or condone, if only things were as it was half a lifetime ago.

"Johann, I know that you've been greatly troubled," he says without looking up. "But I never thought it would come to this." There is anxiety in his voice.

"Don't you concern yourself! This is all my doing. You best disassociate yourself from me." The gloom clings to the soiled stone walls like a newly discovered orphan weeping in the rain. "If only I had a drink."

"I'm ahead of you on that one," he pulls a flask from his pocket and tosses it to Johann who catches it as though someone threw him a life ring. "I'm not sure you know how bad this is. They're not just trying to throw a scare into you. Dietrich is pushing to defrock you."

"Once a priest, always a priest, remember," Johann's smile is missing the joy as the libation drips from a corner of his mouth; each swig makes his body shake in appreciation.

"You know what I mean. You won't minister under Church auspices, at the very least."

"It may be just as well. When I think of Frau Colmarz's young children being whipped while she was being burned at the stake." Johann recoils at his own words, the air seems to be sucked from his lungs.

"The children were whipped?" Franz repeats.

"Dietrich had their arms tied to window bars where they could see their mother. When the torch was set and they were screaming for her, the lash was administered to them." Franz goes pale.

"The devil isn't content with a pact with the mother," Johann continues. "The devil recruits the whole family. We must teach the children the wages of sin. By our severity we possibly may save their souls we are told."

"That's what he meant then," says Franz sitting back in his chair. Johann looks at him. "On the day of the execution Dietrich told me that *wholesome zeal is always preferable to the outward semblance of mercy.*'"

"That's what all the tyrants of history say. That's their excuse for ruthlessness in their quest to exterminate. Mercy, if it is given at all, is just window dressing."

"Johann, I didn't know of the children. I am most distressed." There is momentary silence. "Is this what prompted the fight? You went berserk."

"It festered. But he deceived me. And because of it I sealed the fate of Fraulein von Hoffen. I told her that the inquisitor would be merciful if she confessed to being a witch, that he would not sentence her to death."

Franz considers all he now knows. "So he sends her to the Diocese of Constance where someone other than himself will sentence her to death."

"A bit misleading, wouldn't you say," the sarcasm is palpable.

"And the cardinal, why strike him? The incident with that woman at the inn?"

"Just a reaction to his grabbing me. But there has been another since her, Franz. Ask him what he was doing at Zirl. The cardinal can't keep his pants on."

Franz stands and walks to a corner of the cell; his back is to Johann when he speaks. "These are shameful things. Are you sure?"

"You have known me all my life, Franz." It isn't a direct answer but he does know Johann Carberry and he need say no more.

"Johann, a few weeks ago, when the cardinal mentioned the papal bull Summis Desiderantes Affectibus at Sunday mass..."

"Ja?"

"Well, we were instructed to repeat the Bull at each morning service during the balance of the week. Dietrich told the cardinal this afternoon that he observed that you did not do so."

"He's right about that... You know how I feel about witchcraft."

"He is charging you as a patron of omission. Charging you with neglect in performing your duties to combat witchcraft. Also, for releasing Herr Zimmerman, you will be charged as a protector of one strongly suspected of heresy."

"Well, isn't that jolly. And what does the cardinal say?"

"Not a word."

"Why am I not surprised?" Johann says almost rhetorically.

"I'm greatly concerned for you. I wish you were more concerned for yourself. This is dire, Johann. I don't know what to say."

"I know. I know. And you have been more than tolerant, forbearing of my exegesis, as I like to say."

"Then again, the deportment of..."

"Our cardinal, the inquisitor... the philandering, the lies, the cruelty." There is a long pause. "More importantly, the very existence of inquisitions themselves is a stain on the Church. How will they be justified to history? I can envision the excuse now, they were sponsored by fallible men in error. Yet the same men interpret the Bible; declare what is dogma; right and wrong; tell us how we should live our lives. The truth is, they are the Church."

Franz is not wont to argue the point and changes the subject. "Johann, that blue and pink baby blanket with the gold broken heart on it; Dietrich says that you threw at him. Where did it come from?"

"It is Fraulein von Hoffen's; it was left behind when the hired mercenaries took her off for Constance. Why do you ask?"

"Cardinal Gerhardt picked it up. Then he took a blue handkerchief from his pocket. There were similarities, identical gold broken hearts. He mumbled a name, Anna."

"That was the name of the woman he assaulted at the Boar's Head Inn. Her not pressing charges took the heat off the cardinal even if it didn't stop the gossip."

"Anna. Do you know her last name?"

"Nein, I don't think I heard it... and I never met her that evening."

"Try to remember."

"Why is this important to you now, of all times?" Franz doesn't answer; just looks at him. "I'm sorry, Franz. I'm sure I never heard her last name. I did hear, however, that she was recently widowed."

"Recently widowed!" Franz is visibly shaken.

"What's wrong?"

"Nothing... I must go now." He calls for the guard. "May God be with you... and with me."

"By the way, these schnaps are very good."

 భ

The darkening day is joined by a warm breeze and isolated pellets of rain but the rising moon pays no mind. Half hidden figures pass the lighted windows of retiring shops and disturb the apathetic shadows clinging to them. The snorting of tired horses pulling their wagons give testimony to Innsbruck's slowing heartbeat. Franz rides with his shoulders back, ignoring the occasional glances of those ambling along the cobbled streets, yet taunted by the strength of Johann's convictions. He trots past the flat, empty playing fields onto an ever rising landscape to the castle.

Franz has always been a follower, an organization man, an austere man in an austere profession dressed in austere clothes, save for the hierarchy. A man who faithfully carried out his duties. God works through his Church; he always believed. Now he is doubting the decisions of his superiors and his own eagerness to execute them. *Is brutality necessary to save souls? Is duplicity? Is this what Jesus preached? Has Johann been right all along?* He reflects on these things as he hurries towards his family's domain. *It is so much easier to conform, safer. I do as I am told. It is how one is accepted, how one belongs. I'm a member of the elite. That will all change if I question the actions of the inquisitor. Challenge the cardinal. What did Rafer say when he got prompted out of the seminary so many years ago? He recognizes truth before he recognizes authority. But Rafer faced up to the ultimatum. What will I do? I have few practical abilities. I have so much of my life invested in the Church. It has been my home.*

Arriving at the castle he goes straight to the chest where some of his personal belongings are stored. Returning to the ground floor he heads for the kitchen.

"Franz! It's feast or famine with you. Give me a hug!" He complies. "Is that the baby blanket I made for you?"

"It's not my baby blanket." Pulling an exact duplicate from a bag he says, "This is my baby blanket, broken heart and all." They stare at each other waiting for one or the other to break the silence. Finally Franz says, "It's Fraulein von Hoffen's and she has been taken to Constance to be executed for heresy, for witchcraft."

"Oh my God! Nein!" She reaches for a chair. She stares at Franz in disbelief and tears stream down her cheeks.

"It was you who was accosted by the cardinal, he who has a fondness for a certain handkerchief. Need I go on?"

Anna Keller Buchleitner tearfully relates her bitter-sweet tale of a lonely young woman who was compromised during a fleeting evening of love. Wanting desperately to hold onto her children, she knew that her circumstances would never permit it. Days after giving birth herself, she was recommended to the von Clausens to serve as a midwife.

"Your mother's child died within hours of his birth, probably a heart defect. I saw this as an opportunity to give you a life that I couldn't dream of giving you myself. Your parents wanted another child desperately; they had tried for many years since your brother Willem had been born. As I saw it, it was best for all concerned. And you, a boy, to be raised as a nobleman's son. I sought all the work I could get from your parents so as to be near you." Franz sits with his elbows on his knees and stares at the floor, receiving a new identity. "Yet I was still overwhelmed trying to care for your twin sister. I couldn't take her with me; I would be ostracized for not being wed and no one would hire me."

"And the stigma placed on bastards," adds Franz.

"The children are never illegitimate regardless of what ignorant people say, how can they be culpable? Nor are the parents, who are simply unmarried, compromised by their own affection. This may shock you Franz but I have doubts about passages in the bible. Here you are, a priest, giving your life to the Church, yet according to Deuteronomy 23:2: '*A bastard shall not enter into the congregation of the LORD; even to his tenth generation shall he not enter into the congregation of the LORD.*' A just, merciful God; it makes no sense." Franz's faith is hammered once again.

"Your mother asked me to work full-time for her but I would be required to live on the estate. It was a blessing because I wasn't giving Katarina proper care. It was then that I left her at the convent house in Reif."

"And our father is Cardinal Wolfgang Gerhardt."

"Wolfgang Karl Gerhardt. He wasn't even a priest then, just a bright, handsome, young man passing through on his way to Italy. He didn't know what he wanted to do... or so he let on. He took a fancy to a homely young woman and he captured my heart. Oh Franz, after all these years, I don't want to lose you. And my Katarina. Our Katarina. You must do something." He looks up to see the face of a tormented soul. He stands and pulls her to him.

∽

Franz mounts his horse and heads to the rectory with all speed to seek out Father Hans Dietrich. Toki says that he is napping and asks Franz to get him up for supper. He knocks on Dietrich's bedroom door.

"Ja?"

"It's Franz. Supper's about ready."

"I'll be right there."

"I'd like a word with you first?"

"Ja, come in!" He goes to the closet to dress. It is enough that Dietrich is physically hurting but the nature of Franz's questions add even greater injury to his persona. *How dare he question me for what*

I, a theologian and inquisitor, did. How presumptuous. This is so elementary. "My dear Franz, we are but God's instruments. The measure of punishment will be according to the measure of sin."

"It's all so brutal. Those children. And Fraulein von Hoffen, an unlikely witch if I ever saw one. How can you be sure of what we do?"

"You know the answer to that, Father. The Holy Spirit was a light and interior teacher for the apostles, who had to know Christ in depth to be able to fulfill their task as his evangelizers. It is the same for the Church, and in the Church, for believers of every generation, and in a particular way for theologians and spiritual directors, for catechists and those responsible for Christian communities."

"I know doctrine. It's the brutality that concerns me. I think of a loving Jesus, His charity and mercy. Brutality and love are incompatible with one another."

"You seem to be fond of the word *brutality*. Are you forgetting *justice?*"

"Justice and brutality needn't go hand in hand."

"The devil is a formidable foe. God gives us a choice. We can sin. We can pray. It is up to us." Franz looks unconvinced and obviously has not made his peace with the issues. "These witch trials are a great burden to us all, Franz. I'm going to recommend to the cardinal that you go on retreat. Spend some time in contemplation and prayer." Dietrich finishes tying his shoes and gestures towards the door, "supper awaits."

"I'll get something later." *What am I to do?* he asks himself.

ᐧᔆᐧ

Toki raises hell with the Helmut and refuses to hand over Father Johann's meal to him. Examine it if he wishes but she insists on delivering it herself. She brushes past him to Johann's cell as Impy follows after her.

"Tis against da rules, Toki." Impy is standing next to him and when Toki cocks her leg, the dog pees on his shoe.

"Damn!" Helmut jumps back and shakes his leg. "Here, goes in and takes the damn dog wit you." He unlocks the door then locks it behind them as he goes off to remedy his situation. Johann, puzzled, tries to sort out the commotion but is relieved and delighted to see his new visitors accompanied by a meal heady with the aroma of beef stewed in beer and covered with a scoop of mashed potatoes. At the same time, he has found himself an eager messenger.

Toki finds me at the Boar's Head sitting with Fritz in the tavern area. I quickly learn why Johann missed his dinner appointment with me. Though I am shocked, I don't feel any immediate danger for him. Katarina being moved to Constance, however, is cause for great alarm and she is the only religion I have left. I know I can catch up with her coach even though they had a lead of many hours; I can ride where the coach cannot and faster. Besides, Constance is a long way off. My mind is racing as to who might ride with me. Dolph is a wanted man on the run and probably long gone. Harry can't come because of the added risk to him from his purgation. I don't know the whereabouts of Basil but Snuff and Bear are in the basement waiting for me to join them. Within the hour the three of us are armed and riding from the idle, moist meadows due west along the base of the Karwendel Mountain Range and bringing the dark with us. The brittle night is startled at our hurried intrusion and scolds with a whisper of wind. Dogs are barking in the distance.

The hungry eyes of timber wolves look on with cautious restraint as we descend with an acquired cadence from a vacant road into an unused hollow. The hooves of our frightened horses tear the soft soil as Innsbruck is left farther behind. We later learn that luck is our companion. The wooden front axle on Katarina's coach cracked a couple of miles from Imst and the shifting load caused the diocesan coach horse to go slightly lame. The four mercenaries, however, had been resourceful enough. The axle was bound with leather belts. To lighten the load they jettisoned anything expendable. They switched the coach horse with the towed one belonging to the mercenary driver. It was late in the evening when they arrived at the Black Angus Inn.

We were not far behind. I figure that it is sometime after midnight when we come upon the inn. It lay in semi-darkness on a meandering dirt road, content under a listless sky and an idle moon. On the ground floor there is a suggestion of light behind the colored glass windows, courtesy of two lonesome candles on black wrought iron sconces; the matching chandelier has retired for the night. Wisps of smoke find their way out of the chimney, most likely remnants of declining embers. The diocesan seal on the coach tells us that we have overtaken them and this seems as good a place as any to effect Katarina's escape. But Sigmund, the innkeeper, knows me and it would be best for all of us if I were not recognized. *Thursday, June 25th, will be an eventful day.*

We tie the three horses to trees about fifty yards into the veiled woods. I tell Snuff and Bear to take a room and size up the situation, taking no weapons. Besides, two late arrivals rather than three would be less likely to spook the guards.

Sigmund isn't happy being roused at this hour by the clang of the bell but it goes with the territory. The circular plate forming the base of his candlestick catches the dripping wax as he shoves it about in his torpor. When he holds it up, his round blank face with the grey stubble jumps from the night like a mummer's mask. The features of Snuff and Bear are painted in a combination of light and darkness depending on where the candle is held. "Plenty of room. Only one other party here. Put your horses in the stable! Out back. Knock on the door! The boy will help you."

"Wee awl ready did," says Snuff.

"That will be two groschen each," says Sigmund; pay as you go. I'll register you in the morning, too late to bother with it now." On the way up the stairs Sigmund volunteers, "Have a nice room for you. Don't mind the guard, some female thief or whatever being returned to Constance. Locked in the loft." Snuff and Bear stay close to the wall on the wide staircase and behind Sigmund so the guard can't get a good look at them, perhaps a useless precaution. There is a balcony off to their left overlooking the tables and chairs of the tavern area. Nothing stirs below but a scraggly grey cat licking un-swept crumbs from the floor; he pauses to observe the newcomers; perceiving no threat, he resumes his pursuit.

From the bedroom window Snuff whispers to me that Katarina is confined in the loft; one guard on duty. The loft, I know, is accessed by a pulldown stairway in the ceiling above the second floor hallway.

The normal routine for soldiers is that each guard takes a two hour shift guarding a prisoner; the length of time it would take a small candle to burn down. The one on duty will wake the next on duty and so forth. I had no reason to suppose it would be different this night. Snuff gestures that the guard's candle is pretty low. I whisper to Snuff that I will be back in short order.

Having already taken a black hood, some leather straps and a large rag from my saddle bags, I go directly to the stable. The groom's room is in the right front corner giving him quick access to the stable door in case of guests or fire. It is a warm night, the open window is covered with a screen netting which is easily cut away. The boy is fast asleep not three yards away, face down into his pillow. I climb in slowly and carefully and have him gagged before he can cry out.

I bind his wrists behind his back and then his ankles. There is a post nearby so I lay him at the base of it, bend his arms and legs backwards around it, and lash them together. Confident that he can't stir the horses or anyone else, I close the door to his room behind me and remove my hood.

Moonlight sifting through the stable windows provides enough light to make my way. As I glance around, I see that one horse is standing. I pick up a feed bag and move casually towards the horse trying not to spook it. After strapping it to the stall, I come upon saddles apparently belonging to the mercenaries. As I lead the horse out of the stable, the door creaks to my dismay but it only captures the attention of Snuff. He signals from the second floor that all is okay and in no time the horse and I are past the inn and into the stand of trees where the other horses are tied. It is a handsome Arabian, uncommon in this region, which seems more white than grey once outside the stable.

The diocesan coach is conveniently alongside the inn and I use it to launch my climb up the side of the building and over to the room occupied by Snuff and Bear. Bear takes my arm and pulls me through the window. Quickly they inform me that a guard is pacing the hallway just outside the door and is armed with a sword and dagger. He had been swinging the sword about, when they first came in, as if practicing his technique. Judging from the shadows beneath the door, cast from a hallway sconce, things haven't changed. This isn't good news as it would be difficult to overcome him without arousing the others. We come up with a bizarre subterfuge.

I hand Snuff a bedpan and send him behind the dressing screen to do everything possible; he is very accommodating. Disheveled and holding his nose, he opens the bedroom door and wobbly maneuvers in front of the guard putting the bedpan in his face. "Which way tuh thuh trench, me friend?" Disgusted and intolerant, the guard pushes him away, his hand pointing to the front door and circling to the right. He watches Snuff descend the stairs in the flickering candlelight and close the door behind him.

Minutes later it is Bear's turn. As he heads for the guard, the guard grimaces, holds up his sword and points to the front door and again to the right. The guard no sooner thinks of taking advantage of a chair when there comes a loud knocking at the front door. He puts his sword in its scabbard and huffs his way down the stairs. "Dumkoffs," he shouts as he throws open the door. Bear grabs his shirt and pulls him outside while Snuff smacks him on the head with the bedpan knocking him unconscious. I quickly descend the stairs to lend a hand but my services are not needed.

"Who's the dumkoff?" Snuff snorts.

Katarina is startled when I lower the stairway. Snuff hands up the candle as she stares at me from the darkness. When she sees my face her whole body seems to quake with hope and joy. She scrambles to me and my efforts to hush her are for naught. She sobs and holds me all the while Snuff admonishes us to make haste. Finally he comes up the stairway and starts tugging on my clothes causing me to drop the candle and him to lose his balance; both slam onto the floor. We all stay motionless for a moment listening for anyone who might have stirred.

"What was that?" someone calls. I guide Katarina onto the stairway and then to the hallway staircase. A door opens and a burly, half-dressed mercenary looks out.

"Intruders!" he shouts. "They're freeing the prisoner. Get up! Get up!" He lunges at Bear causing both to roll about only to tumble down after us in a loose embrace. It is bedlam now as the two are in a wild brawl, ambiguous shapes in the meager light. Other doors open and men in undergarments appear. Snuff leaps from the balcony using the soldier below to break his fall, this affords Bear a straight punch to the soldier's temple putting him down. The terrified cat screeches and takes cover under the bar.

The two other soldiers, swords in hand, are now lurching down the hallway. I pull Katarina through the front door only to be met by the first guard wobbling there regaining his composure. A left to the groin and a right uppercut put him back on the ground. Snuff and Bear hurl chairs at their pursuers in a rear guard action. Katarina and I are past the tree line when both of them scurry through the front door. Following in our wake, heads down, they charge across the road with one thought, putting distance between them and their pursuers. Once in the woods, Snuff turns back to see the one guard pick himself off the ground only to see an arrow strike the door in front of him. He pushes his comrades back inside and the door slams shut. When it slowly opens again, another arrow strikes the door with a thud causing it to close once more. With that, Snuff heads for our rendezvous point.

We are all mounted now and Snuff declares our gift from unknown gods. At the same time, I see some movement in our direction. We stop talking and remain still, only patting the necks of the horses to calm them. The archer has eased his horse into the woods to be reclaimed by the night. He slowly comes into view and stops not ten yards from us; we survey each other.

"Anyone need a lawyer?"

"Dolph! You lovable son of a bitch," I say. We all sigh in momentary relief as he comes forward to join us.

"It's great seeing you all but maybe we should hold this party further down the road?"

"Don't worry," I reply, "they won't go far just yet. I cut the cinches on their saddles."

"Yahwold," is the chorus.

"You know that Johann freed me yesterday. I made some hasty arrangements then slipped over to the Boar's Head. Fritz filled in the blanks and I followed on your heels. My friends, it will be a long time before Innsbruck sees me again."

"We might have the same problem. We'll see. Where are you headed now?"

"Jolly old England. A visit with my uncle there is long overdue. Everybody knows him as Commodore Zimmerman, a major player in the maritime industry. If you ever get to Southampton, look him up and you will find me. That's an order. I'll be deeply troubled if I learn you didn't."

"If we ever get to England, you can count on it," I reply.

"The honor has been mine. But I'm afraid this isn't a time for long goodbyes. Would you be going in the same direction?"

"Nein, it's not what I had in mind," I say. He pulls back on the reins. Take care, Dolph," Katarina says.

"My friends, auf wiedersehen!" We reply in kind. Dolph gives us a salute as he eases his horse about and trots away.

"I ask Snuff and Bear, "Did either of you ever see any of those soldiers before?" They look at each other and shake their heads. "Conveniently passing through Innsbruck, I suspect. Hopefully they will keep going after this debacle. But be ready to get out of town quickly if they show up at home. I'm sure they can give a good description of both of you. Katarina and I have other options to consider."

❦

Daylight broke bright and warm. The mood is dark and cold. "You get this straight, my good Father, I don't want to hear another word of your seditious talk." Cardinal Gerhardt is in the foulest form that

Franz ever witnessed. "I already have one priest courting heresy and if you keep on you'll be in the cell next to him. By the way, have you spoken with your brother lately?"

"My brother?" Franz can find no solid ground.

"Willem, he's your only brother isn't he?"

"Well... Ja, ja, of course," he snaps back quickly regaining his composure. Gerhardt gives him a strange look.

"Well, our collections at Mass have been dipping again. Tell him I want to see him!"

"Certainly."

"Cardinal, we have much to do today," says Dietrich trying to move things forward.

"Father Dietrich... Katarina von Hoffen... how long after her arrival in Constance do you expect her to be sentenced?" asks Franz. Gerhardt is stunned. He wasn't told of the transfer.

Dietrich, expecting more recalcitrance and delay, lies to expedite things. "I suppose you didn't hear. There was a landslide. They say her coach and everyone on it have been crushed." Dietrich had heard of such an accident but had every reason to believe it was not Katarina.

"Why wasn't I told of these things?" demands Gerhardt visibly shaken.

"It was an administrative thing, Your Eminence. You have been through a lot lately. I didn't want to trouble you. I sent her on with those Swiss mercenaries we encountered the other day."

"In the future, trouble me. Trouble me, damn you," he angrily retorts. You are to do nothing without clearing it with me. Do you understand?" After a pregnant delay he turns on Franz. "This afternoon, Johann Carberry will be defrocked in the courtyard. Either participate in the degrading or you too will be the object of it. I have responsibilities here. What will it be, Father?"

℃

The cardinal is adorned in his finest vestments, this will be a very formal affair. A half dozen clergy in full raiment had been quickly assembled. Father Johann Francis Carberry, also in all his vestments, stands in the center of the apron that leads into the cathedral. As each minute passes a curious crowd starts to assemble. The Cardinal hands his staff to Father Desmond signaling the start of the proceedings. He arches his arms over his head and brings his hands together only to lower them in front of his chest in a position of prayer. Johann stares into his eyes, looking right through the man. Cardinal Wolfgang Gerhardt is visibly disturbed by this but will not be deterred.

The words Johann hears are the same as those he heard on the day of his ordination; except now a negative twist is put to them. To a casual observer the cardinal is administering the sacrament of Holy Orders. But the incongruity is that the vestments are being removed one by one; not put on. Johann's stole is handed to Father Franz. Then the chasuble is removed and handed to him and so forth until there is no trace of Johann's religious calling. Only then, when all the vestments are piled high on Franz's arm, does Johann look at his childhood friend. Tears well in Franz's eyes as the cardinal orders Johann to face the crowd.

"Johann Carberry, you have been judged by your superiors to be a patron of omission, failing in your duties to actively pursue the eradication of witchcraft and in so doing giving succor to Satan. You have been found to be a protector of one strongly suspected of heresy. Because of these things, I excommunicate you from the Holy Roman Catholic Church. If you fail to repent within a year's

time, you may be charged as a heretic yourself and sentenced to the extreme penalty. At the very least, you shall not be admitted to any office or council nor may you participate in the election of officers. You will be disallowed from the giving of evidence and none shall be held accountable for any business transaction with you. Go forth from our midst."

The clergy turn their backs to him as one; Father Franz von Clausen trembles as he does so and wonders if his faith is accompanied by self-deception. For the first time in his life he feels that he has transgressed his own concepts of righteousness and a look of shame passes across his face as beads of sweat form on his brow. He contemplates what Johann was trying to tell him. Caring and love are what is important, not condemnation and punishment. A stray breeze rustles his hair.

Johann walks unhurriedly down the steps, his indifference is almost mystical, an unfathomable and isolated stillness, his thoughts denied to all as he slowly distances himself from the turmoil. The muted throng clears a path as he goes, only to close again behind him. Fritz Freihofer had been notified of the scene and presses a note into his hand. The eyes of the crowd trail after him until he fades into anonymity among the languid facades of Friedrich Strasse, as though the quarter is embarrassed to cling to its identity. He wanders aimlessly for a while.

ɕↄ

Johann is now something of an orphan but Fritz offers foster care. He gives him a room. Food and drink par excellence are brought to him. This early supper is so sumptuous, that despite the traumatic experience a few hours ago, pleasure pierces the melancholy. But Johann is not about to prolong this imposition.

"Fritz, you are an extraordinary friend. Always there in a crisis."

"It's good for me. Makes me feel good. I do it for myself."

"You're a good man. Thank you for your help and your kindness in this, the blackest day of my life. But I'm going to leave now. I must reassess my life. I must determine the direction I am to take. What and Where."

"You will do that here, I insist."

"Nein. Danke schon. I need to be alone, no distractions" his sad smile is that of a forsaken lover.

"But where will you go?"

"Not far. A several hour walk."

"Walk, my foot. What of your horse?"

"Belongs to the diocese."

"I lend you a horse. As long as you need. You must have a horse when you are in the country. This is one thing with which I will not take nein. Tomorrow I help you saddle."

"Very well then. But this afternoon."

Fritz can see his determination. "This afternoon."

❦

Johann packs the saddle bags with some additional clothing, toilet articles and extra money that Fritz has given him. They meet up again in Fritz's office and then walk together to the stable. The stable boy saddles a chestnut of good disposition. Johann grabs Fritz by the upper arms, shakes him a bit and says, "You are a wonderful friend, the best. How can I ever repay you?"

"I don't look for repayment. But who knows, maybe I need a

favor from you some day. Just be careful out there. You watch out for highwaymen, recent reports." The boy positions the horse for Johann to mount. As he does so, Fritz remembers. "Oh! I carry this package and I let you ride off without it. Some bread, salted smoked ham, honey, wine. Here, I put it in saddle bag for you. And the horse, plenty of grass this time of year."

"Fritz, you're one of a kind, auf wiedersehen."

☙

The sun is hesitant to fall below the horizon but the glinting windows wish it adieu. A wobbly garden gate stirred by a wayward breeze creaks wistfully in the twilight. Only minutes pass for the shadows to darken and for the moon to remind us that it is not a departed friend. There is every indication that it will be a starry night. Johann puts his horse into a trot and realizes an awkward sense of freedom. *Is this a new beginning? Get real, Johann, it may well be the beginning of the end? Then again, it may be both. There is much to accomplish yet every possibility for failure. Luther, right or wrong, was up to the challenge, am I?* As he crosses the bridge over the Inn he hears a commotion in the common off to his right. He has no thought of stopping yet he does turn to look. A man is hanging motionless by the neck from a limb of the gnarled old oak, the one with carved initials of bygone lovers. The river is unusually quiet as if in mourning.

"Father Carberry!" says a surprised young man as Johann bows his head to say a quick prayer.

"Not anymore," says another lacking discretion.

"It's Father von Clausen," a sympathetic, plump woman volunteers, her arms across her abdomen. "There is a sign pinned to him. '*I am Judas.*' We are on our way to notify the rectory."

Johann goes pale; his eyes close and a tear frees itself. He struggles to talk. "Help me take him down," he blurts out, urging his horse forward. He grabs Franz around the waist to take the weight off the rope. The young man rights the fallen table to mount it and cuts him down. The insensitive man, with an apparent liking for garlic, eases the body to the ground while Johann dismounts and kneels beside his friend. He tenderly touches Franz's cheek with his right hand.

"Franz, what have you done… what have I done to you?"

Somewhat hesitantly, the woman says, "There's a note sticking out of a pocket, Father." Johann reaches for it and slowly unfolds the paper, written in Franz's careful, rounded hand.

> *Johann,*
>
> *I forsook you. Maybe someday you will find it in your heart to forgive me for that and for serving the inquisition. You are right; torture and killing in the name of God is sacrilege. I failed my God, my family, my friends and I am unworthy of all. The world will be better off without me.*
>
> *25 June, 1556*
> *Franz von Clausen, OSA.*

Johann picks him up, the noose still around his bruised neck, and lays him across his saddle. He walks the horse back across the bridge lost in the memories of their boyhood. *We were a mystery to each other. I might as well have communicated with a phantom. It was like a marriage where they start talking at each other instead of to each other. Yet, somehow, a certain fondness, loyalty perhaps, persisted that no one dare disturb. He never liked or respected his own father; he was an alien being in his own family. The Church was his real home but even that failed him in the end.*

Several more onlookers, a muddle of humanity, trail behind, watching the former priests through the gloom of the moment. It is a muted procession, as solemn as a funeral itself. Such a tragedy on such a beautiful night, the early stars already making themselves known. The incongruity is ostensible. No one ever spans the gap between the living and the dead.

The cortege stops at the rectory door. Laying him at the threshold, Johann puts the note under Franz's belt and knocks loudly on the door. He calmly mounts his horse and points him away from the courtyard. Toki screams but Johann doesn't turn to acknowledge it. Returning to the site of the suicide, he dismounts and seeks shelter behind a dark, protective embankment. The manifestation of his friend is still suspended there as he contemplates their shattered lives and the shifting world. The cadence of the river seduces him into a catatonic state.

Gerhardt and Dietrich are now at Toki's side. All look to the woman bystander and she explains what had happened. After reading the note Dietrich hands it to the cardinal who follows suit; Gerhardt uncharacteristically breaks into a sweat. He crumples the note and throws it aside only to be picked up by Toki; she will read it at a private moment. Everyone is looking at the cardinal as his mind tries to harness chaos. *Things keep getting worse. One priest defrocked and the same day another hangs himself, both critical of Church practices and me in particular. What else can go wrong? I must get away until things settle down. Sort things out. Let Dietrich deal with this; it's his inquisition. The Visintainer place. And did she return for that bag? So what if she did?*

The cardinal, sullen and distracted, motions Dietrich inside. "Tragically, this reminds me of some very pressing business I put off; totally escaped my mind. Shouldn't wait any longer. I better leave now. I'll be back in a couple of days. You take charge in the meantime, arrangements, whatever. Sorry to dump this on you Hans but I have little choice." He stalks away in orderly retreat and tells little Manfred to inform the stable boy to ready his horse. Then, having packed his saddlebags and affixing them in place, he turns his horse in the direction of Zirl.

೮ා

There are no lights in the chalet that he can see but the moon is casting a pale glow about the place. He ties his horse to the hitching post and steps onto the porch. *Wunderbar! The key is in place. I'll put the horse in the stable after I let myself in.* His ankle bangs a foot stool. "Damn it! Son of a bitch! What a night… where are those god damn sulphur sticks?" *The mantelpiece. Here's a candlestick. Ja, here they are.* He strikes one against the hearth and raises the flaming stick to the candle wick. As he blows it out, I tap my sword on the floor.

"My, my, Cardinal Gerhardt. I didn't expect you back, your lover leaving town and all."

"Rafer!" the cardinal says, dumbfounded, his face reddening as I twirl the sword. He begins to wonder if there was anyone in Innsbruck who doesn't know his business. I pick up a couple of the sulfur sticks and hand one to Gerhardt. Each of us lights more candles, fortunately ones made of beeswax and not the smelly tallow ones. "I suppose your horse is out back?" Gerhardt says nervously. "The place looked vacant."

"And you just happened to be in the neighborhood?"

"This place isn't far from your home, Rafer. I'm surprised you're staying here," replies Gerhardt taking note that I am only wearing a pair of breeches and, also, waiting for me to volunteer information so he can make a damage assessment. "Let me sit down and rest." He takes the large stuffed chair and I the couch opposite.

"And I'm surprised at what a particular cardinal has been doing here."

"It seems that a lot of people have been attributing a lot of things to me. I'm getting used to it." His body settles into the chair with leisured arrogance and his face breaks into an unsure smirk.

"Accosting a widow. What's the story, the devil made you do it? Then a liaison."

"Don't believe everything you hear... besides, attraction to women is innate to the male psyche, wouldn't you say? I'm afraid I'm not exempt. They do have their charms." His restless gaze scours the room seeking threats in hiding.

"Apparently you also have a rebellious subordinate on your hands. It's been said that one of your priests is in the chancellery dungeon. Did I hear that correctly?"

"He set a prisoner free without authorization. He assaulted Father Dietrich."

"Why would he do that?"

Gerhardt's mind is racing and I could only surmise what he is thinking. *What is Rafer doing here? Why the accusatory tone? It must be Johann. They grew up together didn't they?*

"You tell me! You seem to have all the answers, Rafer."

"You rail against witches, yet you resort to a witch to effect a cure for yourself. God's going to cut your life short for that."

"Why is it a concern to you?"

"Katarina von Hoffen, that's why."

"I see. Romantically involved, are you?"

"What you do in your personal life is of no concern to me but arresting Katarina is. I want to cut a business deal with you. And please, don't go sanctimonious on me. We both know better."

"What are we trading here?" He stares with puzzled curiosity, head cocked waiting for the other shoe to drop. His tired eyes cloud with tangible concern as his fingers come together as if in prayer.

"I don't go public with these tidbits, Karl, and it is Karl, isn't it? And add to your troubled storyline. I do have some credibility in these parts. In return, I want a personal favor from you."

"And that is?"

"Katarina, come on out!" Lucky for Gerhardt that he doesn't have a weak heart. Katarina, listening at the bedroom door, walks out wrapped in an oversized towel which has no success at concealing her unprompted sensuality. At first he is flabbergasted at the sight of her but that seems to yield to a sigh in relief. "Surprised?"

"Ja, I am." And then, "more than you know," he mumbles to himself.

"Katarina, why don't you get dressed now." He watches her leave not knowing what to expect next. I watch him for a movement or gesture. The silence hangs in the air like the acrid smoke over a battle-field. Finally, Gerhardt broaches the inevitable.

"She certainly didn't escape on her own. She must be very dear to you, Rafer, risking subjection to the inquisition yourself."

"Then you know that I am prepared to do anything to protect Katarina." I toyed with my sword.

"No need for heroics, my friend. I'm a practical man. I have my reasons. I'll call off the dogs. Just keep her away from Innsbruck. It was reported that she was killed in a landslide anyway."

"Well that story won't hold up for long. I want her exonerated."

"Can't do; the inquisitor, you know. She needs to relocate."

"Can do. You don't understand, Karl," I emphasize the last word again. "Katarina is to be exonerated. I don't want her living as a fugitive. My efforts along this line start with you. You agree to help or else." It is my detachment that rattles him. "Are you dressed, Katarina?" I shout. "I think it is time to move on."

She enters the room wearing a pair of slightly worn, beige riding breeches, a white blouse and red jacket frayed at the collar. "I found these in that old trunk marked donations; better for riding don't you think?"

"They look great. The cardinal here has a life changing decision to make. In the meantime, if you would be so kind as to get our horses ready. I'll be along shortly; wait there for me." She hesitates but senses the heavy tone and leaves to comply. Gerhardt's hand starts to shake.

"Rafer, it's not just Katarina, I want the inquisition to end. You know what I've been subjected to. That dam broadsheet and all. I thought it would begin and end with that Colmarz woman. Things have gotten out of hand."

"Really? I've never heard of an inquisition that didn't get out of hand."

"I only have so much power over an inquisitor, Rafer. If I over-play my hand I will be replaced and then where will you be? He is not all that happy with me as it is."

"You'll find a way."

"You don't know Dietrich…" Before he can finish Johann bursts in and stands there like an avenging angel, the door left open to the night. The suddenness has me on my feet, sword poised.

"Johann, I thought you were locked up?"

"My, my, what have we here," observes Gerhardt wryly.

"The cardinal here released me this afternoon… just after he threw me out of the priesthood," his voice trails after him with a tenor of reckoning.

"My God!"

"What's going on here?" The perplexities of this day have no end for Johann.

"The cardinal and I were discussing his future plans or lack thereof." I glance in his direction.

"Let's get all the surprises out of the way," says Gerhardt. "Hopefully, it will be the last shock of the night. I suspect, Rafer, you don't know about Father von Clausen."

"What about him?"

"Do you want to tell him, Johann? Or shall I?"

"Franz hung himself this evening," says Johann, staring right through Gerhardt. I am stunned and almost drop the sword. "He left a note. Felt he betrayed me for participating at my divestiture and regretted his part in the inquisition." I stand there limp, eyes closed and head hung low. Johann touches my arm. I turn to the couch and retake my seat. No one chooses to speak until Katarina appears at the door alerted by the new arrival.

"Father Johann!" As he turns, she rushes into his arms. He holds her as he would a prodigal daughter.

Shaking off my stupor, I look at the cardinal. "Same deal except that Johann also gets reinstated."

"I can live with that… but in due time."

"What deal, Rafer?" asks Johann.

Gerhardt takes the initiative. "Look! Starting tomorrow, I'll move to stifle the inquisition. It won't happen immediately. Dietrich will resist. All of you go away for six months, a year even better. Do what you want but stay away from Innsbruck. Things will have settled down by then; Father Dietrich goes home; you all return. Deal?"

"And Katarina's conviction is publicly overturned? Johann is reinstated?"

"Katerina's confession of guilt was never made public. It won't be a problem once Dietrich is gone. I'll reinstate Johann; say he was falsely accused."

"And he goes on as if nothing ever happened, says Johann. "Neither one of them deserves to live, justified killings." Things go dead in the water, like a ship run aground and no tide to save it.

"Like it or not, I'm your best bet," replies the cardinal.

"Your deaths will put an end to it now."

"Really Johann. A pause maybe, not an end. And are you really going to kill us? Or is this one of your drunken fantasies? You don't want to make tough decisions so you drink your way to inaction. You leave the distasteful things to others so you don't have to bear the burden."

"Rafer, give me the sword!"

"So you can purify the world? Wake up! The whole realm is full of charlatans, including ecclesiastical ones like me. Taking what they can get from this unforgiving life. Is that too shocking for you?"

"What of divine retribution?"

"Do you think our profligate cardinals and popes believe in the hereafter? If they did they know that they, of all people, would be destined for the most wretched reaches of hell. The hereafter is a delusion for those who cannot accept the finality of their own mortality."

"As much as I hate to say it, you would have a hard time convincing Father Dietrich of that?"

"Fool. Prisoner of a colossal hoax. Like you pitiable priests taken-in by a manufactured institution. How old is mankind? Thousands, maybe millions of years for all we know. If Jesus was divine, don't you think it odd that he only showed up 1500 years ago? And hasn't been back since? Don't you think it odd that he just made himself known to a small corner of the world and ignored the rest? The explorers bear me out."

"Have you no faith at all?"

"I did as a child but I've grown up. Even Aquinas said that one cannot prove the faith and it's foolish to try."

"He also said that one cannot disprove the faith and we should be prepared to defend it."

"Faith is belief without proof. Can you accept faith on those terms Johann? And if it's so obvious that there is a God, why doesn't everyone believe? Religion is a crutch, the universal placebo to cope with a harsh reality. Decide for yourself where truth lies and live your life accordingly or keep looking for something that isn't there. I'll make the best of this life rather than invest in the false promise of another. Some comforts are attainable, if you play the game right."

"Our cardinal is an apostate."

"Report me to the inquisition. Do we have a deal Rafer?"

"Johann has a point. You will sacrifice anyone who gets in your way, including us."

Gerhardt becomes unnerved. "If you kill me, what will you achieve? The inquisition will just intensify under Dietrich. Kill him? The civil authorities will be all over you and the Church will just appoint another inquisitor. Better the devil you know than one you don't." He waits for a reaction but no one says anything. "You couldn't expect as much from any other cardinal under the circumstances. I want an end to this. I'm fighting enough battles as it is and I don't want to be chasing after homosexuals."

"Homosexuals?" I retort.

"Shortly Dietrich will post a proclamation demanding that people come forth and identify all persons known to be homosexuals. Failure to do so will result in automatic ex-communication. Things will get worse before they get better." Katarina and I glance at each other.

"Johann, what do you say?"

"If it wasn't to save his own skin an inquisition would have been the last thing he wanted. He's all about expediency and self-indulgence."

"Will he follow through or will he turn on us? That is the question."

"As he said, I don't believe he wants to deal with another adversary. You being a pillar of the community would make it even more awkward for him. I would have one more demand of the cardinal before I would consider letting him go." Johann stares at him. Gerhardt stares back puzzled and then it dawns on all of us at the same time.

"You want me to resign when all this is behind us," he finally says.

"It's your choice," Johann replies. "And don't underestimate what we are capable of."

He chooses his words slowly. "It has crossed my mind. I'm not a young man. My reputation suffers in Innsbruck. There is a personal issue I must sort out; a new venue would be a possible solution." He lowers his head and stares at the floor... "Agreed."

℃つ

I give Gerhardt the Arabian to ride back to town; I don't want any of us associated with it. Katarina will ride his horse instead. Although puzzled, he doesn't argue the point. Before he rides off he turns to Katarina.

"Fraulein, your age? Would you mind telling me your birth date? You strike me as a Sagittarius."

"December 10, 1517," she replies.

"I was right. You have a good sense of self. You are much like my Anna. Take care my dear. I wish you well. I really do." *Anna, that name again,* thinks Johann.

I turn to Johann. "Why did you come here? You could have stayed at my place."

"And draw suspicion to you and your father with the inquisition going on."

"Maybe Fritz will hire you as my replacement," volunteers Katarina.

"We will be gone indefinitely and I need someone to take over the Inquirer," I add.

"Alright… and I'll feel Fritz out about it. I take it your riding towards Innsbruck." I nod.

We quickly ready ourselves and follow close on the cardinal's heels as our eyes adjust to the dark. Johann, erect in the saddle as any good cavalryman when not burdened with a hangover, takes the lead. A faint breeze tries to reach us through the trees, rustling a few leaves, and the soft thud of our horses' hooves join the transient sounds personal to a forest night. The immediate plan is for Katarina and me to make a brief stop at my chalet and inform Dad of the situation. After a hearty meal, we will pack some provisions and continue east towards Salzburg, timing dependent on circumstances. Katarina raises the issue when we have enough room to gallop side by side on the crumbling trail.

"I hope Fritz will be all right. Does anyone else know?"

"No one ever spoke of it to me."

"Why must the Church make an issue of it? I never met someone with a same sex orientation who was not a kind soul."

"The Old Testament, Leviticus, '*Thou shalt not lie with mankind, as with womankind: it is abomination.*' "

"People have a way of creating problems, if they would just leave things well enough alone. If you hadn't told me, I would never have known, not for sure, anyway."

"It's the '*not for sure part*' that scares me," I answer.

ಐ

Four mercenaries on horseback, two riding double, move at a trot eastward along the main well-trodden road, they pay no mind to an occasional fallen tree or leaning milestone, routine victims of wind, rain and snow. The smell of pine permeates the dry air, a common experience in these parts, nothing unusual about that or the nattering nocturnal noises. The larches and their restless shadows, however, obscure the fork up ahead in a conspiracy to disturb the quiet. The cardinal gallops from obscurity to prominence a few yards in front of them causing the other horses to rear up. Gerhardt slows to assess the situation only to see a crossbow being readied.

"Stop!" a mercenary yells.

Highway men flashes across his mind and he urges his horse to speed but it is too little too late as an arrow finds its mark between his shoulder blades. A few more yards and he drops unceremoniously from the saddle; his rider-less horse slows to a halt.

"It's my horse all right," the apparent leader says. He dismounts and rolls the body on its side. "Mon Dieu! C'est Cardinal Gerhardt."

"What's he doing on a stolen horse?" the archer asks. "I didn't know it was the cardinal."

"Did anyone see him in Imst?" the leader inquires. All shake their heads. "That's the big question. What's he doing out here on a stolen horse?"

"Is he dead?"

"If he isn't, he won't live long with this wound."

"I think I hear horses," another soldier says with some trepidation.

"First we break the carriage. We let the woman escape. Now this." He mounts the Arabian. "Forget going back to Innsbruck. Let's ride!"

&

Johann is the first to see the body lying in the road. He dismounts and cradles the cardinal's head in one hand. I quickly join him, kneeling at the cardinal's side.

"Cardinal! Can you hear me?" he says. "Cardinal?" Gerhardt gasps for air and tries to speak; he barely manages to open his eyes.

"Johann!" Johann takes the blue handkerchief from the Gerhardt's pocket and wipes the cardinal's brow. "Give that to Katarina. Tell her I'm sorry. I didn't know," he murmurs.

"You be quiet. We'll get you back to town," Johann replies.

"What've I wrought?" he gasps.

"Save your strength," Johann insists. "Are you sorry for your sins and promise to sin no more?'

"I have caused so much harm."

"Say an Act of Contrition! I'll give you absolution."

They finish together and a smile crosses the cardinal's face. He goes limp and loses his water. It is extraordinary that Johann was ready to kill him a bit earlier yet now is concerned for his soul. But I have my doubts that the cardinal had a real deathbed conversion.

"By the looks of the hoof prints, whoever they were, they came from the west and have reversed course, possibly horse thieves... or the mercenaries. There is a chalet up the road. We'll take him there. Help me put him across his horse! Katarina will have to ride double with me." Johann moves to remove the arrow. I wave him off.

We continue slowly on wondering what will possibly happen now, no one wishing to volunteer their thoughts. When we reach the chalet I leave the cardinal's body on the front steps and his horse untethered, as though he made it there on his own. Under the circumstances we don't dare allow ourselves to be connected with his death.

Our two horses trot side by side towards Innsbruck once again; we let the stars and moonlight set the tone, all are desperate for tranquility. As we near the outskirts of town, it is Johann who breaks the silence.

"Well, our grand plan with the cardinal was short lived. Rafer, I suppose that you were recognized during the rescue?"

"Maybe not, things happened so fast. They can identify Bear and Snuff no doubt."

"Katarina, this turn of events isn't going to change things for you with Dietrich," says Johann. "But if Fritz lets me earn my keep and I can keep the pot boiling with the Inquirer, I will have found a renewed purpose in life."

"It will be great having you take over," I say.

"My privilege... I'll ride ahead; we shouldn't be seen together."

Johann leans over and hugs Katarina. She kisses his cheek. "Oh! I almost forgot, the cardinal wanted you to have this; said he was sorry... and that he didn't know." Puzzled, she just glances at it and, without unfolding it, puts it in her jacket pocket.

"Fill in the boys," I say. "Katarina and I will stop at my chalet before moving on to Salzburg and then Vienna. Be careful. The inquisitor has free reign for the time being." Johann and I clasp hands.

"May God be with both of you. By the way, Rafer, do you know who the cardinal was referring to when he spoke of Anna?"

"The only Anna I know is Anna Keller, Franz's one time nanny."

"I never knew her first name. She was always Frau Keller to me. Don't see how it could be the Anna the cardinal referred to."

"She later became Frau Buchleitner, when you and Franz were in other dioceses. Herr Buchleitner died a short time ago."

"Oh!" says Johann somewhat surprised. "My, my! Well, both of you take care now!" He wheels his horse slowly about and starts to gallop towards town.

"He'll be forlorn without the embrace of his Church," Katarina says, as we watch him move farther and farther away.

"It's a greater loss for the Church. The Church needs the Johann Carberrys of the world more than the other way around. He is closer to what Jesus was all about."

"It remains to be seen what will become of him... of us."

"Fortitude, my dear, fortitude."

"The world can be such a hostile place... earthquakes, volcanos, tornados, hurricanes, floods, wildfires, diseases, all taking or maiming lives regardless of age or innocence. Loss of loved ones. One species preying on another for food. Man's inhumanity to man."

"It would be wonderful if everyone treated each other as they would like to be treated themselves. The God of any faith would be quite pleased, I would think."

"How is it that people believe in a beneficent God, given the harsh realities of creation?"

"Perhaps the French writer, Michel de Montaigne, said it best. *Men give more credit to things they understand not. Things obscure are more willingly believed through a strange desire of man's wit.*'"

EPILOGUE

This historical novel was woven from fact to examine how doctrinal beliefs evolved and how they came to make up the present fabric of various religious faiths. Who we are as adults, including the religion we practice, is largely a product of how we were raised and educated. Although there are exceptions to everything, it is more typical that we just accept what we were taught to the exclusion of other unexamined beliefs.

Martin Luther

11/10/1483 - 2/18/1546

Holy Roman Emperor Maximilian

3/22/1459 - 1/12/1519

Sultan Selim I

10/10/1465 - 9/22/1520

Abbot Regino of Prum

Unknown - 915

Sultan Suleiman
11/6/1494 - 9/7/1566

Bishop Eusebius of Caesarea
Circa 260 - Circa 340

John Calvin
7/10/1509 - 5/27/1564

Lorenzo Valla
Circa 1407 - 8/1/1457

Desiderius Erasmus
10/27/1469 - 7/12/1536

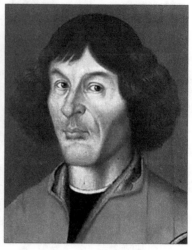

Nicolaus Copernicus
2/19/1473 - 5/24/1543

King Henry VIII of England
6/28/1491 - 1/28/1547

Archbishop Thomas Cranmer
7/2/1489 - 3/21/1556

King Francis I of France
9/12/1494 - 3/31/1547

Leonardo da Vinci
4/15/1452 - 5/2/1519

Gerardus Mercator
3/5/1512 - 12/2/1594

Michelangelo
3/6/1475 - 2/18/1564

Niccolo Machiavelli
5/3/1469 - 6/21/1527

Cardinal Alphonso Petrucci
Circa 1490 - 7/16/1517

Archbishop Albert of Brandenburg
6/28/1490 - 9/24/1545

Emperor Charles V
2/24/1500 - 9/21/1558

Frederick, Elector of Saxony
1/17/1463 - 5/5/1525

King Louis II of Hungary
7/1/1506 - 8/29/1526

Admiral Andrea Doria
11/30/1466 - 11/25/1560

Admiral Hayreddin Barbarossa
1478 - 7/4/1546

Ferdinand I, Archduke of Austria
3/10/1503 - 7/25/1564

King John Zapolya of Hungary
1487 - 7/22/1540

Cardinal Pompeo Colonna
5/12/1479 - 6/28/1532

Charles III, Duke of Bourbon
2/17/1490 - 5/6/1527

Johann Weyer
1515 - 2/24/1588

Pope Innocent VIII Pontificate:
8/29/1484 - 7/25/1492

Pope Alexander VI Pontificate:
8/11/1492 - 8/18/1503

Pope Julius II Pontificate:
11/1/1503 - 2/21/1513

Pope Leo X Pontificate:
3/9/1513 - 12/1/1521

Pope Adrian VI Pontificate:
1/9/1522 - 9/14/1523

Pope Clement VII Pontificate:
11/19/1523 - 9/25/1534

Pope Paul III Pontificate:
10/13/1534 - 11/10/1549

Pope Julius III Pontificate:
2/7/1550 - 3/23/1555

Pope Paul IV Pontificate:
5/23/1555 - 8/18/1559

CPSIA information can be obtained
at www.ICGtesting.com
Printed in the USA
BVHW050750280720
584768BV00021B/595